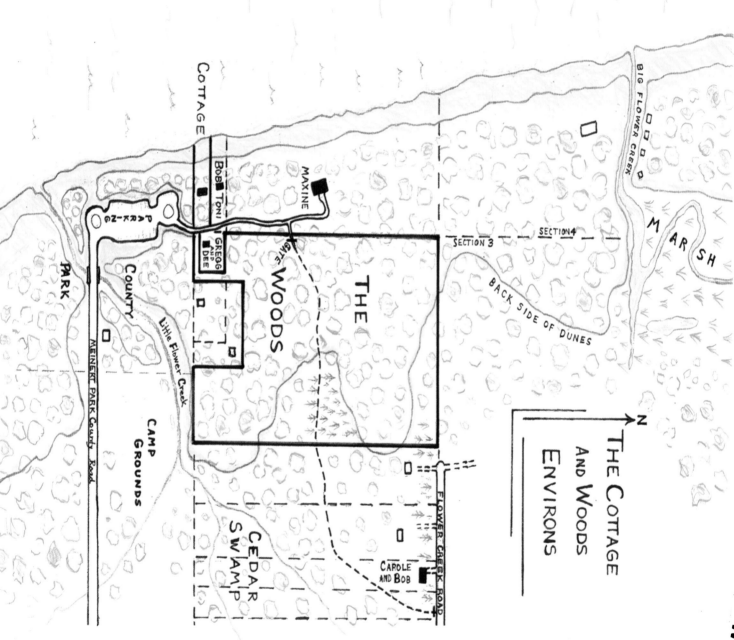

THE COTTAGE AND WOODS ENVIRONS

N

COTTAGE

BOB TONI

MAXINE

GREGG AND DEE

THE WOODS

GATE

BIG FLOWER CREEK

MARSH

SECTION 3   SECTION 4

BACK SIDE OF DUNES

PARK

COUNTY

MEINERT PARK County Road

Little Flower Creek

CAMP GROUNDS

CEDAR SWAMP

FLOWER CREEK ROAD

CAROLE AND BOB

Beside the Inland Sea

Beside the Inland Sea

by

Gretchen N. Paprocki

photographs by Doug Paprocki

Beside the Inland Sea © 2013 Douglas Paprocki (for Gretchen Paprocki)

photography © 2013 Douglas Paprocki

ISBN 978-1-933926-32-2 (paperback) ISBN 978-1-933926-48-3 (hardcover)

book design: Susan Bays, Fetching Design (fetchingdesign1@gmail.com)

A portion of the proceeds donated to The Nature Conservency.

Library of Congress Cataloging-in-Publication Data

Paprocki, Gretchen N., author.

Beside the inland sea / Gretchen N. Paprocki ; photographs by Doug Paprocki.

   pages cm

ISBN 978-1-933926-32-2 (paperback) ISBN 978-1-933926-48-3 (hardcover)

1. Natural history--Michigan, Lake, Region. 2. Nature conservation--Michigan, Lake, Region. 3. Landscape protection--Michigan, Lake, Region. 4. Michigan, Lake, Region--Description and travel. I. Paprocki, Doug. II. Title.

QH76.5.M5P37 2013

                                                        201302766

Arbutus Press

Traverse City, Michigan

editor@arbutuspress.com

www.Arbutuspress.com

Printed in the United States by Versa Press

DEDICATION

Dedicated to all those who work to understand, save, and protect natural areas and ecosystems.

And for those of my family who have shared this journey of which I write in some way or another—or will in time to come.

And for especially Ava and Dane.

CONTENTS

𝒟

INTRODUCTION

Of the planet's ten lakes that are over 10,000 square miles in surface area, half exist on the North American continent, straddling its middle. Immense enough to be called seas, this quintet of connected Great Lakes is the world's largest reservoir of fresh water in its liquid state.

During the second half of our marriage, my husband and I have been privileged to live during periods of nearly one-quarter century along the shoreline of one of those Great Lakes—Lake Michigan. Unique among these greatest lakes of the world, Lake Michigan has, along its lengthy eastern and southern coastline, the largest assemblage of freshwater sand dunes there is to be found. And it was there, in a portion of that wonderful shore-adorned duneland, that we came to reside and be intimately connected to land and lakescape.

The two of us came primarily for the enjoyment of the scenery, as a great many do to the shores of all five of these remarkable inland seas, but soon we were being deeply enriched by far more than visual pleasure. Astonishingly no older than human civilization, the duneworks—these extremely new geological shoreline formations, here forested and diversely inhabited—offered, along with the great lake, a constantly changing array of delight and demands. Arriving at a time of historically high Lake Michigan water levels, we found the demands and challenges of this extraordinary place, at first, somewhat trumping the pleasures for us.

It wasn't long before I felt the need to write about this special setting and of our varied observations, explorations, and unusual experiences there. For in addition to engaging the lake and the forested dunescape, we were to find nearby two very different kinds of wetlands to explore and learn about. I wanted to share with others the sights, sounds, feelings, and new knowledge that came from our first-hand involvement with this coastal world's mosaic of environments.

As our growing discovery and understanding of place expanded, my intent was to provide a sense of what it is actually like to be in that setting throughout all the seasons and to tell of that combination of natural marvels that only this vibrant landscape has to offer—as well as its manifold challenges, an occasional mystery, and the sea's unsuspecting dangers.

While my husband and I came to this Lake Michigan coastal setting for ourselves, we grew to understand that here was something not only exceptional, but quite valuable ecologically. It was important to make this worth more widely known—and there was a real need, an obligation even, for advocacy on behalf of this special and significant living landscape. When a nearby tract of forested duneland unexpectedly came up for sale, we were primed to act on behalf of its preservation. However, the challenges of a land conservation effort were fraught with difficulties and, although our efforts ultimately proved successful, heartaches ensued, and a new stage in our lives was set.

Here, then, is a story of place and engagement beside one of the world's great lakes, bringing to light various aspects of the Western

Michigan coastal world set forth nowhere else. Hopefully the reader will find it the next best thing to being there—in awakening spring, summer, fall, and icy winter—with this Great Lake Michigan, its windswept forested dunes, rich wetlands, and diverse flora and wildlife. It is a relating of varied and extensive environmental change that seems to happen at a faster pace in this meeting of lake and land than in most other locations. And interwoven is the narrative of the dogged search for "our" landscape's amazing defining past—especially the dynamic interplay of extraordinary natural and human history—providing a deeper understanding of, and a broader perspective on, the immense value of those special environments beside the Inland Seas.

WIND

I my way against it.

It wrestled with the ends of my woolen scarf and stabbed through the fibers of my coat. It threw sand at my face as I bent forward to force

I expected wind. Here, it is not just a characteristic of place; wind and wave are architect and owner of the long eastern shore of Lake Michigan. Together they define this spectacular landscape, alternately tearing down or building up dunes and reconfiguring the shoreline.

March is a time of powerful definition. Shore breezes, created by the dissimilar heating of land and the massive body of water, add force to the prevailing westerlies that gather enormous energy as they sweep unimpeded across the unbroken expanse of the Great Lake.

We stood gratefully, my husband and I, in the lee-side shelter of a dozen dwarfed Red Cedars clumped on the prow of a low, sandy lakeshore bluff. We had stopped in a small park in Muskegon County, less than halfway up the western side of Michigan's mitten. This public space was situated where a small, clear stream cut through a gap in the coastal dune system to empty into the lake just beyond. Although the protection of the car was just forty feet behind us, our legs needed stretching after hours of riding, and, in spite of the cold, blustery weather, the lure of the expansive view pulled stronger than the force of wind was able to push us back.

A layered haze on the distant western horizon faded into glimpses of blue, mostly obscured by giant stacks of cumulus fluff that interrupted the scant sunlight and created a collage of color on the surface of the water. Mirroring the afternoon sky, large patches of mottled steely gray surrounded isolated pools of aqua green. Beginning about 300 feet out from shore, the white-capped crests of the wind-generated deep swells collapsed in a series of foamy brews as the bottoms of waves collided with the sandbars of shallower waters. The spent waves rolled toward shore, running up the beach at the end of each successive rush and eliminating any possibility of defining precisely the line between land and sea stretched before us.

Doug ventured down the sandy slope of the broad opening in the frontal dunes, his dark blond hair whipped by the chilly wind. I followed in the wake of his tall frame. Even so, I needed to lean to the northwest to cover the fifty feet of tan beach swept so clean of previous footprints it seemed we were the first to ever reach water's edge. The relentless March wind, and the need to be on our way to home in Indiana, kept our venture here brief, but entranced by the scene and the drama, we vowed to return.

This remarkable coastline of Lake Michigan's eastern curve had beckoned us for years. Doug and I had explored the woods and shorelines of various public places of Western Michigan and northwestern Indiana every summer of our marriage, bringing two young sons along as our family expanded. We joined the tens of thousands of vacationers who annually visit one or another of Western Michigan's lakeside parks to bask in the beauty of a brief summer's moment. Like them, we were tourists, really only skimming the surface. Our many excursions to Lake Michigan provided welcomed interludes, a pleasant contrast to the Corn Belt scenery of our northwest-central Indiana home.

Many years ago, the two of us circumnavigated this long, north-south lake by car—the only Great Lake one can travel around without leaving the country—stopping and camping in various shoreline locations to engage the scenery and venture out upon the cold waters by kayak when the wind was tame. On that tour, we viewed this glacial creation through the eyes of youth, just beginning to comprehend its uniqueness—the marvel of finding in mid-continent an ocean-like sea.

The Algonquins, who earlier peopled this shore, aptly referred to the lake as the "Great Water," for Lake Michigan boasts awesome statistics. As the planet's sixth largest lake, it measures 307 miles long, is 118 miles at its maximum width—though, at nearly mid-length, the reach is under seventy miles—and drops some 923 feet at its deepest point off the coast of Manistee, some sixty miles farther to the north of where we had made our March rest stop. By surface area, this body of water is the world's largest lake entirely within one country.

Just as amazing as this freshwater sea is the narrow band of wondrous high dunes formed of finely worked glacial sand, rising from the beach along the lake's eastern shore and stretching from the southern tip to the lofty, high-perched dunes near Grand Traverse Bay. Dunes are defined as piles of sand deposited by wind, and these eolian hills are part of the largest system of freshwater dunes in the world.

After nearly twenty years of brief encounters with this extraordinary landscape by way of the wandering camper's life, we were in the process of looking for a spot to know as only caretaker/owners can. Actually, "we" is an overstatement. What turned out to be a year-long search for a parcel of northern Shangri-la was the outgrowth of Doug's restless nature. He seemed to be following the same propensity for searching out new places that had driven generations of American males to uproot contented family circumstances and head for "a better life" on the frontier, or some similar place. He had pulled me along on this new adventure of acquisition, if not exactly kicking and screaming, then at least dragging both sneakers in the sand. But, in time, I was warming to the quest.

A small, wooded retreat on the western side of the Lower Michigan peninsula was his original intent, and for months we searched inland along streams and small lakes, starting to the north of the town of Manistee and moving gradually south. Armed once more with a handful of real estate listings, we were spending one cold weekend in March of 1986 searching out the offerings—older cottages, cabins, and vacant parcels. Nothing promising. The places were either way below our expectations or financially unattainable. Discouraged, we were heading home. Facing a four-hour drive, we made that rest stop at a Muskegon County lakeside park. It turned out to be a fateful one. For that windy jaunt onto the Lake Michigan beach to stretch our car-weary legs, our brief experience there, in short order, redefined and solidified a new focus of our searching. We had both become irresistibly drawn to the manifold beauty and drama of this grander lakescape.

As struggling public school teachers with family and mortgage, we had always assumed that a Lake Michigan shoreline abode would be beyond our financial means, so we had been looking inland. But two months later, in late May, with a different kind of real estate listings in hand, and an eye open for realty signs along our routes, we plied the shoreline of western Muskegon County hoping there just might be a lakeside place we could afford. There were similar results as before. What didn't appeal to us, we could almost afford. For many of the lakefront offerings, we were particularly put off by the trend toward recreating the look of suburbia within such a unique natural setting. Yet, anything we liked was off the money scale. Seeking the relief of a mostly unspoiled view, we headed back to the nearly half-mile-long public shoreline of

Meinert Park, the county park with the lakescape that had redirected our search back in March.

To our disappointment, we found a beach greatly diminished in width since our previous visit. While all the Great Lakes go through an annual cyclical rise and fall of water level, this year the seasonal rise of spring and early summer accentuated an already unusually high water line upon the land. On the narrowed sandy strand lay scattered evidence of the action of erosive waves combined with higher water—torn boards, portions of uprooted trees, and mats of dislodged beach grass. Though this day was calm, the flotsam evidence was there telling that the wind, in our absence, had once again been acting up, forcing the rising water to tear loose and redistribute along the shoreline.

South of the park, a community of crowded beach houses clung like barnacles to the low shoreline dunes. An obstacle course of newly constructed seawalls, bulwarks, and jetties immediately in front of them had usurped the beach, attempting to restrain the worrisome rising water of the past year and protect the line of buildings that had been placed too far forward. To what extent this unsightly fortification of the shoreline would hold back the powerful force of storm-driven waves if the lake continued to rise, no one yet knew.

The magnificent view to the north, on the other hand, centered upon a thin curving tan ribbon of sand squeezed between lake and magnificent dunes. It appeared to continue, unobstructed, to a peninsula miles in the distance that slightly tapered westward, gradually diminishing until its point disappeared into the brilliant blues of water and sky. Not alone this warm Memorial Day weekend, Doug and I followed a few other springtime beachgoers as they ambled north along the water's edge, drawn into that subtle drama of rhythmic waves gently washing upon a sun-drenched beach. Beyond the park border, for a thousand yards, there were but four dwellings, none intruding upon the vista. Each was tucked back within the wooded band of maturing forest that graced the high ridge of the forward dunes and provided a towering, dark green backdrop to the lakescape's beauty. It was on this diversionary stroll that we noticed the sign, "House for Sale," tacked onto a slender tree leaning over the edge of the low bluff on the private property immediately north of the park boundary.

From the beach the dwelling was barely visible, nestled back among the hardwoods and evergreens crowning the higher dune area. The increasingly higher lake level and the erosive action of strong wind-driven waves had eaten away the beach foredunes, pulling the sand into the lake and moving the exposed beach farther inland. Here, the slender strip of flat shoreline was now backed by an eighteen-foot, steep incline of bare, loose sand—a wall that stood between us and the route to the house.

With hopes raised, we headed back through the park, turned north, and into the high-rolling forested dunes on a narrow, sandy lane that brought us immediately into dappled shade and gave access to the property for sale. The walk up the tree-lined, curving driveway of sand and gravel to the dwelling's rear side, however, sent our spirits plummeting. A vacant two-story structure protruded awkwardly from where a formerly sloping dune side had been scraped flat. The lower floor was merely a partial basement of unpainted cement-block; the upper, a nondescript box of modest size covered with patchy, not-quite-matching coats of fake redwood paint that failed to hide current and past tendencies to peel. Siding boards were loose, a few with the beginnings of rot at the lower ends. An assessment of the small, roofed entry around the north side rated somewhere between "dreary" and "unsafe." It all spoke of extended neglect.

Across the front of the house, an old cement slab served as a patio, and, most disturbing, right in the middle of where the wide, lake-facing sliding doors opened up onto it, a metal pole extended from the slab to the peak of the roof. Had that been added to keep the gable from inching down upon the glass doors? The electric service entry mast sticking through the roof overhang was severely bent. After scrutinizing stares through the paint-flecked windows, views which boded little better for the condition inside, we had more than a troubling suspicion the place would be a major project rather than a respite. Our emotions ranged from "Something like this should be affordable" to "Are we really this desperate?"

Still, we couldn't help feeling intrigued, especially with the wooded setting of the dwelling and its wonderful view of the lake through the trees, the extensive forested duneland behind, and the relatively few dwellings in the area. Here the buildings were islands in the dunal forest, not the other way around, as we had often come upon. Besides, we hadn't

found anything else in that desirable category—and we had been on our search now for nearly a year.

A few weeks later, to gain new perspective and try to come to a decision, we returned to the house site. After a more thorough examination of the building and the shoreline, and as evening approached, we walked back into the park and up the back side of a front dune to sit on a bench that overlooked the lake. We watched the sun's inevitable slide earthward and saw the calm water change from brilliant blue to silver to gold as the angle of the orb's reflection continued to increase. Mostly, though, Doug and I talked, taking turns as devil's advocate. We had acquired the realty listing and agonized over the asking price. To purchase this place would strain our modest finances and, perhaps, a little of our marital tranquility. Certainly it would be a major challenge to our renovating skills. Yet, like the sun, we were slipping over the edge—a drama of a most subtle and intoxicating kind.

For several weeks we clung to the edge of that precipice, but in early July the decision was made to let go. One hot afternoon we met at the Realtor's office to work out an offer-to-purchase. Matt was a Michigan dairy farmer in everyday life. Real estate was a new side venture for him, and this would be his first offer to submit. He was as nervous as we were. It was a bond that made the interactions easier on us all. We laughed and encouraged each other through the process.

In accord with our uncertainties, our first offer was quite low. For one, we worried over the home's immediate proximity to a well-used park. And that's the reason we decided to spend a night sleeping in the back of our station wagon, parked in the pull-off at the bottom of the steep driveway to the house, under a canopy of tall, leafy hardwoods and the graceful branches of rich-green Eastern Hemlocks. Since the elderly owner now lived in Connecticut and the dwelling had stood empty for some time, our presence would not be an intrusion. We could evaluate first-hand what kind of nighttime neighbor the park would make. It was an altogether different sort of neighborliness that our overnight stay initiated.

Amidst the treed landscape, a small cabin perched atop a lower back dune on the east side of the entry lane, directly across from our

vehicle and only sixty feet away. We hadn't seen anyone around the dwelling. Just the same, not wanting to cause alarm in case the occupants noticed us, total strangers, lingering after dark along the private access road, Doug went up the scant stairs at twilight to inform them of our intentions. He came back to the car with an invitation to breakfast and an apology from the young couple for no spare room to put us up for the night. I could hardly wait for morning and a chance to meet them.

As the darkening of day comes earlier to the enveloping dunal woods, we crawled onto the foam pads in the back of our vehicle for the night long before the waves of sleep could wash away the flood of anticipations or cushion the discomforts of too-cramped leg room and too-thin mattress. We lay awake for some time listening for disturbing sounds to come from the park, but none reached our ears. We were unaware that the entrance had been barred at ten o'clock, a routine practice. Sleep, morning, and stiffness came in their own time, and the appointed hour of this cool beginning of the day found us carefully ascending the nearby cabin's rickety stairs.

Driveway on left to the house for sale and the A-frame cottage next door.

17

Dee, a young brunette of easy smiles and bubbling conversation, met us at the door. We stepped directly into the main living space—and almost slid two decades back into the 1960s. The cabin was like a playhouse—all the makings of a full home squeezed into a 24-by-24-foot square. A homemade wood-burning stove occupied a short wall to the left where husband Greg, sturdy and thick-bearded, had just added a log. A Beaux Arts blue velvet couch rested in front of the windows on the right, and, directly in front of us, a huge, soft, brown bean bag welcomed agile comfort-seekers. An alcove beyond this snug sitting area overflowed with the accoutrements of an infant—crib, changing table, laundry, toys, and one wide-eyed, dark-haired, one-year-old beauty. Her name was McKenzie.

A toddler always eases the coming together of strangers, but conversation and comfort came easily enough on their own. With Greg's fresh-brewed coffee from the wood stove, whole grain toast, and a feast of similar world outlooks, we congenially wrapped ourselves around a cozy table nestled into the corner of a pocket-sized kitchen, spreading homemade preserves and the foundations of a friendship.

Our first purchase offer, a land contract, was rejected. Undaunted, and granted time by a sluggish market—the water level still rising and beaches and front dunes all along the Lake Michigan coast continuing to erode and disappear—we struggled over purchase figures again and again, finally arriving at an offer that stretched us to our maximum. Unable to qualify for a mortgage, we were still proposing a land contract, hoping the new offer addressed the owner's desire for more up-front cash, which we would get from a second mortgage on our Indiana home. While awaiting the response, we planned to camp in the area and pay an inquiring visit to the couple who occupied the small lakeside A-frame cottage next door to our potential home. We had spoken briefly from the beach the month before, but now it was time to introduce ourselves adequately, to seek counsel, and to see if there was a door to neighborliness here, too, as with Greg and Dee.

It was opened wide. As we sat on their deck, framed by several towering White Pines and overlooking the gently sloshing lake, conversation graduated from helpful, to cordial, to warm. Bob, slender and energetic, an information-gatherer and engineer, seemed pleased to be able to offer some statistics about the threatening high lake water. Toni, whose features and manner stunningly brought Doris Day to mind, was more eager to share her affection for their former next door neighbor and her love for the spot that had been their second home and "dream place" for two dozen years. They had built their cottage themselves in the early 1960s and had continued to spend summer weekends as well as their three-week vacation at this site every year thereafter.

In the end, we gathered more than facts about the worrisome rising lake levels and the distant owner of the neglected dwelling. A sense of belonging was soon in our pocket along with a key to Bob and Toni's miniature guest house. Still a year from retirement, they were grudgingly heading home to Jackson and jobs in south central Michigan that afternoon, but we were welcome to spend the night as guests, anyway. The delightful surprise of their generosity and trust made us even more eager for an encouraging response to our offer-to-purchase.

The almost doll-sized guest quarters had one room with two built-in bunks plus a half-bath tucked into one corner. The charming structure had been fashioned years ago to accommodate their young daughter, Amy, when bringing a friend. While I fitted in fine, it was a little cramped for Doug's six-foot frame. But the graciousness of the offer more than made up for any limitations in size of accommodations.

We fell asleep that night convinced we had found not just a piece of real estate, but a unique experience in the making. Our wake-up call confirmed it. I thought at first it was a distant motorboat announcing the morning sun. But my two, sleepy, blinking eyes at the open window were instead greeted by a pair of hovering Ruby-throated Hummingbirds. Feasting on Toni's orange-red Impatiens in the window box, their more than 50-beats-per-second blur of wings was broadcasting a low-pitched hum. "Hummers"' by the lakeshore—I was sold!

Later that day our offer was accepted, and a new and exciting chapter of our lives suddenly began. It would turn out to be a more demanding chapter than any we had known—not counting, of course, the rearing of two sons. Although the years before had led us to briefly explore a wide variety of enchanting natural areas, here, upon these amazing freshwater dunes, we would have an opportunity to become fully immersed in one.

We came thinking we knew about the wind and the Great Water, the dynamics and drama presented by this inland sea we were eagerly engaging. After all, hadn't we visited this Great Lake for nearly two decades? We had traveled to all sides, camped and slept overnight on its soft sandy beaches, climbed the immense perched dune of the Sleeping Bear Dunes National Lakeshore, kayaked its near waters many times, even made a cold February day trip to its frozen southern rim at the Indiana Dunes State Park just a few years before. At the far northwestern stretch of this expansive lake, on a lonely, sunny beach of the Hiawatha National Forest at Peninsula Point, it's likely our second son was conceived. We thought we knew the Lake Michigan setting intimately and well enough.

How little we knew.

REALITY

While grand anticipation accompanied the awaiting of closing, reality moved in with sacks of groceries and bags of clothes as we took early possession of our hoped-for dream spot. We arrived with our two teenaged sons at the beginning of a warm Labor Day weekend, full of the excitement of our plunge into lakeside ownership. And, our first moments were exquisite. The awesome lake, glistening in the sunshine, was at peace with the world, and our concern over the rising waters had been put on hold. Exuberant squeals rose from the park beach as the last holiday splash of the summer ushered in the beginning of our experience beside this great inland sea. We hurried down the narrow sandy trail through the trees to the bluff to spend a few moments soaking in the view before settling in to the many tasks at hand.

Ours was not a permanent move, although we were to explore such a possibility down the road. For now, the school calendar dictated our visits. But we intended to experience the lakeshore year-round, at least twice monthly, if possible, on school-year weekends, with longer stays when vacation schedules and the summer break allowed.

In spite of our entrancement with a place situated on a Great Lake, our sons, now in high school, did not wholly embrace the dreams of their parents, mostly preferring connections and activities with school friends back in Indiana. With college not that far off, their heads were busy plotting futures of their own design. And, in that stage of growing independence, they found this place was too far away to be stuck for

more than a short period with those same controlling parents from home. Still, they came along for our initiation stay, as they would do occasionally in future visits, usually bringing a friend or two. On this trip, they conceded to a stint taming the neglected postage-stamp-sized front and back yards—Jovan swinging the long-handled weed cutter to render the lawn mowable, and Derek tackling overgrown shrubbery—before heading off to explore the high dunes of the public shoreline on our southern boundary.

Arms filled with cleaning supplies, I maneuvered into the building's kitchen entry as Doug began removing the dangerous rotting floorboards from its outside landing. Cobwebs hung in scallops from the exposed beams inside. Well-aged cooking grease mixed with the tars from years of cigarette smoke coated the cedar planks of the low vaulted ceiling above the stove. Degreasing and scrubbing the tiny kitchen from top to bottom became my priority. When I got to cleaning inside the roughly made cabinet beneath the sink, I found only loose boards set across the lower supports to create the cabinet's floor. Removing one of those boards, I faced several half-mummified Deer Mice along with acorn remnants, leaves, and cotton batting the rodents had scrounged from somewhere for nesting. My first close-up encounter with the landscape's wildlife did not hold the type of excitement I had expected.

Hours later, as I felt overwhelmed with unpleasant indoor cleaning and the hole-patching around the sink drainpipe to eliminate joint tenancy with mice, Doug's emotions reached a momentary high. He had moved on to taking brush and bucket up a ladder to tar numerous sources of leaks and weak areas in a neglected roof of rather unorthodox construction, finding himself in a tree-level perch. Above him and the arboreal canopy circled Gulls, periodically disturbed from their beach lounging by shoreline walkers. Looking toward the lake through open branches of long-needled White Pines and broad-leafed hardwoods, the

It was already clear that our land contract holder, the second owner of this house, had not been a handyman. As with so much other interesting information that was garnered from the few neighbors in short order, we learned that Edward was a former professor of Shakespearean literature. He and wife Alice had retired to these shoreline dunes in the late 1960s, living here year-round for the five years before Alice's death. (We were informed that the 62-year-old woman had tumbled down the edge of the lakeshore dune ridge that gave way, and had died from a fractured neck there in front of their home.) For the next decade, this diminutive and increasingly frail gentleman summered here with an older sister. Then, in 1985, an advanced case of emphysema assigned him permanently to the old family home in Connecticut, and his beloved lakeside property went up for sale.

Neighbors spoke of "the professor" affectionately. He "enjoyed growing flowers," and "cherished his books." He also reveled in the lakeshore. Only reluctantly, it seems, did the professor try to fix things. He was evidently one to look beyond the details of such problems, seeing only the inviting setting. It's an easy landscape for perfecting such a habit.

Though described as a gentle man, the professor's favorite tool, if, indeed, he owned more than one, apparently was the hammer. Where a screw had fallen out of a door latch, we found that he had pounded in a nail. And his approach to keeping one of the makeshift upper cabinets in the kitchen from periodically leaning away from the wall was to continue smacking long spikes through the back and into what was mostly semi-solid drywall. In spite of nineteen, large, sixteen-penny nails, we found the unit sagged at enough of an angle to make the storage of dishes precarious. These "cabinets" were useless and would have to go.

panoramic view of the Caribbean-blue water stretching before him and the surrounding lush greenery brought exhilaration, and (he would tell me years later) several times he paused in his work, overcome with a sense of disbelief at being part of such a wondrous scene.

Soon enough, he returned to terra firma and a more mundane reality. For as the weekend wore on, Doug and I were forced to make fresh assessments of the house problems that now belonged to us, and a little of our elation eroded away. In spite of twenty years of experience with home ownership, we agreed that nothing in our past had quite prepared us for this building—or, as we were soon to find out, this lakeside setting.

The vacant lakeshore home begging for occupancy and attention, late summer 1986.

22

The problems that faced us were more severe than a lack of maintenance. There were basic structural concerns to confront. The steel gable support placed directly in front of the living room's sliding glass doors. The ill-fitting and untrimmed windows that leaked sand when the wind howled. The need for a new entry porch off the kitchen. The outdated electrical wiring. The list went on. We were not dealing with standard construction here. If the professor had not been a dedicated handyman, then no master carpenter was the builder.

That unorthodox builder, we later learned, was Wilhelm, or William. As the culmination of an improbable sequence of developments, this German immigrant began assembling this house on rural Lake Michigan dunes in 1963. He was seventy-five at the time, and not unused to difficult circumstances. As a young man in Bavaria, he and wife Erna

had owned a restaurant that succumbed to the economic disaster sweeping Germany in the 1920s, in the aftermath of the Great War. Immigrating to America with wife and a young son, Walter, William started two small eateries in Chicago, only to lose them to the Great Depression. His third business venture began around 1938, when he was age fifty, with he and Erna borrowing money from relatives back in Germany to take the rather unusual step of acquiring rural property in Western Michigan—some ninety-eight acres with farmhouse—bordering the newly-established Meinert County Park on the east and north sides.

In addition to a substantial stretch of forested duneland north of the park, William and Erna's purchase included two tiny neglected log cabins, which the middle-aged couple fixed up, and in a few years, offered for vacation renting. Though not trained or experienced as a builder, the short, stout William cobbled together two more rental units and added extra space to the old, log-framed farmhouse, including its first indoor bathroom. Summer renting did not provide a living income, but it supplemented the wages William received for work he found in town.

In the early 1950s, he also carved three small lots from the southwest corner of their ninety-eight acres and built cabins on them for former summer renters from Chicago who had become friends. Just a short walking distance through the park to the beach, these small summer quarters were an early example of the explosion of retreats and second homes that came to line the shore areas of both Lake Michigan and the numerous Michigan inland lakes in the growing prosperity of the decades of the post-World War II period.

William shaped the small lots and cabins in the wooded dunal setting in his own way, dismissing laments on the part of the purchasers over size of the land parcels and the structures. "That's big enough,"

William and Erna, with daughter-in-law, Elsie in front, and their granddaughter, Carole in back. The three generations are standing between the recently completed Chalet and Bob and Toni's A-frame cottage (in right background), about 1965.

the interior walls were covered with a honey-colored cedar wood, left natural. So warm and inviting. William and Erna named their new home, "The Chalet."

Day after day, month after month, the mild, soft-spoken William had plodded along to build the home overlooking the lake that opinionated and strong-willed Erna wanted. (We were told that, for Erna, there were two ways of doing things: her way—and the wrong way.) In the chill late winter winds of 1966, William was still working away—pouring concrete for a walkway from the parking area at the top of the narrow sand and gravel driveway to the kitchen door. Some family members say it is that work that led to the pneumonia that claimed his life in April, at age seventy-nine.

he insisted. "Bigger would be a waste." The bathroom in one cabin, however, was definitely not big enough. The dimensions of it were so small the tub would not fit, and William had to cut out a section of the newly-completed exterior wall to build a bump-out around it. The smallest of these three dwellings now belonged to our new friends, Greg and Dee.

In 1949, William and Erna had acquired two lakeshore lots on the north side of the park, adjacent to their land and the new little cabins he was about to build. One lot they sold to Bob and Toni eleven years later, and, in a move that surprised friends and relatives, then decided to build on the other. It was Erna's desire, we were told. By this time, 1963, the aged William was well schooled in the art of making do. "Economy" materials were acquired, and various items, such as kitchen and bathroom cabinets, were rustically fashioned by him on site. In one of the bedrooms, he simply turned a double hung window on its side (to fit a shorter exterior wall) converting it into a slider. At the building start, William poured no concrete foundation—thin concrete blocks were simply laid on their flat side on the leveled sand and the larger blocks built up from there for the supporting lower walls, as Doug was to discover.

The man also made do with tools that seemed to be as old as he was. While he did indeed use a level in his construction, a neighbor, who occasionally was called upon for assistance, told us that William would hold it up and eyeball it for leveling—but the tool no longer had the leveling bubble in it. (Perhaps that is why none of the walls ended up fully plumb?) Was it faulty tools, poor eyesight, or just not bothering to measure and calculate that made several risers on the narrow basement stairs unevenly spaced and awkward to descend? Perhaps, at his age, he felt time was short. In one regard, however, the end product was to be quite satisfactory—nearly all of the slightly vaulted ceiling and

Erna stayed in the new home only one more year before offering the place for sale. An exposed dune top facing the windswept lake is not the easiest place to spend a long winter, particularly for a lone elderly widow. Edward and Alice bought the lakeshore home in 1968, and Erna moved to the warmer clime of Florida.

Now, the idiosyncrasies and unfinished business of this building belonged to us, and we faced the reality of a long, difficult process of tackling manifold improvements. Each trip to the lake was to entail far more work than we had earlier anticipated when analyzing the place as potential buyers. But we had come to a setting of compelling beauty and wonderment, and occasional moments were found—no, insisted upon—to tentatively explore the broader landscape and do a little frolicking in the lake before the water turned too cold, for autumn was at hand.

To the north, a little more than one-half mile walk along the beach, we early on discovered the outlet of a modest-sized stream, named

Big Flower Creek, we were told. Looking inland from the confluence of stream and lake, we could see that the creek channel passed through the forested duneworks for some 300 yards, but then it abruptly turned north, preventing sight of what was further upstream. Some day, a little trespassing would allow us to find out. Other than occasional quick walks in the woods behind the cottage and short visits with neighbors, work demands left little time during our weekend visits for much else in way of engaging our new landscape. However, those evenings that promised a riveting sunset were clearly our signal to wrap up the long workdays a little earlier than usual and prepare to indulge in the display.

The reality of innumerable home improvement needs, however, was not the only challenge presented to us upon taking ownership of a place beside this inland sea. As in a dark secret, the forces of nature were very soon conspiring to present us with yet another reality that was far greater than we had bargained for.

Historically high lake levels, pushed by strong winds, tear into the front of the shoreline dunes, fall 1986.

WORRIES

They came naturally to deliberate people like us. That is the reason Doug spent our first day of possession on the roof—a decision that turned out to be quite fortunate. Not long afterwards in September, in our absence, a series of storms brought record-setting rains to Lower Michigan. In just three days, Muskegon County set an all-time precipitation high for the entire month of September with 8.6 inches of rain. Thirty miles to the northeast of our location, a 13-inch-deluge washed out area dams and bridges and rushed new waters toward an already over-full Lake Michigan.

The late 1970s and the first half of the 1980s had set the stage for this fullness. During that time span, the Lake Michigan basin experienced successive years of above-average precipitation. Then, a period of extreme rainfall throughout the Great Lakes occurred in 1985, pushing water levels to record highs on all except Lake Ontario, the farthest to the east. Beginning in our property discovery month of May, 1986, five consecutive months of above-average precipitation steadily added to Lake Michigan's encroachment upon its long coastline.

In the Great Lakes basin, precipitation begins to increase, from winter lows, with the onset of springtime. The amount of seasonal rainfall generally does not peak until later, in early fall, with September usually registering the highest monthly precipitation. True to form, our first September beside the inland sea leaped right in there, superlatively leading the rest of the months. On September 19, President Reagan

declared twenty-two central Michigan counties (and three in northeastern Illinois) to be a Federal Disaster Area. The estimated damage in Michigan topped a quarter of a billion dollars.

Although there was no visible harm to our building to add to that statewide dollar estimate, the shoreline bluff had not been so spared. Before the rains and deluge, precious little in the way of beach had extended beyond our bluff line. The waves generated by the September storm easily covered that narrow tan strip in relentless quick dashes and washed away tons of sand from the dune base. A yard and more of our lake-facing bluff, with its top-edge vegetation, collapsed and slid down into the persistently gnawing water. Carried out by retreating waves, the sand vanished under the rising water, to be hidden beyond the shoreline in submerged rows of new sandbars. Now, even when the lake was calm, there was essentially no beach, the water line reaching inland further and higher.

The leaning 10-inch-diameter tree that had posted the beckoning "House for Sale" sign that we had responded to in May lay prostrated against the bluff slope along with several of its dozen companions. Next door, Bob and Toni's stairs down their bluff area to the beach had collapsed as well, the second time this had happened. Immediately to the south, the high water had drastically cut into the larger dune forms in the park. And at the park's approach to the beach, half of the sheltering, dwarf Red Cedars that we had stood behind six months earlier were washed away. The seawall fortifications south of the park were continuing to protect the beachfront cottages there, but just barely. With the normal season of intense storms approaching, the situation seemed certain to grow worse.

We had recently learned that a blizzard-like storm on December 1 of the previous year had created the steep sand bluff backing our drowned beach. That raging event had roared across the lake at fifty miles per hour, the howling wind pushing waves of more than fifteen feet to attack the shore like a giant, insistent bulldozer. In many areas, the water scoured and totally washed away the sand and vegetation of the low, rolling frontal dunes and tackled the higher dunal slopes behind.

"The gales of November were late by one day," noted the *Muskegon Chronicle* after that storm, "but the consequences throughout western Michigan were devastating, particularly in communities fronting

Lake Michigan." South of the city of Muskegon, four lakefront cottages, the foredunes in front having been swept away, collapsed from the pounding surf then undercutting their bluffs and foundations. Lakefront damage was severe all along Lake Michigan with some locations reporting storm action claiming thirty horizontal feet of duneworks.

On into the first half of 1986, as we were searching for property, rising water had continued to carve into dune slopes everywhere.

Repeatedly, in places along the dune-edged shoreline in both Michigan and Indiana, ten or more feet of bluff at a time collapsed into the growing lake, occasionally carrying a house with it. We had seen several of these remains on our search forays, homes probably built in the mid-1960s, years of record low lake levels when many cottages and houses were short-sightedly placed too far forward on the shorefront dunes. The scenes had made us worriers extremely wary of buying a home close to the shoreline. (But how close was too close?)

Now, ten months after that big December storm upheaval, on our trips north as new shoreline owners, we were seeing results of wind-wave action on an even higher Lake Michigan. Some dwellings, shored up and left perching high on stilts after last year's damage, currently had waves licking at their "legs," while others sat teetering on eroded bluffs.

Great Lake water levels experience pronounced fluctuations with the seasons. The average difference between the summer high and the winter low for Lake Michigan is normally twelve to eighteen inches. *Normally*. But these were not normal times. Last winter's lake level *lows* measured appreciably higher than the average summer *peak*. This fall, as in the months before, the lake reached new record elevations, three feet above the long-term average—and was not to hit the seasonal "summer" crest until October. And the period of extreme late fall weather, so characteristic of the Great Lakes—with the turbulent transition from warm to cold over the dissimilar adjacent bodies of water and land—was

yet to come. Just months before, we had been entranced by the Lake Michigan drama. Having bought tickets to the show, expensive ones upfront, it was as if the lake and its associated elements were now saying, "You like drama? We'll show you drama!"

What, and how much, we should or could do about the situation were questions that kept us in as much turmoil as the churning waters at the base of the eroded bluff. Our house was still one hundred and thirty feet back from the receding bluff edge and the devouring waters, and we wanted to keep that safety buffer as fully intact as possible. Nor did we want to lose any of the intervening vegetation that anchored the forward dunescape, discreetly screened the dwelling from the beach, and served to make the site appealingly natural. With the new turn of events, and what seemed to be coming, we now turned to worrying that the home we thought very likely safe, when pursuing it, was not far enough back from the rising water after all. If thirty feet of duneworks could disappear at a time in a storm, as in the recent past elsewhere, what could happen with the lake level now even higher in such a weather event—followed by others? The water was already easily able to lap at our bluff base without storm conditions.

And as if all that were not enough to edge up our lakeside anxiety, the September storm had presented us with a disturbing revelation. With the collapse of the leading edge of our sheared-off bluff, we found, to our great surprise, a huge squared-off timber sticking three feet out of the bluff slope, approximately two feet up from the base. And, several hundred feet to the south, inside park property, a log jutted out of a much higher sheared-off bluff, at about the same level up from the beach floor.

Doug jumped up and down on the protruding section of the squared timber to see if it could be loosened. It never budged, evidently embedded deep into the 18-foot dune slope. Within a few days, dried sand had collapsed down the bluff incline and reburied the exposed end of the large timber, not to be seen by us again.

There could be only one explanation for the existence of this wayward timber and the protruding log in the park in their unexpected buried locations: the lake water had once been higher than now and had deposited these wooden items on an earlier and somewhat higher beach that stretched many yards further inland where currently the frontal

duneworks began to rise up to our dwelling. Clearly, the lake could drive much closer to our house location—for it once had, and not all that long ago, either. The depositing event had to be within a historical timeframe, not a geological one, as the entombed timber was a human-fashioned product.

With what we now knew, should we do some fortifying, too, as those cottage owners to the south of the park had done? Yet, as lakefront neophytes, we had absolutely no experience to guide us. We only knew something of past events and processes, but no way of really knowing what would likely happen or how to prepare for the foreboding possibilities.

Our concern was not entirely a case of new-owner jitters. On one of our visits to consult next door, Bob passed along a copy of a monthly Great Lakes bulletin put out by the U.S. Army Corps of Engineers at Detroit. Basically, the Brigadier General of the Corps gave instructions to our very receptive minds to definitely worry. In "Great Lakes Levels Update, No. 17," he wrote, "Shoreline residents should pay attention to the weather situation. If severe storms occur this fall and early winter, the amount of damage could be very severe. Properties never damaged before may now be subject to damage. Again, I cannot overemphasize the need for shore property owners to take immediate steps to organize and plan now, in advance of any major storm events." The lake was giving a crash course in the power of natural forces, but we were not ready for any exams![1]

---

[1] The U.S. Army Corps of Engineers publishes a "Monthly Bulletin of Lake Levels for the Great Lakes," and because Lakes Michigan and Huron are connected hydrologically through the Straits of Mackinac, the Corps reports the water levels of the two lakes as being one set of data. However, I only refer to Lake Michigan when citing lake levels. Interestingly, being a single body of water hydrologically, Lakes Michigan and Huron together comprise the largest lake in the world by surface area.

Armed with determination, we began, in October, a strenuous effort at attempting to stabilize the bluff of our one hundred feet of shoreline. The Corps had said to act, but it had not told us what to do. We had neither the finances nor the inclination to construct some heavy bulwark on the beach as cottage owners south of us had done. So, Doug decided to try a non-structural solution of his own devising.

We bought a dozen bales of hay from a local farmer and three 50-foot rolls of slatted snow fencing. These I helped heft onto Doug's back, and in a bent-over forward lean, he carried them, one by one, the seventy-five yards starting from the rear driveway, up over the house-site dune, and down to our bluff, where they were rolled down the 18-foot, eroded slope. During our weekend stays in October, we staked the bales at the toe of the bluff to receive and absorb the force of the waves as they licked at the dune base. Sections of the fencing were driven into the sand and staked just forward of the bales to help anchor them in place.

widow of seventy, she stopped by regularly to check our progress on projects and to lend neighborly advice—wisdom gained from seeing (and enduring) more than two decades of seasons cross these shores, the last decade living alone. A no-nonsense, slightly severe woman, Maxine held and offered opinions on how to deal with septic systems, pumps, flowers, roads, gates, and other items with authoritative finality. Living high and far back from the beach area, she disapproved of building seawalls and groins. Having over 1,700 feet of lake frontage, it was impractical for her anyway. It was best, she maintained, to just let the shoreline go through its natural cycles of tearing down and building up. She asserted that our dwelling was far enough back.

We appreciated the reassurance and most of the advice. Still, these were unusual times, and we felt duly compelled to worry over the famed "gales of November" and the approach of winter. The fury that pushes polar air relentlessly through this mid-continental trough stirs up giant waves. With even higher water than last winter, the results of new major storms would certainly be devastating. So, periodically, we were on site to gauge the continued press of wind and water on our denuded forward dune slope and its modest phalanx of hay bales and fencing at its base, augmenting the protective lineup any way we could.

Consumed as the two of us were with the shoreline work and the house repairs, our first autumn along the great lake and its forested duneworks crept in and then faded without our full mindfulness. It did not entirely escape us, though, that this cooling down period, particularly October, is a celebration of the senses here. We toiled against a varied backdrop of deepening aqua hues of the lake, vibrant oranges and reds of Sugar and Northern Red Maples, the pale harvest gold of the Beeches, and the ever-rich hunter greens of the delicate needles of Eastern Hemlocks. The strong, bright sunlight of our summer prelude to

Maxine, our neighbor who lived year-round on shoreline property north of Bob and Toni, approved of our efforts. A sprightly, light-of-frame

lakeshore residency had lost much of its intensity and harshness in daily retreating further south and slipping lower in the sky, radiating into softer and more colorful tones to enhance the outdoor décor. The sensual offerings of the surrounding forest mosaic and the increasing crispness of the air aided our energy level. But, too quickly, the aroma and sound of new-fallen leaves crunching underfoot signaled that the autumnal season had peaked and was soon to depart.

Along with the migrating birds that had headed south to far-flung wintering habitats, Bob and Toni had closed up their little A-frame cottage to spend the winter at their residence in southern Michigan. Increasingly, our trips north to the lakeshore were to a depopulated scene. As days shortened and temperatures cooled, seldom did we notice anyone visiting the park or walking the narrow beach. Only very occasionally did we see widow Maxine, who lived more than an eighth of a mile to our north, or Greg and Dee behind us, both of whom worked in town.

As those first months of our engagement here beside the inland sea, a time of both travail and splendor, came and went, we kept asking, "When will the water quit rising?" And along with our scanning of the

Roadway leading to Maxine's lakeshore home to the north, with Greg and Dee's cabin in upper right, opposite our driveway going up the slope to the far left.

entrancing autumn color palette, now fading, we kept a vigilant eye on the northwestern sky, anxious over the coming weather.

"Mountain range" of frozen water at lakeward edge of ice shelf.

WINTER

Out of the northwest sky, above a cold steel-blue sea, the first act of winter moved in on dark gray clouds, whipped high and thick as mounds of holiday potatoes. They filled the sky with an expectant heaviness and then a darkening that seemed to say, "Seek shelter." Their payload leaked intermittently until gathering winds tore the pillowed softness, spilling downy stuffing in a steady flow of transforming white. By morning the cold front had spread the narrow strip of beach with snowy icing, and wind-blown sand had marbled the surface with a dusting of burnt sugar swirls that invited one to feast on new vistas. Winter might not be official by the calendar for a handful of weeks yet, but, on this mid-November morning, its elements were already at hand, requiring accommodation to a harsher reality.

Actually, the coming of hard freezes here is delayed in comparison to places farther inland and even much farther south. Slower than the land to cool, the immense body of lake water—the second deepest of the glacier-gouged Great Lakes—warms breezes that moderate coastal temperatures into the fall and winter. Because of the predominant wind direction from west to east, readings can be four to five degrees warmer here than on land directly across the lake in Wisconsin. An even greater temperature differential exists between our coastal area and that farther inland, and the effect will continue into January. The phenomenon is reversed in spring, with the cooled lake delaying that season's warming hand, and summer here will generally be a comfortable ten degrees cooler

than even half a mile in from the shore. This tempering effect of the lake extends roughly twenty miles inland and has enabled residents of the far western side of Michigan to establish a long, narrow, coastal belt of orchards and vineyards over the past century and a half—an important industry for this part of the state.

Although our lake frontage measures a mere hundred feet, on any winter-like day such as this one, we appear to hold exclusive domain over a mile and more of beach. Even on calm afternoons, I explore unencumbered by sight or sound of other humans. Calm, however, is not a word often associated with November here. With the deep lake still clinging to a measure of summer's stored warmth, and masses of cold air pressing winter into the world above it, the result is massive movement of energy in the form of that familiar, excitable element, wind. Storm fronts entering this turbulent mixing zone are greatly augmented, receiving an enormous boost of heat energy from the warmer waters below to fuel the storm action. Tempests can be conjured up any time of the year, but November storms are especially sudden and powerful—exceedingly dangerous to any who would be venturing upon the lake during their emergence. To sailors of the inland seas, the "gales of November" are fearsomely famous, with its ocean-size waves. More boats have gone down or crashed upon the shores of the Great Lakes during this month than at any other time of the year.

Following the sudden and mysterious sinking in Lake Superior of the giant iron-ore freighter, the Edmond Fitzgerald, on a November night in 1975, Canadian singer-songwriter Gordon Lightfoot wrote a haunting and popular memorial song to the event and the twenty-nine crew members that perished. On a day that began clear and relatively calm on this largest of the Great Lakes, a storm suddenly emerged and grew with a great ferocity—the gales of November had arisen. Caught up in the maelstrom before it could make it to shelter in Whitefish Bay, the

729-foot-long freighter began taking in water, and during the early night, vanished into the massive waves without warning or a distress call. Many other wrecks occurred that day as well, but none to match the *Edmond Fitzgerald*, the most recent of the major shipwrecks on the Great Lakes—and the largest vessel ever lost on these seas. Lightfoot's "Wreck of the Edmund Fitzgerald," one of the most poignant story ballads ever penned, is built around multiple references to "the gales of November," emerging once as "the witch of November come stealin'."

By our Thanksgiving trip to the "cottage," our simplified name for William and Erna's "Chalet," those infamous November gales thankfully (oh, so thankfully!) had not materialized—not yet, anyway. Although the November lake level set another monthly record, the peak finally had been reached some weeks earlier in October, and the water level now was actually several inches lower than that new record high for Lake Michigan. That didn't keep the wind and water from occasionally acting up and eating under the hay bales bit by bit. Nor did it prevent sand from further slipping down the bluff slope. But the breaches in our defensive line-up were patched as best we could with the acquisition of more hay bales and another section of snow fencing. We gathered branches, boards, beach grass clumps, and whatever else the restless water deposited along the narrow beach strip and tossed it all on the lower slope behind the bales to help catch and stabilize the sand that drifted down as it dried, losing the surface moisture that helped hold it in place on the steep, tilted plane.

We knew, though, with this full lake, that roaring waves wiped up by any gale now would simply howl at our pathetic attempts to fend off its demolishing work. The best we could expect from the fencing-hay bale lineup in a real storm would be a slight diminishment in the inflicted damage. The wiping up of a truly powerful storm, sustained on a heavy

dose of atmospheric amphetamines, would mean farewell to the bales and fencing—battered to pieces, the blocks of hay would be spirited away with the fencing, along with tons of the bluff slope sand.

As the days of our concern passed by, temperatures continued to drop under the increasingly colder skies. On into December, periods of below-freezing days sent the wet edge of the beach sand into a hardened state. Gradually there emerged a layering of thin shoreline ice as waves washed onto the beach and a portion solidified. Well into the month, colder temperatures began the freezing of the shallow shoreline water. This skim of ice gradually thickened and expanded lakeward into an embryo "shelf," becoming more than a foot thick. Without us then really knowing it, our salvation was underway. The dreaded gales of November (or early December) had not materialized in their usual manner, and now there was emerging a solid guardian form out of the very substance that could render the havoc we feared.

Doug and I arrived late in the day for an extended stay near the end of December, during the Christmas school break. The strong northwest wind, driving a thin snow, and the churning wave action that moved in during our first night was to build and continue. During the following morning and afternoon, we focused upon indoor chores—working mostly on upgrading the small corner kitchen by constructing open wood shelving to replace the wretched wall cabinets. The weather outside, however, was not to be ignored for a moment. The constant wind coming unimpeded across the lake grew sufficiently violent to make the building move enough to creak; shingles flapped and tabs tore loose, and we heard them bounce across the roof on their way to the back yard, or farther.

Trees around us bent inland, their tops thrashing about, generating a rising concern that one would come crashing down on the building. And from off the lake there had developed an unflagging background drone

34

that matured till it was as if there were freight trains roaring endlessly past the cottage front. Insidiously, a fear emerged within us that those "trains" could blast in upon us at any moment with a torn loose branch hurled through a section of the twelve feet of patio door glass facing the lake—or with the force of the wind blowing one of the glass units in upon us. What could we do to cover a breach in the building's perimeter? There was no plywood sheet or other such material available in the cottage to stop an incoming onslaught through a gaping opening.

By early evening of that first full day, we could stay encaged no longer—what was happening on the beach and to our bluff? And what would it be like to be down there, testing the raging elements—instead of continuing to huddle indoors, protected by the cottage? Cocooned in down-filled layers and with hooded heads, we stepped out into the blizzard, pushing streaking horizontal snow and going the back way through the park to reach the beachfront theater.

The sea was in an uproar. Out of the darkening lakescape and bellowing wind came white-capped charges of high water relentlessly rolling shoreward. All was in motion, as we braced against the power of the wind and the nearly deafening sound. It was immensely fascinating, and even a little frightening—like looking into incessantly emerging jaws, fully as tall as we were, rising up out of a watery hell and raging to reach and engulf us.

We peered north from the park beach into the flying snow, and, to our amazement, despite the height and ferocity of the waves, we could see in the dim light that each rush of foaming water was barely reaching the hay bales at the toe of the bluff, before retreating backwards, defeated. Instead of destructively blasting away at the vulnerable bluff, the huge waves were first slamming into the near shore sandbars and then hitting the ice shelf that had been gradually forming outward into the lake during the previous weeks. Energy expended, the charging avalanches of water came upon the narrow beach exhausted and diminished. As a portion of the cold, seething liquid splashing up and onto the shelf and the beach then froze, the coastline was receiving an expanding seawall to hold the watery beast at bay, locking its destructive force within a frozen vise. Constantly buffeted and beginning to get chilled, we gratefully embraced the revelation that our bluff was apparently saved—for the few winter months ahead, anyway.

Doug locked his arm tight around mine to help me stay upright, and moving as one, we blew south with the wind and flying snow to briefly inspect the closest cottages beyond the park before the dark of night fully descended. There the beaches had long been gone, the strong surf having scoured the sand away from the fronts of the human-placed seawalls, leaving the water too deep to be frozen yet. Waves slamming into the fortifications sent heavy spray hurling up and over, scaling cottage steps

On our third day, the fury having diminished, we ventured out again to check the stormy sculpting of the lake's now frozen rim. Slushy water just beyond the developing shelf had been lobbed onto the ice sheet as opaque or slightly translucent soft-ball-sized chunks of ice. "Come look," I called to Doug, as we proceeded along the hardened shoreline. There, amidst the more normal ice debris, an array of window-clear pieces, smoothly rounded by swirling water into convex disks before being hurled ashore, provided six- to eight-inch magnifying glasses, enlarging the grains of sand embedded in the ice shelf—as well as my perspective on nature.

On succeeding days, the former beach edge became a cobblestone path of the rounded ice globules, hard on the feet and treacherously slippery. In the period ahead, more and more fluid was converted into an expanding world of solid matter, with waves breaking over previous creations of shore ice to build ever higher piles of frozen spray. The and even reaching the front doors of a few of the deserted dwellings. Ice coated stairs and decks, and giant icicles hung from some of the railings and roof overhangs.

In comparison, we felt very fortunate. It was past time for us to give William and Erna well-deserved credit for the judicious placing of their coastal dwelling. They had built the Chalet in the same period as the establishment of many of these ice-coated cottages, when the lake level was very low. But the couple had not succumbed to the temptation of locating right up close to the beach. Having lived in the vicinity for a quarter of a century before building their coastal home, they had learned of the substantial variability of the waters of this inland sea.

To return home along the frozen beach, facing into the northwest gale, was near impossible, so we headed inland to walk the somewhat protected swale behind the front row of dunes—more than ready for the warmth and shelter of our creaking cottage. It had been exciting and invigorating to challenge the storm elements, to face the roiling sea up close, and we returned in the white-streaked darkness with a modest sense of satisfaction in having engaged this new and unusual experience.

The two of us had stood safe, however, upon the beach, out of the raging water's maw, mere fascinated spectators upon the stormy scene as evening was turning into the full gloom of night. But what had been the fear engulfing those on the Edmund Fitzgerald and the thousands of other ships that had been caught upon this Great Lake and the others in such cold, watery upheavals, many, many much worse? It must have been a horror gnawing deep into their souls, particularly in the blackness of night, times that oft led to no light of morning.

natural seawall continued growing at its front face, building lakeward. And with it now extending over twenty-five feet out into the water, no more was the rampant sea able to reach the bluff—or even the thin line of beach.

By our return in mid-January, rows of icy mounds near the solid shore stood guard above a still-growing shelf that now extended nearly a hundred feet out into the sea. I wondered if the ice had ever truly stretched solid across the entire lake, as I'd been told. Outer frozen domes were reaching ten to twelve feet in height so that, from the beach, any view of the water disappeared to be replaced by a low, rounded Smoky Mountain-style skyline. We had to stand back atop the shoreline dunes or climb forward upon the first row of icy hills of the shelf to see the liquid lake beyond. The sight of this substantial ice shelf, like a low range of white mountains running up and down the coastline as far as we could see, held us in awe.

Awesome, too, was the twist in the lakescape drama. Just six weeks before, water was lapping unimpeded at the toe of the bluff. The development of seasonal gales at their normal time would easily have breached our hay bale defense and wiped it and yards of bluff line away. Now even the most vicious wave attack could not come within one hundred feet of the land. In its cycle of life, the shoreline, that dynamic interface between water and land, had been hardened into a stable and stilled landscape—for a time.

There was also a different kind of calm to the setting. Gone was the thunder of huge waves hitting the near shore sandbars on their

way to land. And missing as well was that gentle, pleasant slapping of water lapping at the shore. All the watery sounds to which we had become accustomed were now silenced or being generated well away from the shore, the bluff, and the cottage, out beyond the mighty fortress that had arisen. And what we could hear under windy conditions was remarkably muffled by that intervening wall and distance. For the time being, we were experiencing a very different aural world, and a welcomed one.

There was also a new quieting within, for our concerns and anxieties of autumn and early winter had been greatly calmed as well. Living in a wholly new climatic and landscaped world, we couldn't help but wonder what other winter discoveries awaited us beside this ice-bound inland sea.

VENTURES

From my perch atop the dune bluff down from the cottage, a gray tulle fog discreetly obliterated a secret meeting of sky and sea somewhere far beyond the ice. It painted a monochrome backdrop for the silhouetting of the rounded frontal "peaks" of the ice shelf formed by the raging waters of the earlier stormy days. The distant open water felt no stirring of wind, no rising of waves, just an unusual and immense silence. It was not an empty silence, but the kind one listens to very attentively, and absorbs. Though a Saturday, no one else invaded the expanse of frozen wonderland. Occupied by warm indoor activities or errands of necessity, others must have considered a venture to the beach and lake, if they thought of it at all, as a pretty dreary and uninviting enterprise on such a day. I enjoyed their absence, although I would happily have shared this sweet solitude with equally quiet and appreciative others.

This early February day had first appeared overwhelmingly as a tri-color morn of black and gray and white. But it was far from dreary with its scattered dabbling of other hues that emerged in the growing, diffused light. A few remnant beach grass clumps punctuated the lower bluff slope with graceful golden fountains of slender leaves. Behind me, bright maroon stems of shrubby Red-Osier Dogwood crowned the top of the snowy bluff whose sloping side was richly patterned with wind-placed sand atop its shallow white blanket. The stand of twenty-foot-tall Balsam Poplars teetered on the bluff edge to my right, each trunk clad

with a greenish-tinged gray skin. Only in winter, with the overwhelming dress of greenery gone, do I adequately notice that nature has painted the bark of woody species with a wide range of colors.

I long lingered at the bluff edge, entranced by the stark, yet subtle, landscape. My reluctance to move was rewarded. Off in the distance, a slender, pumpkin-colored Red Fox with black leg stockings suddenly appeared, trotting steadily with purpose along the middle of the ice shelf, heading north on that barren terrain on some appointed rounds of which I had no knowledge. As solitary animals, the long-limbed Foxes travel alone. Thankfully I was not as preoccupied as the diminutive Canid with the long, fluffy, white-tipped tail, or I would not have noticed this fellow adventurer of the morning.

Our teenage sons had accompanied their parents on this trip and had quite a different deep winter adventure in mind. Restless with the cabin fever young men are prone to acquiring, they had determined to go snow camping later that day. Being of that gender and age well-known for sensible ideas, they were not to be dissuaded by radio forecasts of zero-degree weather. We gave a reluctant, "Okay, but come back if it gets as cold as they say." The two loaded their packs with supper, sleeping bags, and small tent and headed off in late afternoon into the snowy world, full of the challenge of a new type of youthful undertaking.

Their destination, they told us, was to be a little less than half a mile down the frozen beach, inland through drifted snow to the huge blowout carved from the high sandy dune in the county park, then south into the steep wooded slopes beyond.

As evening and then night wore on, outside temperatures did indeed move toward zero. Doug and I both hoped and expected that our Arctic explorers would return momentarily, but neither hopes nor expectations came to pass. We went to bed in a state of parental anxiety about how the boys were faring and what we should perhaps do about it. We dozed fitfully. There was simply no way to keep our thoughts from contrasting our warm, safe indoor condition with the frigid circumstance of the dark outdoor world. At two o'clock Doug could stand it no longer and got up to check the thermometer—just below zero—and made the decision of what he should do.

Wrapping body and concerns inside layers of warm clothing and high boots, he headed out, flashlight in hand, into the still, snow-shrouded world. Frigid air stung his lungs, but labored movement through foot-deep snow soon warmed him as he made his way south over the uneven terrain and up into the bowl-shaped blowout of the park dunes. Here he was able to barely pick up the campers' trail and follow it up a steep slope where it disappeared into the darker woods.

His flashlight was not adequate to find the trail again among the trees, and Doug began calling out their names. "Jovan?" Only silence answered. "Derek?" After repeated and louder attempts, concern changed to disturbing thoughts. He continued through the deeply rolling, forested dunescape, and then finally, in a low swale, his light fell upon the dark outline of a small tent nestled under the drooping, green-needled branches of a grove of Eastern Hemlocks. He called again loudly, without answer.

Hurrying down into the wind-sheltered dip, his mind conjured up the alarming thought, "What if the moisture from their breath had frozen on the inside walls of that small closed-up tent, making it air tight, and they were suffocating in their sleep?" He vigorously shook the tent as he crouched down, anxiously inquiring, "Are you guys okay in there?"

A groggy voice was slow to reply. "Yeah. What's up?"

"Well, I'm just checking. Are you warm enough?"

"Yeah. We're fine."

"Really?" Doug pressed as he assessed the situation. "Do you really want to stay the whole night? The temperature is down to zero."

"Sure," one yawned and snuggled contentedly back into his hooded sleeping bag, with just his nose sticking out.

Doug returned home red-cheeked an hour after his mission was begun, his color a mix of skin's reaction to cold air, the blood-flow of exertion, and the glow of having a parent's worries displaced by contented circumstance. He reported to me that the boys had been found in surprisingly comfortable slumber. They had chosen their sheltered spot well. Finally, greatly relieved and thankful, I could go to sleep in my well-chosen spot—under a thick comforter.

The campers arrived ravenous at breakfast, jokingly complaining about some rude awakening in the middle of the night.

On into February, there occurred a slight thaw, and it seemed that the ice shelf was beginning to recede. Former twelve-foot-high mounds of solid ice appeared to be diminishing slightly. More than a half dozen weeks past the winter solstice, increasing sunshine was reaching the lake water and its frozen rim. And from underneath, the band of ice was likely beginning to decay as the top was slowly melting down. Our cautious explorations onto the shelf and outward to where we could see the forward edge revealed that small caves and open tunnels had been carved into the front wall by the alternating angled currents of warming liquid. Waves, sloshing in through the tunnels and onto the ice, left water freezing around the openings, fashioning rising cones. With more powerful waves, streams of spray erupted skyward through the cones and onto the shelf. Miniature volcanoes and geysers strung out along the coast served up another winter wonder..

Out here was emerging a new lakescape world. However, it was not a place to be for much longer. For beneath this unfreezing terrain, more violent waves produced a deep rumbling. And there were tremors we could feel underfoot. Previously Doug and I had ventured out to those

40

cracking sounds that came from the shrinking ice shelf, however, were warnings, not invitations to venture that far. The warming sun was transforming the icy formation, increasingly destabilizing its solid structure—it was definitely time for *all* to stay on firm ground.

On the calmest of late February mornings, I was drawn to a seat at the top of a makeshift ladder that Doug had laid down the bluff slope to the beach, not realizing I would be an audience of one for an incredible unfolding performance.

The sea of water beyond the diminished icy rim showed only the gentle breathing of the sleeping giant. Trees dared not move for fear their rustlings might awaken it. The sun-energized air, however, fairly crackled with crispness. Movement briefly appeared with a brace of ducks skimming the lake surface, but spying no breakfast here, moved on silently, their departure punctuated by the raucous call of a distant crow. Life looked forward toward winter's demise, knowing there were still weeks to go.

To my eyes, the icy shelf atop the lake appeared motionless, but the musical sounds that reached my ears created visions of dramatic

solid hills with little concern other than falling on that rugged, slippery surface, but now I deemed it not safe to explore any longer, though Doug continued to push the envelope for a time. As the month wore on, the thinner ice along the shoreline edge was melting into a long narrow channel, creating a shallow moat between the beach and the ice wall beyond.

Briefly, Old Man Winter raged again, reconstructing bergs by throwing slabs of free-floating ice upon the frozen hills. Yet, more and more, the gradual warming was bringing the demise of our brief ice age and was inviting me to venture outside more often. The groaning and

The symphony of late winter began with gentle burbles and gulps under the thin shoreline ice. Unexpectedly, it erupted with a percussive cracking that seemed to tear the more massive form apart, though no change was visible to the eye. Then came the chirping woodwinds. One could easily imagine tiny feathered masses, helpless beneath the ice,

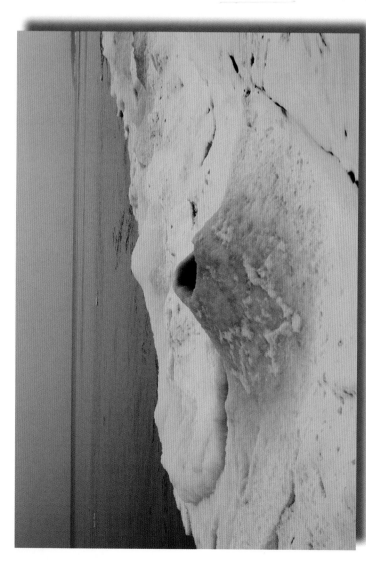

calling for rescue. The initial hesitant call was repeated in ever more assertive variations as the sound traveled the length of the shelf, moving from south to north.

Next entered the strings. No variation of pitch, just the vibrating like old wire stretched taut across a metal tub. It was a short solo part strummed perhaps a dozen times, not to be heard again. Then silence.

The second movement transported the ice music from jug band to Star Wars as the laser guns were fired from the north, their whining sound speeding rapidly past. The answer was from more conventional arms— rifle-like percussive cracks of the ice sheet that ricocheted down the shoreline several times before fading into the distance.

Again silence. Silence so penetrating I became aware that even though I was sitting still, my breathing was causing the strings of my hood to move against the nylon jacket I was wearing, making noise like someone softly crunching through deep snow behind me. I turned to be sure no one was there; then, holding the strings silent, I waited, motionless, perhaps five minutes, for movement three to begin.

Burbles came, also splitting cracks, as the intensifying sunlight weakened the very structure of the ice sheet. The next instrumentation called for chimes made of aluminum pie plates—a flurry of strikes, then brief silence. A long, low rumble of timpani built the suspense for a whistling climax like an explosive covey of quail. Finally, subdued, but prolonged and clearly discernible, digestive gurgles spread out in every direction, rippling into the distance as this movement ended and silence reigned once more.

I do not know how many more movements this day's symphony offered, how many would be played before no audience, with no happenings within and beneath its surface. The music I heard this day was a symphony conducted by the shelf itself and orchestrated by the sun. Symphony seems the proper term as the performance occurred in movements—and from movement in the true sense—splintering separations in this huge sheet of ice. Though it had sounds of New Age, it was definitely old-age sound, as old as the first thawing of thick sheets of glacial ice eons ago. I cannot relate the physics—the dynamics of stress that caused it. I can only describe its song. Like true art, it changed my perspective forever. Ice as a totally solid, cold, lifeless form is an illusion.

applause. Needing to head toward warmth and the mundane demands of lunch making, I marveled at the extraordinary opportunity to enjoy this magnificent concert uninterrupted. No sight or sound of human intrusion upon the stage. No markers to define historic time frames. Just a few ageless moments alone with ice-age wonders.

Much of late winter is wind and unforgiving battles of Gulf and Arctic temperature competitions, leaving gentle days along the lakeshore in the minority. Growing weary of drawn-out winter's lakeside irruptions, Doug and I sometimes sought a respite in the snowy woods of the inland back dunes that spread out behind the shoreline cottages and north from the park. Suffering a little wintertime cabin fever, and not currently needing to be engaged in bluff protection, there was also the desire and some time to explore. So, for a handful of times into our first lakeside winter, we ventured further afield into this transformed coastal landscape that, during this season of darkness, was oft made lighter day and night by the sometimes laying down of an insulating blanket of white.

Inland from the icy shoreline and into the dunal woods, we might seem peacefully alone on a wintertime walk, but the evidence is otherwise, for there are hardy and resourceful year-round residents in the forested neighborhood, out and about even in the coldest of months. I had previously seen that Red Fox traveling out on the ice shelf, venturing beyond these far more hospitable woods that is its home. For those varied, active wintertime creatures, coping with the cold meant an autumnal fattening up, growing thick insulating downy feathers, or developing heavier fur. For our winter outings we sort of borrowed variations of all three strategies.

A stout-bodied Porcupine, with strong, curved claws, having ventured from its burrow or hollow log, had stripped a tall, jagged, three-foot section of bark from a dying Hemlock in its efforts to secure a meal of inner bark. Chips from this favored food source were scattered on the snow below like feathers from a plucked chicken. A Pileated Woodpecker had also scattered chippings from its carpentry work, produced with its chisel-shaped bill anchored to a hard, thick skull. A large oblong cavity hacked out of a dead Paper Birch told of a search for ants. Later, on a larger tree, a more rounded hole and a deep tunnel will be excavated by a breeding pair for springtime nesting by this member of the largest remaining species of the continent's woodpeckers, highly distinctive with its brilliant red, sharp-pointed crown. To Doug, the Pileated's high-pitched territorial call sounds like a highly agitated, misplaced chicken out in the woods.

Lines of small, five-toed prints revealed the bounding of a Weasel across the thin snow, the slender, diminutive hunter in search of even smaller mice—or any other prey this somewhat pathological killer could tackle. The speedy, ferocious carnivore is the scourge of many creatures, from small animals to birds the size of Turkeys, slaying far more than it can eat, if it has the opportunity. In winter, this most efficient destroyer of small rodents is camouflaged in white fur and is known as an Ermine. A fierce killer, it, in turn, is killed for that beautiful fur.

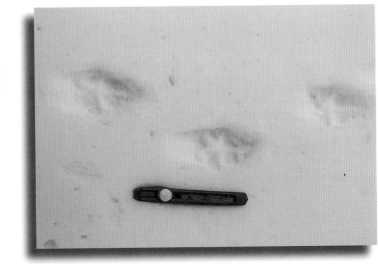

At the bottom of a nearby Red Oak, half-eaten acorns and the discarded husks of beechnuts were strewn atop the snow just beyond the small melted area which sun on dark trunk had caused. The diners, ones who survive winter mostly below the snow cover, were small enough that no prints gave away their comings and goings, but messy dinner habits betrayed them. Did the hungry, driven Weasel, soon to lose its winter white coat, also notice these tiny rodents?

White-tailed Deer are another matter. In the snowy forested duneworks behind our cottage their trails well-used—the very ones that we usually chose as well. We followed their deep two-pronged prints up the pass between two dunes and wound our way to the ridge trail (also theirs), side-stepping the piles of dark, oval-shaped, berry-sized droppings, so obvious in the whitened world of winter.

They had strayed downslope from the path to eat a few Hemlock tips and to browse the tender top twigs of a freshly fallen Bigtooth Aspen. Their heavy travel to this regular feeding spot had cut a path through snow to spring, exposing a lush patch of stubby, bright evergreen Clubmoss, a primitive, ground-level plant. This was not deer food; but on the more open flatlands on the far back side of the dunes, White-tails had pawed through snow to find an even more primitive plant, the pale light-green lichen so prominent there in that infertile sandy expanse. Their search for this less desirable food, commonly called deer moss, indicated a hard winter or too many Deer—or both.

This winter, no long stretch of snow remained unmarked by prints of White-tails and their bedding spots were many. Within these wooded dunes we came upon large ovals of melted snow exposing brown leaf-litter in more protected areas. In deeper snow, pads of thin ice remained where they had made their beds—melt from their body heat, which had then refrozen after they arose. We concurred with the choice of a

haven of grouped evergreen Hemlocks in a swale, a somewhat sheltered microclimate, but we wondered at their selection, at other times, of an exposed ridge. Possibly, in less harsh weather conditions, these had been chosen as lookout posts.

While Doug and I were out and about for exploring and a measure of pleasure, the wintertime movements of the durable woods creatures are for survival. We could see that they were all on a driven quest for food. Earlier fattening up and heavier growth of down and fur are not enough for non-hibernating animals to make it through the winter. Survival is dependant upon an incessant finding and uptake of energy sources through this extended harsh season. We coldly observe in our outdoor ventures, they must eat.

As new paint often transforms a room, the white-washed woods of early and mid winter had offered vistas so different, so open, it was easy to feel we had found a new place even when we were on the same trails the two of us had walked before the coating of white had been applied—a whitening miraculously emerging from icy crystals of clear water. But trails that with early and deep snows were transformed into ventures to fantasyland now failed, after nearly three months, to transport us out of our developing winter-weary state. Even here in the subdued forested duneworks, we felt an ongoing coldness. And the backdune tranquility we had enjoyed through much of winter had now been swallowed by a loneliness that caused us to help shovel the lane after a late snowfall and follow Greg and Dee to town to square dance with strangers into the nighttime.

We had had enough of buffeting wind and hours of roaring waves that led into too many interminable cold gray days and long dark nights during our trips north—enough of winter. Despite its fascinating and enriching experiences and varied revelations, we longed for climatic

44

change, knowing the huge reservoir of cold lake water stretched out in front of the cottage landscape would make it slower to come here along the coast than further inland.

around with the other hardy residents of the wintertime forested dunes. Relatively few can do this, instead of needing to migrate south to conditions less harsh.

The smaller non-migrant species depend upon various methods of finding hidden dormant insects, their eggs or cocoons, and various seeds and nuts. Some birds even store seeds in the fall and early winter, caching food for later feeding. The larger birds, such as owls, are predators dependent upon small mammals—and some of the smaller birds—that are out and about through winter in search of their own food supply. When winter weather moderates or food supplies are generous, fat reserves are built up, providing more body insulation and supplies of energy for leaner, harsher times. It's not about my type of hunger. It's eat, eat, eat, or freeze—and some do. Breeding will generally have to wait for hints of that universally desired spring.

The Black-capped Chickadees, along with their look-a-like southern cousins, the Carolina Chickadees that inhabit our Indiana landscape, are most unusual creatures we have found out. They're not built to feed up and down the bark cafeteria, but are able to hang upside down on branches while foraging, virtual acrobats working their examining way through twigs and branches. With such thorough probing and the superior avian eyesight, Chickadees glean every food possibility from their tree searching, gulping down what less agile birds can't reach.

They seem possessed of a great curiosity. But more importantly, these small, intelligent birds are capable of making complex behavioral decisions, especially in their caching of seeds in fall and wintertime, a form of energy storage that requires remarkable spatial memory and sustains them through the cold months. During this period, they are gregarious birds, flocking together in small family-sized groups. And, in their seasonal stable social systems, Chickadees employ an extraordinarily complex call system to keep the group together and to convey a wide range of information among the flock members. According to researcher, Jeffrey Lucas, biological sciences professor at Purdue University, Chickadees "are an example of a species whose vocal repertoire has a number of characteristics of a true language." Professor Lucas believes this unusually complex vocalization system is rare among all species, non-feathered animals as well as birds.

The lonely leaves of winter. Graciously, young Beeches retain their dead, but attractive, leaves well into winter, the only deciduous trees of the dunal forest to do so.

By late March, our diminishing, protective barricade of shore ice had totally succumbed to the work of warming temperatures and wave demolition. Except for shadowed, hidden collections, the ephemeral snow coatings were recently gone, but the feel of winter still was lingering. The ice shelf's dissolving into the sea should have been marked by us with a "thank you" farewell

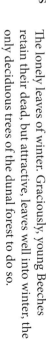

ceremony, for its birthing just ahead of the late December storm had been our bluff's saving grace. And as that icy formation had grown in the subsequently colder weeks, we were treated to a fantasy world on our doorstep that was the highlight of our wintertime experiences. Too often a gesture of appreciation is thought of too late.

With the guardian wall gone, we worried about what was again in store for us regarding lake activity and our bluff slope. We were now receiving the "Monthly Bulletin of Lake Levels for the Great Lakes" from the U.S. Army Corps of Engineers and had learned that through this past January, 1987, Lake Michigan had set sixteen consecutive monthly lake level records. The highest water level, since the keeping of more accurate records beginning earlier in the century, had been set in October. Although the subsequent November through January monthly levels came to be lower than that of October, 1986, they still were higher than the records for those months that had been set the year before. Thus, our first half year of residency beside this inland sea had coincided with the highest monthly water levels—for the months of September though January—for this century. I suppose it could be said we came at a historic time, certainly an extremely interesting and challenging one.

The Bulletin also noted that an even higher lake level period had evidently been attained exactly a century ago, in 1886. And we had very possibly seen evidence of that historical activity back in September, our first month here. Immediately following that month's record-setting rainfall, it was quite a surprise to find that huge squared-off timber sticking out of the newly eroded bluff slope, revealing that the beach had once extended further inland at a time of a high lake level. As we analyzed the import of this discovery, it was disappointing to have had sand collapsing down the bluff to rebury and hide this relic of the past.

Following the watery depositing of the large timber, there would have been decades-long building up of the frontal dune on top of the old timber and former beach—and then time afterwards for the clump of trees to be established on the crown. This geological process within a historical timeframe—evidently just a century in length—was yet another lesson for us in how dynamic and shifting this lakescape environment is. In fact, natural coastlines are the most dynamic of land forms in their shaping and reshaping.

For the present, the lake level had been declining since October, for five straight months, and was now nearly seventeen inches lower than that record high fullness of the fall months—back to the water level of when we first had viewed the lake at Meinert Park, one year ago. This decline was following a substantial decrease in monthly precipitation. A beach that had at times been down to a matter of feet was now measured in yards. This was certainly encouraging, but not adequately reassuring, for a strong spring storm could send high waves rolling up that still very narrow sandy strip and attack our bluff. And a normal annual rise that occurs in spring and early summer was very likely to bring the water level back up. Crisis clearly could return—in a big way. Doug and I just had to wait, contain our uneasiness—and hope.

Welcomed newcomers, Mergansers fished the cold, now-open waters of the lake, diving for breakfast, then popping unpredictably into view for brief moments. This created great frustration in trying to catch these sleek, multi-colored ducks in the lenses of our binoculars. Fast underwater swimmers, these Common Mergansers are "saw-bills," having saw-toothed bills with pointed serrated edges, top and bottom, which aid in grasping slippery small fish. Mergansers are lovers of deep clear lakes such as "our" inland sea and, having wintered further south, were moving on north, where they will be one of those few waterfowl species that, interestingly, nest in tree cavities.

Into early April, a court of Golden-crowned Kinglets arrived, probably coming only a short distance from their more southerly wintering grounds. Almost as small as Hummingbirds—a mere three and one-half inches from beak to tail tip—these highly active insectivores picked off their lunch from the entry stairs as we lunched just inside. They had found tiny white insect cocoons attached to the edges of the wooden planks. Shortly, each in turn would leave on smooth roller coaster flight from ground to tree, then dive toward low-creeping Yews. Not seen again, they were on their way further north to spring-summer breeding grounds, perhaps as far as the boreal spruce-fir forests of Canada.

Finally, my metaphorical hunger was being nourished by the lengthening days and the gradual atmospheric warming. And the increasing appearance of wild things in the lakeshore drama warmed me psychologically, as well.

There was yet one unsatisfied hunger as March came to an end, for I increasingly longed for new growth, a greening of the landscape, to hide the drab, faded litter of last fall's showy leaf displays that still choked the ground between trees and shrubs—and to dress and brighten the forest's dominating dark wooden structures. I visually devoured the first Snowdrop blossoms to emerge through ground still laced with a patchwork of melting snow along the cottage's sheltered slopes. The white sepals of this low plant hung like three drops of milk, it is said, from their short stem. These welcomed harbingers of spring were a legacy of the professor, who had planted the tiny bulbs of this Eurasian species near the cottage, with a few remnants having naturalized on the adjacent wooded front slope.

He, too, had hungered for spring. Beyond the white Snowdrops, newly emerging stems of gray-brown, sepia, maroon, and red were already tipped with their compact treasures—buds promising the gift of

renewed life soon. When it comes, the broad green brush of spring will transform the envisioned shape, as well as the color of these dunes. And I was more than ready.

The "fiddleheads" of a Woodland Fern emerging in early spring from the leaf litter of previous seasons. The furled tops of the new fronds (the stems and leaves) of perennial ferns get their name from a resemblance to the scrolls on the ends of string instruments. The fiddleheads are harvested by some for eating, with the taste of the cooked vegetable said to be like that of asparagus.

Trillium erectum, commonly known as Red Trillium and Wake-robin, an early spring-flowering perennial of eastern North American woodlands. In folk medicine, it's called "birth-root," as the astringent roots were once used to ease childbirth. The plant has had a long history of use by Native Americans and was considered to be a sacred female herb.

SPRING

April provides just nibbles of spring this close to the cold lake. I watched the growth I longed for come in hesitant steps. From underground, beneath the wooded slopes near the cottage, low-growing Hepatica of tri-lobed leaves were among the earliest native wildflowers to test the possibilities. Their soft pastel shades appealed to a variety of insects also just emerging from winter hiding. Having gone dormant for the winter by dieing to the ground, these emergent herbaceous perennials, as well as many others, had thereby gained protection from deep cold, breakage, and excessive drying. The sprinklings of ground-hugging, rootless mosses were acquiring a brighter green. And the slender, pointed leaves of the Siberian Irises that the professor had added to the edge of the wild landscape were also coming forth. Although the eight-inch-tall, white-petaled Dutchman's Breeches, both flowers and foliage, will disappear in a matter of weeks, the greening of this coastal world was finally underway.

Mid-April again brought tossing gray waters lined with white-topped ridges of foam and rolling waves that now fully worked their way onto the marginal beach. No longer blocked by the hard grip of winter's hand in the form of a shoreline ice cover, wind and wave returned to their restless business of redesigning the forward edge of the coast. But this time the wind-powered waves were usually low, slow-moving swells,

carrying fresh sand upward with each rush of water, and dropping it upon winter's released beach. Of course that "fresh" sand was the "old" stuff that had been taken away in the previous year and earlier. It came from multiple offshore sand bars that had formed parallel to the beach—low underwater "dunes." With the lowering of the water level, these sand bars were now giving up some of their largess to the land. The resulting granular accretion created a very slowly widening expanse of newly spread tan, gradually raising the beach level, as well. This was more like it! And it beckoned Doug and me to walk—and to share some relief.

Near the water line the sand beneath our feet was solid. Farther up the incline of the narrow beach, the new deposits were soft, and with each step, we freed bubbles of air buried beneath the freshly created layers. The pressure of our weight brought a pattern of holes bursting open around each booted foot as the pockets of air escaped their burial chambers. While fellow humans were seldom encountered out here during this yet-still-chilly period, the landscape was not always deserted—nor was it today. Gulls had been returning to the shoreline in growing numbers with the disappearance of the ice and snow and were now often at flock size, usually in several loose groupings in our area, facing stoically into the crisp breezes when "hanging out" along the beach.

On winter days that had not been severe with strong winds, snowfall, or really frigid temperatures, we usually had seen at least several hardy Gulls soaring on their graceful backswept wings above the shoreline area sometime during the day. Perhaps they were scouting to see whether the water's edge was unfrozen and suitably available for food finding—or just reconnecting for a time with their more normal environment. Where they and their companions who stayed for the winter had found shelter away from the lake, we did not know. But it was probably in the vicinity of the county landfill some eight miles inland, for these birds scavenge for food there year round amidst the dumped garbage before it is covered over. We have also seen them foraging in farm fields, especially after the earth-disturbance of plowing, going after worms, insects, nesting mice, and any other small life. Unlike our specialized woodland avian residents of winter, those Gulls that make it through the long cold season here do so by being opportunistic, omnivorous scavengers, eating animal, vegetable, and insect items whenever and wherever they can find them.

As the two of us ambled along the shoreline there was gull company not far ahead. Approaching the resting area of these robust birds of purest white and light gray, we watched the nearest flock members begin migrating on foot further forward of us, quickly followed by the next closest ones. Very soon, the whole troupe of thirty was smoothly doing a two-step up the narrow beach, as Gulls have longer legs than waddling ducks, for example, and thus walk easily. Their feet are narrowly webbed and they can swim buoyantly, but do virtually all their foraging on land.

Although we tried not to seem threatening and hugged the water's edge, the time came, as we were gaining on the birds' faster pace but of much shorter steps, that one or two decided it was best to take to the air. Seemingly as a commanding cue for the rest of the squadron to take off, they all arose and headed up the shoreline, landing several hundred yards ahead of us. As we again approached, invading their comfort zone, the routine was repeated, until the third time the flock circled around to land at our back. On our return, the process recurred. Although relatively approachable, these Gulls still didn't trust us to simply quietly pass them by, and took to their evasive maneuvers.

Gulls are our most regular and numerous companions along the coastline, bird-wise or otherwise. Although group-oriented among themselves, they don't seem to appreciate our company, as we do theirs. Most people refer to these long-lived shorebirds as "sea gulls," but among the world's fifty gull species, there is no individual species or grouping of birds that has that actual name. Gulls can be found far inland from oceans and seas, near lakes and smaller bodies of water, and we have seen them in the middle of the continent along an Iowa reservoir. As they are primarily land foragers, feeding and spending much time away from water, they could as well be called "land gulls."

The dominant species of the Laridae Family here have been the large Herring Gull and the smaller, but similar appearing, Ring-billed Gull. As with most gulls,

these two species are omnivorous, eating just about anything, which helps make them adaptable to diverse environments—and generally abundant. However, they were not very numerous at the beginning of the twentieth century, for gulls were extensively hunted for millinery plumage and eggs, a plight faced by many bird species then. After making a comeback, Herring Gull numbers in the Great Lakes region were again diminished during the 1970s by water pollution. While once the only breeding gull species of the Great Lakes, they are now outnumbered here and in the larger region by the Ring-billed Gull, distinguished by its somewhat smaller size and thin black ring around its yellow bill near the tip.

As scavengers, "our" Gulls search the water's edge for marine organisms, large and small, particularly liking the carcasses of fish that periodically get washed up—and over which they sometimes noisily squabble. It's not unusual to see one Gull with food in its yellow bill being chased by another trying to steal the morsel. Beyond that, I have not witnessed the aggressive competition within gull groups that others have described, calling gulls "a bunch of ill-tempered opportunists."

When I watch these light-bodied birds floating on the water they appear to be just bobbing along. It turns out that gulls are so buoyant that, unlike the Mergansers, they are incapable of diving under the water's surface.

On into May, the vision of spring made its defining appearance, despite the coldness of the lake water and the lingering coolness of the air. *Trillium grandiflorum* sprang from trenches and marched down the forested dunal hillsides, the snowy white ranks occasionally broken by a dominant *Trillium erectum*, uniformed in deep maroon-red flower. As the last of the dominant Trilliums discarded their faded pink-tinged petals, Columbine emerged at all flanks to succeed the departing members of the Lilly Family. The gentle storming of the wooded dunescape was advancing, and choruses of frogs and toads gave vesper cheers from the wetlands behind the dunes.

Warmth continued to ease in gradually along with the changes underfoot. Although the daily length of sunlight in May is comparable to that in mid-July through mid-August—the heart of summer—temperatures are usually more like early fall, here beside the still-cold inland sea. Yet, persistent sun eventually has its way. With rays ever more direct, that nearby star softened the bite in the air and coaxed leaves from bursting buds with the lengthening and ever-warmer days.

It has been determined that this increasing daylight activates certain chemicals in plants which trigger growth processes. All plant species produce such growth-regulating phytohormones, but each species responds to its own solar-related rhythms. For early plants, a late spell of cold weather here can delay their emergence, but if we have an unusually early period of warm weather, they will not come forth until their external solar signal is of the proper day-length. Actually, laboratory experiments have determined that what a plant really measures in its development is the length of the continuous period of nighttime darkness—which, of course, is dependent upon the amount of seasonally available daylight.

While a plant's initial growth spurt relies upon its small supply of stored food, full seasonal growth requires the emerging leaves with their photoreceptors to intercept and absorb solar energy by the green chlorophyll pigments, which fuels the wondrous assembling of simple air molecules and water into a burgeoning food supply—chemical energy stored in bonds of sugar. With the extracting of carbon from the gaseous carbon dioxide compound of the atmosphere and the expelling of the oxygen, this photosynthesis within plants is the source, directly or indirectly, of energy (food) for nearly all life on earth. We humans, for example, consume the carbon embodied in plants—and the animals that have eaten plants—recombining it with the highly reactive atmospheric

oxygen, "burning" us into activity and growth. We expire when we can no longer carry on the vital combustion of carbon and oxygen within us.

Leaves, then, are the lungs of a plant. In the case of trees, each leaf has thousands of tiny controlled pores on its underside, called stomates, that take in one form of atmospheric gas and release another. But more than that, the leaves, "fueled" by the sun, are the engine of a plant, making its own food and delivering it for growth.

In latitudes where plants die back to their base in a colder period of the year, the sun is the great resurrection god. Of course, it is the callous diminishment of heavenly radiant nourishment in the first place that cyclically withers this world requiring annual rebirth.

On the sun-drenched beach, not far above the water line, a newly emerged Sea Rocket became the first brave pioneer plant to settle this newly established hostile environment. I sat in the sand beside this native of the Great Lakes, as well as North American ocean shores, gently pressing the fleshy, water-retaining leaves between my fingers as if associating myself with it would give us both encouragement. I marveled at how this six-inch annual withstands the onslaught of wind and waves, swamping and drought, to resolutely complete its life cycle with dainty four-petaled lavender blossoms that will mature into the miniature, green seed "rockets" that prompt its name. The ripe jettisoned seeds of this radish-like succulent may land near enough to the water to be carried away by rolling waves and be left high upon some distant beach to begin the cycle anew. "Somewhat like us," I thought.

By June, greenery was conquering every upland stretch of land. It had moved in graceful, temporal sweeps from the ground-level herbaceous layer upward, from the early spring ephemerals—woodland-floor wildflowers whose only chance at adequate light and bloom was early in the season—through understory leafing out, and lastly to the canopy ceiling of the deciduous, or "hardwood," trees. Unbelievably, what had been stark and bare—except for the evergreen Hemlocks and White Pines—just a month or so before, now stood full and lush, the dark vertical lines of the entire community of tree trunks overlain and surrounded with the bright, rounded contours of deployed leaf.

In deciduous forests, where plants annually lose their leaves or die back, this is the general pattern of spring's leafy uprising. For the full forest community to exist, the sun-collecting greenery must come out of the starting gate first at the ground level and work its way up to the high canopy. If the crowns of the tall trees leafed out first and filled in the opening to the sky, those lower plants would be starved for the energy-giving sunlight needed for growth. There are some exceptions to this pattern, but on the whole, this is how the process has evolved to work, how it must work.

The completing of this grand photosynthetic display of leafing out was matched by an opposite development. By this time, the few species of spring ephemerals, such as the Dutchman's Breeches, the Spring

56

Beauties, and the later Trilliums—those delightful wildflowers who had led the verdant charge—had had their brief appearance in the early spring season's increasing sunlight and now were finishing up their time on earth, so to speak. Having set seed and quickly photosynthesized a year's supply of food and stored it in underground bulbs, rhizomes, or tubers, their foliage was withering under the closing, sun-hogging canopy above. Faster than any other forest plants, these low-level perennials had done their thing—their "whole thing," as one observer put it—while they had had their chance, and soon no vestige of these transitory spring leaders would be visible to us, until the welcomed close of the following winter.

Interestingly, the foliage of the hardwoods that crowned the dunal landscape, and provided the full greening for which I had been waiting so long, already had been in existence even before we had arrived for residency last September. For deciduous trees are, in the current summer, already establishing next year's leaves. Developing in miniature form and contained in tightly-wrapped buds, the embryo leaves are held in abeyance for emerging the following spring when they can quickly begin maturing to take advantage of a limited growing season. All through long winter I had had the greening of spring all around me—but could not see it.

The arrival of more cheerful colors and the full establishment of a forest spring was visually overwhelming, but the season of grand emergence awakens every sense. For more than a week, the fragrance of the professor's Honeysuckle shrub by the cottage permeated the air as did the sound of Bumblebees attracted by the nutritious abundance. I spent long moments in the warming sun listening to the song of a thrush busy feeding among the tangled stems. Against the house a stunted Rhododendron, another legacy of the professor's, hinted at its upcoming fuchsia display. And beneath its several graceful, arching branches, one of those biological curiosities that can do a gender reversal, Jack-in-the-

pulpit, began his/her sermon: "Spring is a treasure worth the wait." The treasure was strung out like pearls.

Doug and I have always enjoyed identifying plants and animals we encountered. The process of name-learning forces a focus upon the details of nature and helps link the observer to the natural world. While previously only a casual "birder," I now began to keep a bird journal, encouraged by the increasing opportunities of the springtime setting to observe, identify, and learn more about the many winged species that had been arriving in our coastal landscape. Back in autumn we had been far too preoccupied with shoreline and cottage demands to have much noticed our avian neighbors. The singing of males to attract mates and to defend territory, cues that call our attention to their presence, had diminished by the time we had taken up lakeside residency. Besides, some bird species had already begun migrating south. And the rest of the migrants were busy overeating to store up a whitish-yellow fat under their thin skin necessary to fuel their long flights to distant wintering locations.

So as we were assiduously settling in along the lakeshore during our first fall, much of the animal life not earthbound was depopulating the scene. The two of us took little notice that, as the avian migration proceeded and closed out, there was a silencing of the forested dunescape. Now, with harsh winter having morphed into inviting spring, a new cycle of migration brought varied company into our environs to join the resourceful and hardy souls that had stayed—and were fortunate enough to have survived—through the difficult cold period.

A brief off-shore visit from five squat Bufflehead ducks provided the first journal entry. Three were tuxedo-clad males with wide, white earmuffs on oversized, squarish heads. A committee design, no doubt, but one with style. I felt lucky to see these cute travelers out on the lake, our smallest duck and another tree cavity nester. This was just a quick these newcomers to the dunal woods turned out to be species making incredible, twice-yearly journeys of up to thousands of miles. Flying from distant southern wintering locations to northern breeding grounds, and then back again, these diminutive, delightful Neotropical songbirds are participants in one of the great migration systems of the world. The Canada Warbler and the Blackburnian stop for a day, but move on from here to even cooler climes to the north. (Like the Wood-Pewees, the Blackburnian Warblers don't actually winter in a tropical habitat, but along highland slopes of the Andes Mountains.) There are colorful others that may well stay—the Yellow-breasted Chat, the Black-throated Green Warbler, the Rose-breasted Grosbeak, the Indigo Bunting, and various Thrushes. How special were these sightings, for virtually none of the migratory species of the cottage area were ones we encountered in our semi-urban Indiana location.

As with the growth activation in plants, bird migrations are attuned to changes in the position of the sun and the corresponding daylight hours. In spring, light receptors in avian brains are stimulated and reproductive organs enlarge, releasing hormones which trigger a complex set of seasonal behaviors, including an urge of migrating birds to fly northward from wherever they have spent the winter. Their biological clocks have them returning to nesting grounds here and further north on predictable time schedules. Yet, if the earlier arriving migrants encounter a period of frigid or snowy weather once here, their instincts will not send them back south, and they may suffer near-starvation, or worse, in the inclement conditions. On into late summer, with the shortening daylight, sex hormones diminish, the desire for reproductive behavior ceases, and migrating species "follow" the retreating sun back southward.

Interestingly, there are a lesser number of bird species in the Southern Hemisphere that are also flying south as "our" northern visitors are doing so in our autumn. However, they are traveling to a far-southern stop, however, on their long seasonal journey to the lakes and rivers of Canada's north woods from perhaps as far south as the Gulf of Mexico. Like the Mergansers that had appeared weeks earlier, the Buffleheads are diving ducks that go underwater for food, rather than "dabblers" that feed mainly by dabbling their bills in the water's upper layer.

As with the waterfowl migrants, the olive-brown Ovenbird is another long-distance "runner" coming north from the Gulf Coast area, but this species regularly stays for the summer. A terrestrial wood-warbler, it has no interest in the water and shoreline area and is heard from the forest beyond or occasionally seen scurrying across the leaf-littered floor foraging for insects. I caught a rare glimpse of one in the low branches of the Hemlock outside the kitchen window, with its bold black streaks on white breast, a light brown back, and a thin orangish crown matted from the light rain. I was pleased with this ground nesting warbler's choice of "our" woods. Some day I hope to find the unusual nesting structure of this rather secretive species from which its name is derived: a small, domed-over hovel of grasses, little twigs, and leaves on the forest floor, looking like a Dutch oven, with a little side opening for an entrance to the cup nest inside.

The Eastern Wood-Pewee travels even further to grace "our" woods with its clear and plaintive calls. This flycatcher is one of more than one hundred species of birds who spend their winters in the tropics and mountain areas of Central and South America, but return to the forests and woodlands of eastern North America to breed and nest each spring. Labeled Neotropicals (as wintertime residents of the New World tropics), many of these long-distance migrants follow the Lake Michigan shoreline north.

As I listened intently and stalked the avian calls and songs for sightings to identify, it was a springtime revelation to learn that each of spring for breeding—and then returning north toward the equator for their wintering grounds during our spring.

In mid-May, two pairs of Scarlet Tanagers paused momentarily near the cottage on an overhanging Red Oak branch whose newly-emerging leaves were still too small to obscure the orange-red brilliance of the males. The beautiful songbirds fitted restlessly in the mist between the high perches of Pines and Oaks foraging for insects. Though soon out of sight, their nasal "chick-bing" call gave away a continuing presence in the surrounding woods throughout the morning until they moved on to some luckier landscape.

If by one chance in a million, I would see one of the Tanager males on its fall journey south to Central America, it would be hardly distinguishable from its mate. Like the female of the species, the previously intensely colored male would now be a drabber olive green, though its outer wing would still be black. Not all birds go through such a transformation, but all go through the process that, in many species, can bring a radically new attire—the molt of feathers.

Feathers are a body covering unique to birds, providing temperature regulation, protection, and coloration for display and camouflage, and, of course, are instrumental in flying. But these remarkable covering structures, weighing more than a bird's skeleton, periodically must be replaced. As with the beaks and claws of birds, feathers are composed of keratin, a family of insoluble, structural proteins. Keratins are widely used for body parts in the animal world, with the most familiar function being that of our hair and nails. While I periodically cut my proteinous hair and nails because they continuously grow and become too long, feathers, once fully grown, become shorter, damaged, and less functional and must then be dropped off with new ones

re-grown. Usually the worn feathers are replaced over a period of time in staggered fashion.

For those birds that change colors, their basic plumage occurs in winter, then, sometime in late winter to early spring, the beauty salon opens up and the birds emerge from a feather molt with their summer complexions for the breeding season. For the males of many species, the alternate plumage is especially bright for mating display. But once the demands of summer breeding cease and before a strenuous migration south begins, the energy and nutritionally demanding process of feather replacement once again occurs, though some species wait to molt until after they have reached their post-breeding wintering grounds. For those species that remain in or near the same area year around, their molts may not alter their basic appearance. Our resident gull species, for example, undergo no noticeable seasonal color change, male or female—nor is there coloration variation between the genders, and we can't tell which is which.

On an end-of-May walk in the duneland forest, I spotted a male American Redstart surprisingly high in a tall, slender Black Cherry tree. It fluffed its sleek Halloween orange and black attire, seemingly in greeting to me. Later that afternoon, I was granted another of my "first" sightings—a Hooded Warbler, a lower-dwelling insectivore, sitting atop brambles pioneering in a small clearing. It sang a clear, loud, and melodious song in support of spring's favors. A distinctive bird on limb with a black wrap-around hood and bib over brilliant yellow, it flashed its white-spotted tail in flight. I felt favored to view it—and grateful to those who spend a lifetime gathering the information I can read and learn so easily from the identification books when I return home. Eagerly, I added the Hooded Warbler to my growing list.

Many of these lovely, highly mobile creatures, commonly categorized as "songbirds" for their usually melodious vocalizations, are or just to scan the sky. It wasn't unusual to have company far above, with several of our gull neighbors circling over the water and the cottage area, gliding and maneuvering adeptly, often announcing their high-up presence with raucous calling.

Cuddling unobtrusively atop the bluff in the cool twilight of a June evening, now our usual ritual ending to a long day of chores, Doug and I reflected upon our experiences of a coastal spring, especially its welcomed relative calm, and how it had contrasted with the trauma of our first fall. The few beach walkers had already headed home, and as we lingered in the dimming light, a Red Fox and her three kits, now over two months old, ventured out from the frontal dunes to scavenge dead fish from the water's edge. The kits had left behind the days when food was brought to the den by doting, temporarily pair-bonded parents, days when they merely practiced playful pouncing with beetles, butterflies, and each other. Still puppy-like, the kits were learning now to forage for themselves and practice other adult behaviors. By six months they will need to find their meals of vole, rabbit, carrion, insects, or berries on their own. But this evening along the beach, romping still seemed of stronger interest.

Our perch was tucked low to the bluff crest, nestled near the Balsam Poplars, and we continued to sit patiently, at one with the landscape. As with the appearance of the vixen and her entertaining kits, we were often rewarded for that. Occasionally Deer came down out of the dunes in the evenings and warily crossed the expanding beach to briefly frolic in and out of calm waters, not ever knowing they were being intently observed as they came and went. Once, in early spring, twelve migrating Tundra Swans passed nearby in low, staggered, single-line formation. With necks outstretched in flight, the powerful rhythmic flapping of their wings fills the air with a tone like a heavy whistling, much as a strong wind moving through a narrow opening; and until more

threatened at both ends of their incredible journeys. The most common wintering grounds in the Caribbean and southern Mexico are undergoing massive deforestation. The vital forest breeding habitats of the summer range here in North America were greatly diminished during the past

two centuries with the extensive advance of human settlement. What was subsequently left of the great Eastern American Forest remained primarily in small sections—woodland fragments. While some of the forest cover has grown back, it is matched by increasing fragmentation of wooded areas elsewhere—and being ecologically diminished in the process. Biodiversity of native species in forest fragments is low in general and that includes songbirds. It has been found that the small areas disrupt the natural social behavior of Neotropical birds and reduces the breeding success of many of these migrants in several ways.

Over the past half-century, it has been documented that more than two dozen migratory songbird species have suffered long-term declines in population size. The most recent estimates by the Audubon Society are that more than a third of the 340 species of Neotropical migrants in the Western Hemisphere are experiencing ominous declines. In addition to habitat losses, migrants face many newer obstacles in their seasonal north-south marathon trips, such as flying into the vast array of human structures continually being erected into their flight paths, such as tall communication towers and wind generators of electricity. Collisions with such structures alone bring the untimely death of millions of birds annually. The concern is more than a loss of their intriguing songs and colors. If we don't insure a place for these Neotropical migratory insectivores, who will eat the gypsy moths and the tent caterpillars, the mosquitoes? Who will control the pestiferous insects?

The warm days and jacket-needy evenings of June tugged me out-of-doors continuously to work in the yard, to walk the shore and woods, recently, they were tagged "Whistling Swans." The smallest of the swan species—still with a wingspan of nearly six feet—some of the Tundra Swans follow this shoreline on their long flight from Chesapeake Bay to breeding waters in the treeless high Arctic.

During one cool period that discouraged human visitors to the shore, we watched from a distance through binoculars as a dozen Great Blue Herons ever so slowly waded the mouth of the creek to the north while the setting sun provided an ever-changing backdrop of amber, magenta, and lavender to highlight their elegant dark silhouettes. Only weeks earlier, these large migrants had arrived from their wintering wetlands in the southern half of the country. Unaware of our spying, as we handed our binoculars back and forth, the nearly four-feet-tall waders atop their stilt-like legs gracefully stalked supper in the shallow water for almost an hour. Ever so cautiously, each hunter waited motionless or slowly moved about, ready for the lightning stroke that spears the unsuspecting prey with a stiletto bill. Then, just before darkness blanketed them, the Great Blues silently drifted aloft on slow, powerful waves of their giant wings and, with necks drawn into an S shape while in flight, headed for the wetlands and nesting trees, just upstream and behind the dunes.

Spring is a continuous parade of little and not so-small marvels packaged in the evolved extravagances of nature. Here, for us, it has been a mostly private showing. Too soon, the winter-abandoned settlement of cottages south of the park was being sprinkled with the bright colors of flags, towels, and deck chairs—and then will come the noisy, polluting water toys. As summer's sun brings a migration of people to park and shore, solitude will too often disperse in its wake. For the moment, though, we sit in evening silences, and on nights not fully clouded over, watch the long sunsets in their varied and expansive displays above the vast, open lake stage. Only our planet, I have read, with its thick but transparent atmosphere, experiences the rich sky palette of colors that often transitions day to night. While Mars has a twilight, its thin gaseous envelope is incapable of producing a heavenly display like that of our unique world.

We are privileged beings here. And our day-ending delight begins after the glaring, blinding sun of daytime becomes a viewable reddish-orange ball in its approach to the horizon. One evening, we watched as unusual atmospheric conditions modified the setting globe into a squarish, glowing ziggurat as it settled down on the straight-lined edge of the far distant horizon, and then continued to change shape as it sank slowly behind the darkened watery stage. With the dipping of the sun out of view, the horizon gained a brilliant fiery glow, and the rich hues of twilight swept out across the sky canvas, with light, soft clouds high above us becoming tinged with pink and magenta, enlarging the display.

It takes clouds "sitting" above the horizon for the hidden sun's rays to paint upon to make a dazzling sunset, we've found. On such a huge stage, there is frequently so much beauty I have to turn my head from side to side and gaze up to take it all in. It can be overwhelming.

One time of lingering luxuriant twilight, a vibrant purplish haze stretched in a sky-wide horizontal band, matched by one of slightly different hue reflected upon the lake's vast liquid mirror, and between them was trapped a thin ribbon of aqua blue. Like the aqua ribbon, I felt wrapped in beauty, reluctant to relinquish the sensual feast of these waning days of long-awaited spring, our first beside the inland sea.

62

SEA

❦

Samuel de Champlain, French explorer and geographer, became the first European to describe the Great Lakes. Arriving on the shore of Lake Huron in 1615, expecting its vastness to be the Pacific Ocean, he tasted the water, found it was not salty, and entered into his journal that this was *la mer douce*—a sweet water sea. It is easy to understand why. In spite of the unsaltiness, their size and the dangerous conditions that can develop upon these lakes justify the designation of sea.

The breeze that skimmed across the sea-like water of Lake Michigan on this July day rippled the leaves of the Balsam Poplars rising in a broad clump from the rim of the bluff. There were now but eight slender trunks still standing, several others having fallen to the undermining of the last fall's erosion enemy. The outer roots of one upright tree clawed the air at the bluff edge where once they had clutched sand, but the hay bales we had hauled to the base ten months ago and the brush laid against the slope were continuing to stabilize the bluff and keep the remaining trees in place. Doug fastened a hammock between two of the larger Poplars, creating a shady retreat from summer's hot beach, a perfect cocoon for a bookworm.

I sat in the hammock's gentle swing, but I was not reading. I found it hard to concentrate on anything but the distant red and white triangle sliding smoothly across the blue expanse of water, propelled by that same force that helped shape the coastline. Son Derek and a high school friend he had invited to join us for this long Fourth of July weekend were sitting below a colorful sail in a Sunfish. The small sailing craft had belonged to the daughter of our next door neighbors, Bob and Toni, and they had recently offered it to Derek. For him, the timing could not have been more perfect. He had just read Thor Heyerdahl's *Kon Tiki*, and to learn to sail suggested adventure.

After an evening studying a booklet on the basics of sailing, and a half-day of practice, Derek captained his 13-foot craft with confidence. Too much, for my comfort. The Sunfish seemed but a dot on the immense lake. Where Derek saw adventure, I sensed danger. It was hard to separate my anxieties from his growing need to venture out on his own. Hard to let go. I fretted until my sailor glided silently into the shore. Hunger is my most reliable tether.

By this July of 1987, the lake level had continued to drop for more than half a year. This phenomenon was in tandem with eight consecutive months of record low precipitation in the Great Lakes basin, with higher than normal evaporation rates. These two factors, basin precipitation and overlake evaporation, are, according to our Corps of Army Engineer reports, the dominant influences upon lake levels. So, just as the water level had previously climbed unrelentingly during most of the preceding year, we were now experiencing the opposite condition. A complete turnabout that had this summer's water elevation, instead of normally rising this time of year, descending—and to a level that had not existed since well before starting our property search over two years ago. And with no major storms since the fading of the protective ice shelf to do damage, the beach was duly expanding, to our grateful relief.

But the very modest beachscape that lay between my hammock repose and the Poplar stand and the blue sea edge below was not the

topography of our shoreline area that had preceded the many months of rising lake levels and the accompanying severe erosion. Then, there had existed low, undulating foredunes with beach grass and other plants, the homes of insects and other creatures, between the shoreline and the bluff. Now, there existed merely a gradually broadening tan strand, flat, grassless, and generally lifeless, coming right up to the bluff toe. There was still plenty of stolen sand out there under the water. Would it be repatriated in due time? Or would there be yet another turnaround and watery steal? That possibility was always in our minds—not the deep worry of the past, but still a persistent concern.

As summer's sun warmed land and water, the lake's siren call beckoned us all. The public beach filled with frolickers, and boats dotted the horizon. It wasn't unusual to see people playing volleyball in the park on the new, flat sandy expanse. I, too, bared my toes and, like the Great Blue Herons, waded the shoreline shallows—not for food, but for the refreshing feel of cool water splashing against tired legs. With summer water temperatures often staying in the sixties, it is seldom warm enough for me to actually swim. Doug dons a suit about twice a summer. The professor, we were told, ceremoniously plunged, if only briefly, most afternoons from Memorial Day to Labor Day. We, however, depended less on the written calendar and more on nature's cues.

Normally, the lake is thermally stratified by the end of June. The bottom layer remains an almost constant cold. But, during July and August, the temperature of the upper layer climbs to its maximum. At this time, a week or two of intense sun warms the surface to seventy degrees or more and southerly breezes sweep this warmed water toward

our beach. Hurry in to take that dip! By the next morning, it may be chatteringly cold. If northeasterly winds appear, they will skim the warm layer from the top and hurry it toward Chicago. Upwelling currents then bring colder water from deeper down to fill the void, leaving the shallows of this eastern side chilly once more.

On any day, though, the lake provides visual enjoyment. It is a beautiful sea. Its color on a sun-filled midday is the Caribbean blue of a tourist brochure. The lake is not just a reflection of the sky above, but a different color of its own. The true color, of course, is clear. Few sediments mar clarity here. Extremely young by geologic measure, the lake is an oligotrophic body of water—cold and clear, sandy-bottomed, rich in oxygen, but nutrient-poor. As a consequence, it is relatively unpopulated by life that might add its own wash of color.

The alluring apparent color is a function of the physical properties of light and water—the refraction of light into the visible spectrum as it breaks the surface and the absorption of the longer wavelengths. Blue has a shorter wavelength and a higher rate of electron interaction than most colors. Thus, it is slowed down and deflected more. Deep, clear water allows the greatest penetration of light and the greatest deflection of blue wavelengths, creating the glorious shades we are treated to here. When the edges of blue waves end in spray, however, the light spectrum is scattered, and blue disappears into frothy white tips. In late afternoons of light breezes, refracted sunlight turns rippling water into a glorious sea of holiday sparklers.

Winds and barometric pressure play rather freely with surface water here. Friction between the moving and lighter air fluid and the denser lake fluid almost always is generating waves of one magnitude or another across the water surface. Occasionally, on a larger scale, the powerful interaction of the two fluids produces wind setups and seiches. Sustained strong winds can move surface water across the lake so that it tips or rises along the direction of the wind. The downwind side temporarily "sets up" with a higher level than the upwind shore. Sudden strong air movement and differences in barometric pressures can cause seiches—tsunami-like surging displacements of water from one side of the lake to the other. The lake level quickly raises several or more feet on the downwind shore, followed by the reflexive slosh back and forth, going through several oscillations as the liquid seeks its normal level. Our eastern side of Lake Michigan has seen seiches that have temporarily raised the level of water onto the shore as much as ten feet in a few hours.

The initial impact of higher seiches can be dangerous to small craft, fishermen, and bathers. All of the Great Lakes experience seiches, but one of the more deadly ones occurred on Lake Michigan in June of 1954. Powerful winds that quickly arose out of the northwest sent a six-foot surge of water against the Indiana shoreline at the lake's southern end. The rebound of the water was sent westward to the Chicago area, where it suddenly raised the shore area water level eight to ten feet and swept dozens of people from piers, drowning seven of them. Earlier seiche edge waves on the lake in 1929 and 1938 overcame beachgoers, drowning a total of fifteen swimmers.

There are also pronounced currents within the lake. This elongated body of water, second deepest of the five Great Lakes, is divided into northern and southern basins by the lake's most important geological feature—the Milwaukee Reef. This mid-lake reef formation creates a submerged dividing line across the lake, running roughly from Milwaukee on the west to between Grand Haven and Muskegon on the eastern shore, just a few dozen miles south of us. Within each large basin, a slow current of about four knots travels in a huge clockwise swirl. And then there is the action of the moon's gravitational pull on each of the five inland seas, resulting in tides. Although all of the lunar tides are quite small, Lake Michigan has the largest, with a rise and fall of 1.7 inches.

A variety of books and reports try to remove some of the mystery from this huge, ocean-like reservoir of glacial legacy, and, if one is to play in its midst, an understanding of its workings is important. For most of us, though, our knowledge is skimpy, and the phenomena remain outside our full comprehension. Time and again, this is a situation ripe for tragedy.

Such happened on a hot, sunny July afternoon just to the south of our cottage a number of years into our lakeside tenancy. With National

Weather Service small craft advisories in effect, boaters stayed in dock. Powered by a strong south wind, 7-foot seas surged at an angle to our sun-warmed shore. The constant crash of breakers filled the air, accented by boisterous squeals of joyful park bathers who, tempted by the muggy winds, mingled with the refreshingly invigorating surf.

Then, disturbing new sounds came to be heard above the roar of sea. Sounds that began in the distance and converged at the park beach. Sounds of trouble. Engine whining, a twenty-five-foot Coast Guard inflatable craft plowed the thrashing sea, coming south from Little Point Sable. A Muskegon diving team raced north along the shoreline in a four-wheeled beach craft. Then an emergency Aeromed helicopter thumped insistently overhead, scanning the near-shore waters in front of our beach, up and down, north and south.

The water is relatively shallow for quite a distance here, with the multiple rows of undulating, subsurface sandbars creating long runs of tumbling breakers, with the ordered motion of waves degenerating into turbulence. But the outer bars can suddenly drop off to a depth over a person's head. A man swimming in this day's strong surf some distance out had disappeared within them. No one had noticed him venture too far; no one had seen him slip beneath the foaming waves. When his wife turned to look for him, he was gone.

Because our dwelling sits more than a hundred feet back from the bluff edge and trees screen our view of the park beach, we were not at first cognizant of the unfolding drama. We did not fully understand it until after rescuers had found the man's body a quarter of a mile north, carried to within fifteen feet of the shore by the pounding waves.

That same afternoon, twenty miles to the south, a group of young people were playing catch in the frothing water. A stray toss landed lakeward, beyond the gathering of friends. The young man who went to retrieve the ball did not return.

Both men were unsuspecting victims of the lake's physics. Along the shore, strong surf is accompanied by a powerful retreating current of water that creates an undertow. On days of unrelenting waves, swimmers who move beyond the shallower water, who reach a spot where a sandbar drops abruptly to greater depths, can be pulled under by that current. Sadly, these two had not anticipated the overwhelming power of moving water under such conditions. Four years later, "riptides" and undercurrents claimed seven swimmers in one weekend at beaches further south along this coastline.

While I am drawn to the beauty of the lake, in living beside this great body of water I have learned it has many moods that demand respect. Again and again, year after year, others who also have been drawn to this enticing water world, to enjoy a few hours or a fun vacation, have suddenly met disaster. As the experienced Coast Guard Chief who participated in the search and rescue mission for the swimmer who drowned on that windy July day in our area declared: "I've grown to expect the worst from this inland sea they mistakenly call a lake."

Of course, mariners on the Great Lakes had long ago learned that lesson. "Freshwater is less dense than salt water, so lake waves rise quicker and run faster and can be harder for a boat to negotiate than the long rollers of saltwater seas," explains another man who has sailed the Lakes. For Lake Michigan especially, the stirred-up waters of this long north-south lake create unusually tempestuous waves with narrow and deep troughs between the crests that hamper normal maneuvering of boats, even by experienced hands. The number of craft and their human occupants lost upon this one great lake alone total in the thousands, many of these going down without a trace. An accounting of the twelve worst ship disasters on the Great Lakes up to 1950, based upon the

The two-masted sailing vessel had left Chicago the day before the snow-laden gale tore across the lake. Headed for its home port of Muskegon, the *Conway* was blown off course northward and ran aground on sand bars not far from shore, in a location we could easily have seen from our beach. Much of the boat was torn apart and debris, including its load of corn and oats, was later found widely scattered. Over the following weeks, corpses of the crew members were found along the shore to the south and north of the wreck, one body having gone into the mouth of the creek to our north where we had watched the Herons wade. The last crew member, not discovered until December, had to be cut out of the shore ice. "The witch of November [had] come stealin'".

As with other stretches of the eastern coastline of Lake Michigan, our shoreline vicinity witnessed the result of shipping disasters over a period of many decades. Only three years after the *L. J. Conway* tragedy, the local newspaper reported in early December, 1889, that "considerable lumber and square timbers has come ashore opposite this point [just to the north of our cottage area] this fall; also portions of vessels or steamers, which show that there have been wrecks at some point on the lake this season." In commenting on the number of shipwrecks, the paper's editor wryly added, "Plenty of 'em."

Could it be that the large square timber we briefly saw protruding from our bluff during the high lake water of September, 1986, was from the shipwreck debris reported in the 1886 or 1889 newspaper stories? The very high levels of 1886 would have eroded the shoreline at the time and

number of lives lost, revealed that nearly half had occurred on Lake Michigan, more than on any other of the lakes

The most casualty-laden era was in the 1800s, when smaller, wooden sailing ships and early steamers were the norm for carrying cargo and passengers. "Last week...witnessed one of the worst storms that has swept Lake Michigan this long while, and the haulocaust [sic] of marine disasters is appalling," was a report in mid-November, 1886, from an early local newspaper in our area. Incomplete tallies at the time had the loss of ships and cargo at over a quarter-million dollars and forty-two lives. One of the disasters of that "wild November gale" occurred just a mile or so north of the cottage, with the wreck of the schooner, *L. J. Conway*, and the drowning of its crew of five.

prepared the way for the depositing of debris inland where the timber we saw was entombed in the bluff sand. If not in the falls of 1886 or 1889, it was surely some other time in that period of commonly occurring shipwrecks—coinciding with a high lake level—that the timber would have been strewn up on what was then a lonely beach extending many yards inland from the base of today's bluff.

I enjoy the lakescape; I am usually enthralled by its ever changing drama, but am now deeply aware that its playlist includes tragedy as well as happy offerings. I am not tempted to venture far from the shoreline into this aquatic environment. I prefer to stay where I can still feel the sand between my toes. When Derek and Jovan and friends take to the sea, I warn and worry. Water is the first element of life; it can also bring life's end.

SAND

On the Fourth of July, a small community of cottages some distance north of us and beyond Big Flower Creek positioned their holiday festivities such that the fireworks were visible from our beach. Encouraged by the pleasant, light sweater evening, Doug and I set beach chairs in the sand beside neighbors Bob and Toni to view the performance. With the sun at the furthest northern reach of its annual path, and clocks set for Daylight Saving Time, the ten o'clock beginning of the aerial fireworks show at this northern latitude came before dark had settled over the lake.

The bursting colors of human-launched explosives against the long, lingering twilight of the early summer sky held our attention for only minutes. The four of us soon realized that the sky itself, a vast panorama stretching over the vast water, had captured our gaze. The developing dazzling displays of brilliant reds and fuchsia from sunset's afterglow, with later blushes of pink and lavender, so riveted our attention that focus upon the somewhat distant human attempt at aerial splendor and bombast was all but forgotten—lost in the expanse of compelling vibrant sky. As twilight deepened, the delighting colors shifted, delicately tinted cloud layers imperceptibly moved, and the lighter blue overhead richened and then darkened keeping the celestial show new as it played out in slow motion for nearly half an hour. Unmatchable are these summer twilights over the lake we have found—perhaps, the grandest and most gorgeous displays of magnificence possible.

The evening of celestial beauty capped a special day for celebration—the nation's birthday, and mine. The fact that we now had enough beach for sitting could be added to the celebratory reasons.

Having weathered the minor storms of winter and spring, the bluff had suffered no loss of sand other than some surface slide to the base, as the slope sought its natural angle of repose. And as our first summer beside this inland sea progressed, and the water level continued its abnormal decline for the period, more and more of a beach face was being exposed with the water's retreat. Summer waves were also continuing the process of carrying suspended sand onto the broadening expanse, adding fresh layers as they rolled up the gradual incline, dropping their miniscule load, and sliding back down. We fervently hoped this dual beach-building process would persist in putting more of a safety zone between the often restless water and our bluff.

One warm, calm day, I brought a magnifying glass to study the myriad pieces of miniature rock accumulating on the gentle slope of our beach. I have walked several beaches and know they do not all look the same. Florida's Gulf coast is white; some California coastal sand is gray. I have read that certain beaches along the Oregon coast are green, and volcanic Hawaii has some black shorelines. Color is determined by the type of material that erodes to form the small granules. The material varies, but it's all considered sand by its particular diminutive size, regardless of its composition, color, or source of origin.

Sand of Michigan beaches and dunes appears light tan from a distance, but a close examination of the individual grains showed a rich mixture of colors and minerals. As I picked up a handful and let the tens of thousands of particles fall through my fingers, I sifted the product of these summer twilights over the lake we have found—perhaps, the grandest geologic processes that began millions of years before.

Michigan sand is predominantly (87-94 percent) composed of translucent quartz, understandably so, for quartz is made from the two most plentiful elements of the earth's crust—silicon and oxygen. Our Michigan sand has a lot of company, for close to seventy percent of all sand on the planet is composed of silicon dioxide. It had its ancient beginnings in crystalline igneous bedrock that resulted from the patient, millennia-long cooling of magma deep underground. Coming out of the depths, and over eons, some of it reformed into the sedimentary and metamorphic rocks of granite, sandstone, and quartzite. At least four times during the Pleistocene Age, massive, miles-thick glaciers moved southward across the northern portion of the continent, gouging, scraping, crushing and grinding rock, then leaving it when retreating north each time in piles of rubble which confound the ability to conclusively count the ice incursions.

Distributed further by post-glacial river flows, lake currents, and wind and wave, now a portion of that same ancient quartz, in infinitesimally huge numbers of very small pieces, rests upon our beach, coats the nearshore bottom in undulating forms, and is spread for miles inland. Beyond the coastal dunes, the glacial legacy of sand is so enormous and extensively spread throughout Michigan that the state has been described as "a big sandbox."

Weathered from the granite, sandstone, and quartzite of glacial till, the smoothly rounded, frosted grains flow silkily through my fingers when dry, pat to a fine smoothness when wet, and in-between, when barely damp, fluff to a soft meringue. Once worked down by the ravages of time to sand size, these quartz particles, hard and very resistant to chemical attack, will be extremely persistent, withstanding further most natural forces that might seek to disintegrate them.

The remaining ten percent or so of the granular materials of this beach provides the depth of color with flecks of light brown, sienna, iron red, green, white, and black—minute pieces of minerals weathered from rocks containing feldspar, epidote, garnet, hornblende, calcite, magnetite, ilmenite, orthoclase, zircon, and tourmaline. Names evocative of beauty and mystery. Many are silicates, combinations of the plentiful quartz and various other elements. Wind and, to a lesser extent, moving water have battered and rounded and sorted the varied sand grains over the ages so that now fine particles of one-fourth to one-half millimeter predominate on the beach.

At times, a second type of sorting occurs. Angled waves sometimes will cut away at the shoreline, leaving a vertical face, and there I have found horizontal stripes of tan, burnt red, and black along the cut edge—proof of water's ability to sort and settle out minerals by their densities. The black sand, twice as heavy as the durable quartz, easily settles out and is visible most frequently in streaks or bands in the wet zone of the beach. It is very fine and sticks to my feet like an oil slick (which originally I thought it was), but it is my favorite. After collecting and drying a mix of sand, we give visiting children the task of separating the black grains from the other colors—easy work with the help of a magnet. The children's efforts are for the fun of watching the black grains with a metallic luster readily jump from the mix.

The black sand is magnetite, an iron-rich oxide mineral that quickly clings to the magnet, for the black grains themselves are magnetic, the most so of all naturally occurring minerals on earth. But the ferricmagnetic mineral is more than a beachside curiosity. It is an important iron ore, common and widely-distributed around the globe, and used in many industrial processes. As with the origin of quartz sand, magnetite came long ago from the bowls of the planet.

Of greater interest to me is the biological functioning of magnetite. Migratory birds use the earth's magnetic field as one of their orientation and navigational aids in their wondrous long-distance journeys. Unlike the sun and star positions also used by birds for finding their way, but not always visible, the magnetic field is continually available. But to be geomagnetic avian navigators requires some sort of internal magnetic compass, which in turn necessitates a magnetic substance in birds. Not many years before we came to our sandy beach of varied ingredients, it was discovered that one of those granular constituents, magnetite, in tiny crystals, was the magnetic material that was aligned in the heads of many bird species, enabling them to navigate using the earth's magnetic field. In addition, this ferricmagnetic mineral has been found in the brains of bees, termites, fish—and humans. Quite a connection for this component of our sandy landscape.

As the new accretion to the beach continued, the summer sun and winds readily dried the tan surface. And there was now our enhanced realization that wind, which generates both the powerful waves that steal sand and those gentler ones that grudgingly give it back, can also directly move it around, constructing or deconstructing on various scales. We occasionally watched westerly winds, which must blow at least eight miles per hour, transport sand across the beach toward the bluff base. Coarser grains might just roll along the surface in an action called "creep." Medium and finer particles would be lifted by the wind and bounce across the surface, colliding into more sand in a chain reaction known as "saltation," a process largely responsible for most sand transport. These violent impacts are also largely responsible for knocking off the rough edges of the grains. Having become relatively rounded and smooth, the sand granules are further resistant to abrasion—and to becoming smaller.

When winds hit the dry beach at an angle, as is most often the case, the surface sand moves either up or down the beach, somewhat parallel to the shoreline—with some of the blowing grains coming to rest against driftwood and other objects and a portion gradually easing its way inland to the bluff base. With sustained, strong, dry winds coming at an angle, working their way along the beach, sometimes finer particles become airborne, accumulating and remaining in suspension as they ride inches to a foot or more above the surface. Joining the other traveling grains, energetically bouncing along by saltation, the particles become a visible moving haze. A miniature sandstorm! There have been times when walking the shoreline, with very strong winds of nearly gale force at our back, we could not return facing into the wind because that granular rock came blowing into our eyes. Retreat was accomplished by walking backwards or up into the dunes, away from the windswept beach.

Thin lines in the picture are tracks of numerous grains of airborne sand being blown away by a strong wind from the little natural sand sculptures on the beach.

Sand is magical. Joining up with wind and/or water, it forms expanses of flat beaches, undulating dune fields, and an unending, shifting variety of curvaceous shapes in deserts. Sand accumulations offer, along bodies of water, some of the more inviting lounging places humans seek out, as well as presenting some of the most inhospitable environments on earth to enter. Extremely hard as individual grains, yet forgiving in aggregate. Soft when I scope it up, either wet or dry, from the beach, it can be transformed into solid rock under great compression. When grains of quartz sand have become well-rounded and smooth, as upon our beach, they are capable of producing sounds—"singing" and "booming"—when displaced under dry conditions.

My bare heels rubbing across dry sand when walking the shoreline can create squeaking noises, sometimes called "singing" or "whistling." Scientists have determined that the compression of treading on dry sand, in which the granules are quickly forced down and out, produces friction emissions of high-frequency, musically pure notes, of very brief duration—the squeaks I hear. In deserts on this continent and across the globe, shifting sands in large dune fields can emit sounds of great variety. Avalanches, in what are called "booming" dunes, produce acoustic reverberations that can be either low or quite loud and can sound like musical instruments, drums, cannon fire, thunder, moans, and a host of other noises that last from seconds to minutes.

In late winter, there can be rare combinations of elements working upon our beach sand that conjure up remarkable little sculptures. Small areas of the sandbed become a stationary potter's wheel when the moist granules have frozen. And, then, with a slight warming, the wind begins

76

carrying away the unfrozen, dried sand from around more solidly frozen clumps. Carved by the wind-potter's shaping force, an unbelievable array of small forms is brought forth at different times as the surrounding dry detritus continues to be blown away. Varying works of art emerge from differing conditions. The sculpting wind can be lazy, leaving only fields of miniature "dune" humps or tiny boulders, or be far more creative, producing pointed and truncated cones, cylinders, pyramids, "pancakes," "chocolate drops," and a "village" of little round, pointed-top "huts." The most amazing we're seen have been beautiful pointed "toadstools" with flared skirts, "growing" forth from the drifting sand.

Once, on the south side of the creek outlet to the north of us, the piled sand just back from the water's edge was being worn down by the ever-active wind. Coming upon the site, we were for the moment lucky

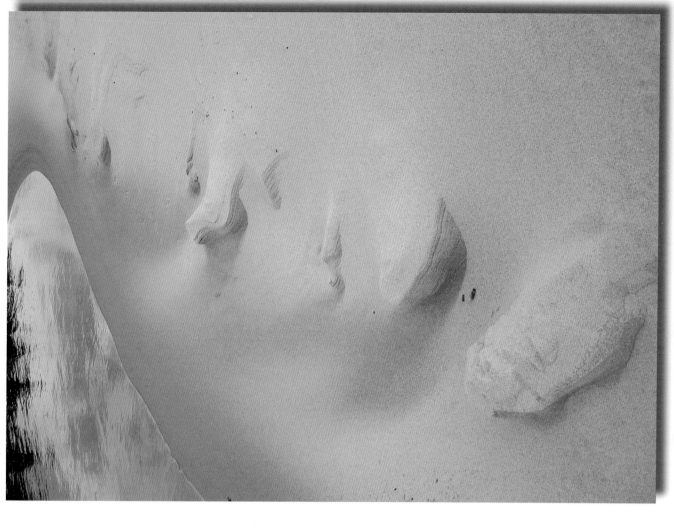

"Ancient stoneworks" being uncovered from the "drifting sands of time."

"archeologists." As the granules were being blown away, there remained several portions of compressed sand that protruded out from the pile like the eroded stone blocks from an ancient building of a past civilization—now being uncovered from the drifting sands of time. The newly revealed, rounded-off "stone blocks of ages past," however, were creations of conditions of but only months or a few years ago. Come stronger winds or a rain, and the "ruins" would quickly be no more.

So commonplace is sand, yet so marvelous. And isn't it somewhat ironic that the glacial ice, that did the gouging, scraping, crushing, and grinding of very hard rock to create the soft sand I walk upon, started out as soft-fallen snow? And, further, that infinitely huge numbers of tiny snow crystals begat infinitely large numbers of tiny sand grains?

The long period of above-average precipitation and record high lake levels that had set the stage for our residency along the shoreline in the preceding year continued to send reminders our way. During that period, rains had sent many items—some natural, some human-made—down swollen rivers into the lake. And the periodic high-water storm waves, generated over many months, had stolen much from unprotected shorelines, until the coming of the ice shelf. With that shoreline barrier's demise and the retreating of the lake level, the booty was free to come ashore all along the sandy coast. Through spring and summer, and for months afterwards, waves continually brought a share of the varied flotsam to our area, washing it upon the broadening beach.

Years of working with recycling programs made Doug a natural beachcomber. He came back from walks with arms and pockets full—and often something on his shoulder or dragging behind him. Smaller wood pieces, smoothed and fashioned by their endless tumbling in the surf and sand, provided interesting shapes. Logs were used as slanted fins on the beach to direct windblown sand toward the bluff. Boards were set out in the sun to dry for construction use. Larger driftwood pieces became seats on the beach or sculptures in the cottage yard. A long spire-like piece was planted not far from the hammock and became a favored perch for birds just back from the bluff edge. During one period, we were continually finding tennis balls washed up on the beach. Where did these come from? For me, the best wave gift was a cable-stitch sweater of periwinkle blue. Washed, it found a place in my drawer of favorite things to wear. Unfortunately, a lot of what we removed from the beach was outright trash—even to a recycler.

Over the years, we occasionally had found small pieces of broken glass from bottles on the Lake Michigan public beaches that we visited. The once clear, sharp objects had become frosted with rounded edges. We were surprised then to realize how abrasive moving sand can be. The hard glass, itself having been made almost entirely from quartz sand, had been tumbled in the water along the sandy shoreline and then scoured by wind-driven sand after being left high and dry on the beach—sandblasted, in effect. We now collected and accumulated these little oddities during our beach walks, with the frosty pieces of various colors ending up on a cottage shelf in a long narrow tray that Doug fashioned from a section of cupped driftwood. A real find was frosted deep-blue glass, such as came from the old Milk of Magnesia bottles and colored by the hard, brittle metallic element, cobalt. As the years went by, both the cottage and our small Indiana residence came to be a little over-decorated with "found art."

section of the bottom of an old wooden boat became exposed at the mouth of Little Flower Creek, which flows through the park on our south side. Truncated ribs poked out from the keel—perhaps the shipwrecked remains of a schooner from another century's terrible storm. The local newspaper was notified, but there wasn't enough of the wooden skeleton to identify it, and subsequent turbulent events buried it once again.

Huge logs that had been churned from former landing or burial spots at distant eroded beaches wandered along the lake's coastline, and occasionally one washed ashore at our location. We saw possibilities in these, and a few times even waded out to direct a floating carcass to our beach. One weekend, two young lads from the park had commandeered a five-foot-long section of an old tree trunk that had appeared out in the low surf. The smooth log was nearly thirty inches thick and cut flat at both ends. The boys came bobbing along atop this half-submerged raft in front of us, and Doug offered them a dollar apiece for the derelict log. They readily accepted, and we all brought it to the water's edge. As the four of us struggled in the dry, soft sand to roll it bluffward, luckily, a pair of sturdy teenaged boys happened along the beach, ones eager to show their manly strength. In joined, strenuous effort, our assembled team gradually rolled the bulky item up the beach incline, away from the water's reaching grasp. Sometime later we moved it further inland, upended it into a hole in the sand in front of the bluff, and had a fine new beach perch.

Infrequently, the main portions of sizeable trees would appear along the shoreline, shorn of most branches and usually bark naked. These might float on by nearly submerged, but at times one would end up at the shore's edge, the splayed out root stock caught in the sand on the bottom, and the top roots sticking upward like arched arms appealing for help. The trunks, some nearly up to twenty feet long, might be pointed out into the lake or lay alongside the water's edge. As often as not, the next big wave event would lift it away from the shore and send

Storms are a beachcomber's delight, sometimes in a big way. After one particular event that shifted shoreline sand around, a 10-foot skeleton it to someone else. At other times, large waves would repeatedly lift the wooden mass and forward it, foot by foot, further upon the beach, where it might spend years cooking and freezing in cycles before being entombed with drifting sand. Very likely this had been the story of the large timber momentarily sticking out from our bluff.

Boat sections, trees, boards, clothes, fishing gear, auto tires, hypodermic needles, a dead deer, and a multitude of other debris—even once a car fender—have all ended up along the shoreline in our vicinity. We've hauled away what we could. And as the parade of varied items appeared during the higher water years, particularly, it dawned upon us that the shoreline and beach have always been an on-going dumping ground and ancient, sandy graveyard. Thankfully, not always including human debris.

As our first seaside summer transitioned into our second autumn, we were pleasantly amazed to find the lake level continuing to decline at a relatively fast clip. By the end of September, 1987, the water level was two feet below that of a year ago—and just one foot above its average level for this time of year. But we could never really feel at ease. An extended rainy period could once again bring lake levels up and reverse the welcomed downward trend. We had now seen it go both ways in a relatively short time; why couldn't extreme conditions as quickly return, we persistently reasoned. So, watching the capricious lake level continued to be one the main focal points of our attention as we advanced into our second year.

The beach that had been forming in the past half year was generally a scalloped one, cutting in at one place, and a little down the shoreline, swooping out a ways before curving back inland. In many stretches, the sandy ribbon would be no more than twenty-five feet deep, although at the park, with its larger forward dunes and greater abundance of sand, the beach there was usually at least twice that width. With still no wide expanse of exposed sand, we wondered at first why the high waves generated out on the lake didn't have a full runup on the beach incline. The apparent answer soon dawned upon us.

Most of the stolen sand was still out there underwater, in a series of parallel sandbars. And, with the significantly lower water level, they were not that far below the surface. During the summer, we could wade out some eighty feet and more on calm days and still be only waist deep in water, standing on a bar. It became evident to us that the powerful deepwater waves coming landward were running into that series of low underwater "dunes," expending their energy in sending water splashing upward, before rolling onto the beach, greatly subdued. This phenomenon harkened back to the taming effect of early winter's ice shelf formation. Scalloping of the beach was due to those waves coming at the shore at an angle. In both cases, waves smashing into those offshore bars were blasting sand forward to the shoreline, carrying the granules in suspension, with some being deposited—gratefully, from our viewpoint—onto the beach with each runup.

Like a great grandfather clock, eternally swinging its time-keeping pendulum back and forth, the in and out of the waves over the shore sand goes on and on. Unlike the clock, the beat is varying, sometimes strong and at other times nearly stilled, but the rhythm is one of eons, ever since there have been seas and land. A complete ice covering may hide the watery movement for a cold moment, but underneath is a throbbing heartbeat.

With autumn settling in, the sea level still continued its months-long decline, reflecting closely, for the first time in more than two years, what would be its "typical" seasonal activity. Gratefully, Doug and I welcomed the slowly extending tan beach follow the receding water line.

And while assessing that environment, we became aware that the mobile, wind-transported sand was collecting in piles against numerous driftwood pieces scattered about on the beach, sometimes even covering them completely and leaving little humps on the flat sand bed. And as the wind blew inland across the growing beach, eolian sand was gradually building up against the bluff base, beginning to bury the hay bales and forming low sloping mounds in front.

It occurred to us that we were now observing the beginnings of dune building, on a miniature scale, of course, but geologic activity, nevertheless, at work right before our eyes—and working in our favor.

Fantastic! And were we not also getting a lesson in the construction process for the past creation of the massive coastal duneworks serving as the backdrop for our current frontal dune birthing?

For the sand building at hand, how could we mere humans get into the mix and hurry it along, we wondered. From feverishly putting up bluff-side defenses our first fall season, we were now contemplating, an extremely eventful year later, how to establish an offense, outward onto the beach. We wanted to see more of that magical sand spread out and piled up in front of the bluff!

SUCCESSION

Through fall and winter and into the early spring of 1988, the water level graciously continued to decline, the wind was to blow without any damaging storm events, the beach expanded, and the sun-dried and wind-blown sand continued to build up against the sloped bluff, fully entombing the hay bales. A wind that during our beginning shoreline residency was seen as Shiva the Destroyer was now Brahma the Creator, a rebuilding force in our favor.

Learning from the natural embryonic dune building, we sought to hurry along the process of beach sand accumulation in the months after the ground had been released from its winter freeze. Purchasing snow fencing once again, we began our newly devised offensive strategy by staking several fifty-foot fence sections from the near beach to part way up the bluff face. Spaced roughly fifty feet apart, the slatted-fence lines were placed perpendicular to bluff and water. The goal was to entrap as much sand as possible as it blew up and down the beach.

The method began to work immediately, and, with the additional strategic placement of boards and collected driftwood pieces here and there on the beach, we were getting the rudiments of low foredunes faster than we could see elsewhere along the shoreline. As the drifting sand gradually built up against the placed impediments, we periodically pulled the porous wind fencing up so it wouldn't be buried, but would continue to entrap sand.

With that project underway, a cautious optimism about the shoreline scene began to prevail, and Doug commenced in our second April to build a small sitting and observational deck at the top edge of the bluff with a 32-foot-long stairway down to the beach, with younger son, Derek, helping on one weekend. It was definitely an act of hope, for we remembered that Bob and Toni had twice lost smaller bluff stairways to high-water waves just two years earlier.

As 1988 progressed, we were increasingly encouraged, for the lake level, after May, persisted in its somewhat amazing descent until it was near its long-term average by the end of the year, something that hadn't occurred for a decade. Parallel to the retreat of the water was the ongoing gradual growth of the beach landscape, both outward and upward. Again learning from natural processes (and some shoreline management publications), it appeared to us that we could further help the establishment of foredunes by placing select vegetation amidst the newly accumulating sand.

With sore backs and sunburned faces bearing witness to our labors, we accomplished the planting of native beachgrass one surprisingly warm day in early April of 1989, one stalk at a time. A thousand pieces of dead-looking grass plants, acquired from the area's Soil Conservation Service, were shared with the two property owners to our north. To plant our 400 pieces of grass, Doug used a narrow spade, stabbing into the lower bluff slope, then pulling forward, as he dropped one plant into the slightly moist sand behind the blade. Working along the emerging foredunes, I wielded a broken broom handle instead, making a foot-deep hole in the sand to receive the fifteen-inch stalks. Over the next months, hundreds of stems of lifeless-looking beachgrass eventually greened, rooted, and began to send up new shoots spreading outward.

We had planted Marram (American beachgrass), the most prominent and important colonizer of foredunes of the Great Lakes and along Atlantic Coast beaches. A dune-builder, the grass grows in clumps, several feet high, "catching" wind-blown sand grains and creating mounds around themselves. The Marram clumps inhibit further shifting of the caught sand with a rapidly spreading mat of net-like roots and rhizomes just below the surface. Then, fresh, spike-like shoots spread outward and stab through to light and begin to establish new clusters in each direction. These perennial clumps continue to extend their stems further upward, persistently outgrowing the accumulating sand. The outward and upward reach is matched by the growth of long, wiry roots deep into the sand in search of moisture—further stabilizing the piling up of the drifting granules. As long as there is beach area and a supply of sand to be swept along by the wind, Marram grass and foredunes grow together, advancing toward the water like an imperceptibly crawling, expanding mass. New terra firma—for a while, at least.

In their second year, tall seed stalks developed, emerging from the center of the grass clumps and rising above the mounds of narrow leaf blades. At their tips, greenish brushes up to one foot in length hung full of a powdery pollen in August that turned into the color of a golden wheat in fall.

Another spring planting of 500 Marram stalks the following year led to an impressive result of helping stabilize our bluff and in assisting the development of young foredunes. This time, we extended our planting a distance into the park, where the higher bluff there was still not stabilized. Throughout the winters, we viewed the rich amber color of the nearly three-foot-tall Marram clusters on the hummocks they created, a welcome reminder of their faithful service.

By the end of our fourth summer, 1990, low, undulating, and vegetated foredunes with soft contours had arisen along the inland expanse of the still enlarging beach. We had joined the "geologic forces" at hand and augmented their creating of a new topography. Although our efforts were meager in the grander scheme of things, it felt good to be working (as we saw it) with nature. As the ever-spreading beachgrass streaked the bluff and the young foredunes with green, other vegetation took hold as well. And each new plant provided another resting place for wind-blown sand, furthering the development of the emerging forward duneworks.

The coming forth of a new land form and associated vegetation upon the expanding beach brought the realization that there were a series, a succession, of different "zones" that stretched from the water back to the far end of our particular coastal property—all within the

350-foot depth of the lot. And with the new, miniature dunal formations and the appearance of plants previously unknown to me, I began to take closer note of our landscape's distinctive botanical makeup. Keeping a journal, I catalogued various species that seemed to define each of the environmental zones. My notepad and several vital field guides that enabled me to identify the many plants I did not recognize were seldom shelved, ever laying ready on the cottage table by the door. And considering all that came to be observed and studied, we could think of no other landscape presenting as many environmental changes in such a short distance as does a march inland from the lake's edge here.

My walking the beach barefoot in warmer weather always includes taking in the first zone. It is the flat, constantly wet and varying "swash" zone, or wet beach, where the water eternally rides in and out and nothing in way of vegetation has a chance to grow. Continually changing as water level and wave action vary, it is a feeding area for many shorebirds, with incoming waves dropping small mollusks, remains of fish, and other food items as the water flows back lakeward.

While an impossible habitat for vegetation, the swash is inhabited. My magnifying glass can't detect the microscopic creatures, but I have read, to my great surprise, that there are probably hundreds of species here within the wet sand—many kinds of bacteria and other organisms that have names seemingly from science fiction stories. They are designated as *meiofauna*, survive in a very difficult world, and are like no other group of living things. We should be extremely grateful for them as none of us would likely want to walk the beaches if these unseen organisms were not at work. For as geologist Michael Welland has observed: "Without meiofauna, the sands of our beaches and lakeshores would be stinking, toxic places, with organic debris rotting unconsumed and dangerous bacteria rampant. The microscopic creatures of the meiofauna feed off this debris: they keep our beaches clean."

The normally narrow and mercurial swash zone is a transition between the sea and the dry beach. In what I see as something of an oddity, this vast body of water exists beside a desert-like zone. At least some of the time, for when the lake level is low enough to provide for a sizeable dry beach, the hot summer sun can bake the sand to temperatures too hot for me to walk on barefoot. While this zone is relatively flat, the wind shifts the dry sand around, mounding it against objects in its way, sweeping some further inland to make foredunes, and occasionally creating low sandstorms, all as in a desert. There are times on some summer afternoons I just don't want to be out there in that hot, arid environment.

Usually a harsh habitat, with its temperature extremes, strong winds, and absolutely nothing that we would normally call soil, few plants can take hold on the dry mineral sand bed. I had previously become familiar with the brave little Sea Rocket that springs forth in sparse plantings, the lone species to early appear in this beach zone. It is able to withstand that hostile environment—sun-baked in the summer, frozen in the winter—but for a short growing season, with the water-holding capacity of its succulent stems and leaves. No perennials can sustain themselves in such a desert-like and oft-changing environment.

Out of the desert sands of the drift beach arise the eolian foredunes, only a little less desert-like, just a little less dynamic an environment than the wet and dry beach zones. Hot or cold, if the dry beach is indeed dry, wind can do its building of dunal structures. These low forward dunes are formed and destroyed on a cyclic, though irregular, basis, depending upon lake levels, as we were now well aware. The dry beach and foredunes are highly active zones. Geology works fast here.

Some time in the mid-1960s, during the century's historic low lake levels, a telling photograph was taken of William and Erna's new sand, leaving a sheared-off 18-foot-tall dune face that is our bluff. Now the sand dune drama was playing out a new restoration act. And we could understand that the story of sand cycling back and forth between the sea and the land was not just one for our time, but one for the ages.

Although we had hurried our foredune growth with snow fencing and the planting of Marram grass, elsewhere, up and down along much of the shoreline, the same development was soon after occurring. The combination of eolian sand transport and the emergence of the "pioneer" Marram grass species was slowly providing new beach formations. On its own, Marram colonizes beaches from remnants left after dune destruction, from rhizomes snatched from one area and water-carried to another shore location, and from seeds dispersed by wind and water. Once established, these living "sand fences" are tenacious, capable of sending their root tendrils deep into the foredunes they are helping to create where the roots can absorb silica, the material of quartz sand itself, to strengthen the tall green blades against the blowing, abrasive sand. Burial stimulates vegetative growth, and the slightly more hospitable growing conditions provided by a field of Marram grass encourages additional plant species to take hold in the foredunes.

Following the establishment of Marram grass and the foredunes, other species sturdy enough to survive this slightly less harsh environment were cataloged. One was Sand Cress, deceptively fragile in appearance, with a fine, ten-inch stem rising from a low rosette of toothed leaves, and one of the first bloomers, with tiny white flowers in late May and early June. Splotches of slender Sand Reed Grass later appeared among the older mounds of Marram. It, too, is an early colonizer and stabilizer of new sand formations, but unlike the Marram grass, which is endemic to sandy coastlines, Sand Reed Grass is widespread across the continent and really a prairie plant, preferring open sandy soils. As

lakeshore home, now our cottage. From out on a wide beach, somewhere near the water's edge, the sunny scene looks back to the Chalet (and Bob and Toni's A-frame) with the intervening duneworks in the foreground. In the pictured landscape, there is no drop off of a bluff, no need for a

32-foot-long stairway for getting down to the beach area. The piled sand just rolls down from the higher location in easy, stretched-out, undulating slopes of low foredunes down to the beach zone—just right for a nice stroll to the water. Extensive foredunes here two decades before we came to the lakeshore—totally absent when we arrived.

Our guess is that hundreds of tons of those foredunes of the mid-1960s were destroyed in the succeeding decade during the high lake level period of 1972-77. And the rest were washed away not long afterward, as the water rose even higher in the historic lake years of 1985-86. Then, absent the intervening foredunes, eroding waves ate away at the higher

a tall, hardy prairie grass, it is sod-forming and is grazed by cattle and cut for hay—not a plant I would expect to also emerge amidst lakeside foredunes.

Inland of the low hillocks of sand, where conditions had become a little more stable, appeared the gray-green Wormwood, finding welcoming spots at the lower slope of the bluff. Growing as a solitary item, Wormwood produces tubular, greenish-yellow flowers in July. Its stalks reflect the hot sunlight off tiny hairs that cover the bitter stems and leaves, an adaptation designed to retain moisture.

Moving up to atop the bluff and immediately behind is the beginning of the dunes proper, a fourth zone, with a far larger array of plants—and all but a few different—than in the shoreward zones. Not much disturbed by erosion, except where the bluff edge had lost several yards, many of the species were well established prior to our coming, although the wealth of vegetation did increase as our residency went by. One of the seemingly new species came riding the upper edge of the bluff several years after its stabilization, with a few isolated splatterings of bright, deep yellow. A June decoration, Hairy Puccoon presents clusters of flowery tops and clumps of fuzzy, drought-resistant stems in the form of a small bush. A plant also of dry prairie sites, the rather cute "puccoon" designation comes from a Native American word for plants that yield dyes, as puccoon roots produce a reddish-purple color.

About a month later, another yellow-flowered species of eighteen to twenty-four inches appeared, four-petaled rather than the five of the Puccoon, and with a pronounced x-shaped stigma. Evening Primrose opened as its name implies, sharing its light-yellow color with late-in-the-day walkers, like myself. It wasn't long before it began to descend down the upper bluff slope.

No question about it, the rich yellow of the Hairy Puccoon makes it the brightest, cheeriest flower of the dunescape.

Delighted with the new growth from the beach inland, and desperate to protect this hard-won vegetation, Doug and I gave patient explanations of the problems of erosion and the process of dune-building to park beach walkers who strayed from water's edge and headed over the new foredunes or who let large, untethered dogs run duneward, sometimes bounding up and down the bluff slope. Trampling shifts sand downward and tears tender connecting roots, preventing new vegetation from becoming adequately established on fragile slopes and in loose sand.

Education is a slow, time-consuming process—a realization we brought with us by profession. Some people listened intently and apologetically; others gave ear without seeming to care, and moved on. A few argued loudly, claiming even privately-owned beaches and foredunes as public space and thus available for them to use as they chose, even with recreation ("wreck-creation") vehicles. In reality, the public's rights of passage are restricted to pedestrian uses, within definite limits, along Michigan's Great Lakes beaches.

As for ourselves and our visitors, we all moved up and down our 18-foot-high bluff face only on the stairway Doug and Derek had carefully constructed, proceeding to the water along a short, winding path through the growing foredunes. The stairway, elevated slightly above the sandy incline, came to catch blowing sand and helped stabilize the slope at that location, encouraging plant establishment. And, at the top of the stairs, near the edge of our small deck, there appeared a plant known as Scouring Rush—so named because its thin, bamboo-like green stems, abundantly coated with gritty silicate particles, made them useful to pioneers for scrubbing and cleaning utensils. Earlier, Indians used the rough, abrasive stems to polish wooden tools. And the Japanese still use the extracted silicates for fine polishing of wood.

Scouring Rushes are a type of Horsetails, the most primitive of the ancient fern families. This particular species is all upright stems, its primitive structure of multiple half-inch-thick, segmented, hollow tubes poking up two feet from the sand; and without true leaves, the cylindrical green stems perform the photosynthesis necessary for its upward growth. Like the related ferns, Scouring Rushes reproduce by spores, not seeds. For me, this flowerless remnant of the long-ago Carboniferous Era encouraged handling, as its hollow, inch-long, jointed segments pull apart and snap gently back together—like the pop-bead necklaces of my youth. As with Marram grass, this "living fossil" is a perennial arising from rhizomes that descend deep underground, extracting small quartz-based crystals from its sandy environment.

During our first years of lakefront residency, arrays of Riverbank Grape vines began extending their reach lakeward to drape the shoulders of the bluff, while in the small open area directly behind the bluff deck, Sand Reed Grass waved its slender, delicately branched lavender tops with the slightest of breezes—probably the seed source for its emergence in the foredunes. Here, too, are scattered clumps of Marram grass. And Little Bluestem Grass and tall, nodding Wild Ryegrass with its drooping, fuzzy seedheads had found an occasional niche atop the bluff. Enough grass types on hand to surprisingly view a portion of our lakeshore environment as somewhat prairie.

Amidst the varied grasses, the talon-shaped and purple-dotted, creamy blossoms of Horsemint and Milkweed's droopy popcorn-ball clusters of pink flowers stand out. Horsemint arranges its leaves in ascending levels of whorls around a square stem and has a typically minty aroma. Milkweeds are the favored host plants of Monarch butterflies, the fleshy leaves providing the principal food for the generations of this butterfly's larval stages—and a toxic chemical protector from predators, cardiac glycoside.

In early September, when the warty gray-green pods of the Milkweed were filled with the silkiest of parachute seeds, I stood among them on the sandy bluff to watch the annual aerial parade southward of hundreds of Monarchs who follow the shoreline as a navigational pathway, some fluttering within reach and others riding high on thermals created above the water's edge. The passage would be spread out over several days and include thousands, feeding along a nectar trail on their way south. All of these striking orange and black butterflies were on the same valiant, long-distance migratory journey to a few, small winter retreats—remnants of the Oyamel Fir forests on mountainsides of the neovolcanic belt in central Mexico, a place this generation of butterflies had never seen. Not until 1975 had the wintering destination for the Monarchs east of the Rocky Mountains been located by scientists, nearly four decades after a search had begun.

Although tough and adaptable, these attractive insects cannot survive northern winters. And, rather unique among the more than twenty thousand species of butterflies and moths, Monarchs became long-distance migrants. Unlike birds, however, the amazing insects passing me on their autumnal way south will not be returning to their northern place of birth next spring. After wintering and mating in Mexico, these individuals will head back to temperate North America early next year, the females soon laying eggs along the way on Milkweeds and then dying. As in all metamorphizing insects, the hatched larvae become the primary eating stage before miraculously transforming into fluttering beauties.

Three generations, each journeying further north or eastward, but lasting only about six weeks in the winged stage, will come forth, with a fourth being the honored ones to achieve a measure of longevity. Only these fourth-generation Monarchs, the great, great grandchildren of the individuals I was watching, will make the next southern trek of several

thousand miles. Actually, with the way they flutter about in search of nectar to fuel their journey, the miles chalked up must be several times that. How each generation can know their partial route in the great circle that none of them ever sees in its entirety is simply astounding. I cheered the current generation on and gently collected the limp, wind-tattered bodies of those few whose journey ended here.

It is atop the bluff where the first woody plants exist. While prior to the 1985-86 erosion, the Balsam Poplar grouping had not clung to the bluff's edge, but this was their position now as the most forward trees of the landscape, just a few yards north of the deck. Early on, we could not really pin down whether they were Poplars, Aspens, or Cottonwoods, all closely related, until we took a branch to a naturalist. She broke open a sticky end bud and had us smell the spicy aroma. It was Balsam Poplar.

These small trees produce root suckers from buried stems, and on our bluff this resulted in a rather circular, cloned clump around an open center of roughly ten feet across. These trees also produce new stems from parts that get buried, we found. Some years after the bluff stabilization, we noticed first one, and then a second, little tree emerging from the slope. They were new Poplars sprouting from the several trees that had early on fallen downslope from the main clump and were now entombed by sand. Sometimes an unusual situation can place trees a little forward from where they normally would first emerge.

On the south side of the deck and nearly to the bluff's sandy edge there is one lonely Eastern White Pine, a species usually found a little farther back. This open, exposed location certainly provided the sunshine that pines require to germinate and thrive. A mere six feet tall when we came, with its base slightly buried by blown sand, it was probably about ten years old, and thus became established in the mid 1970s during a wet period—and when the edge of the bluff was at least several yards

further lakeward. We watched it add another foot of height, more or less, each year, filling out into a nice Christmas tree shape. Spread out beyond the Poplars and the Pine along the bluff's top edge there are also a few stunted Red Oaks, like the Pine, requiring sunshine for germination and growth. But this is not a suitable location for Oaks to thrive and they remain at shrub size. Of course, none of these trees were "living on the edge" prior to the erosion of the recent past.

Retreating just yards inland from the bluff's edge, I identified several scattered shrubs that can tolerate the build-up of sand around them—Sand Cherry, burgundy-stemmed clumps of Red-osier Dogwood, and the woolly-twigged Dune Willow. Here and further in are two species of very small trees that appear to be members of the Prunus genus, cherries of some type. Frustratingly, the tree and shrub identification books don't allow me to pin down the specific names, though one may be a Northern Dwarf Cherry. This is the aggravating bane of us non-professionals, with species identification of many observed plants, birds, and animals often not seeming to fit any of the guide book descriptions. Sometimes happens to the trained specialist as well, I'm told.

Some eight to ten yards further inland from the bluff's edge, the ground dips into a slight swale that runs for roughly twenty feet before rising to become the first high dune features and the cottage perch. With its spotty, miniscule accumulations of humus, the swale is overgrown with the weedy Bracken Fern, but there is also Starry False Solomon's Seal, prolific vines of Poison Ivy, and other lower-level species—among which there is an alien. Spotted Knapweed, now widespread through much of the eastern United States, particularly along roadsides and in waste places, has made it into this special environment.

This small area is home to the most universal of any of the plants we find in our entire dunescape. The hardy Bracken Fern inhabits many poor soils spread over the world, perhaps the only fern species that

tolerates sunny and drier conditions, and here the band between the bluff edge and the inland rise of the swale is still mostly open to the overhead and western sun. Once established, the Brackens send out widely creeping rootstalks deep enough underground to withstand drought, heat, and cold. Stalks are sent up, each with a flatly branching trio of triangular leaflets at the top that create a sort of an elevated "ceiling" across a dense patch of the coarse plants. Here they grow only two feet high or so, but Doug and I have threaded our way through extensive patches that reached up to our waists. While we protected every bit of the sparser growth associated with beach and bluff slope, here I used gardeners' clippers to keep open a narrow sandy path for bare feet.

Amidst the smaller plants of this interdunal depression are the tall, forward representatives of the once great coastal forests of western Michigan—White Ashes, Red Oaks, numerous young Sugar Maples, and a few small White Pines. All the trees being rather young indicates that this swale is not that old of a formation and has been undergoing a case of succession, with trees moving in to replace some of the earlier vegetation.

As the back slope of the swale quickly begins its rise to become part of the higher and more stable inland duneworks, the number and size of tree species substantially increases. The forward swale species are joined by a Black Cherry, Hop Hornbeam, Beech, and further up, Eastern Hemlock—and towering over them all are nearly a dozen tall White Pines, the largest perhaps seventy years old or more. With the beginning of the backdunes zone comes a mixed forest habitat with a much greater flora emerging. Here, in the increasing arboreal shade, the sun-needy, weedy Bracken Fern gradually gives way to scattered clumps of the graceful Marginal Woodfern, and the first woodland wildflowers appear, as well as a plethora of other plants not seen lakeward.

Up from the swale, Doug cut a gently winding stairway of timbered risers and sand among this still rather young forest to climb the somewhat short and steep rise to the yard and the cottage front. And here is the final stage of succession for this coastal environment, where the larger trees of the cottage setting announce a mature, though by no means old, forest—a "climax" vegetation. This diverse botanical association, one that now includes shade-tolerant and shade-loving plants, will maintain itself, in theory at least, for the long term—barring some catastrophe, natural or human-made.

From the cottage, nestled amidst the larger lakeward specimens of this northern forest, which stretches inland nearly a half-mile, I could look back to the inland sea and recount the zones I had learned to distinguish. A total of five habitats, all existed at this time within less than 200 feet!—and why couldn't I count the sea itself as a sixth zone? This appeared to me to be an amazingly rapid progression, or succession, of environmental change, from "early successional," or "pioneer," plant species out front to a mature forest community of the nearby backdunes. With a little imagination, a brief walk inland from the water and on to the wooded cottage landscape can seem like a condensed journey through different lands.

Significantly, such a trek inland brings not only a different category of growth with each increasingly older physical environment, but also leads to expanding biodiversity. Along with a generally fuller vegetative cover, larger plants, and a greater biomass in each successive zone, there appears a greater number of animal species. Moving inland, we find more songbirds, for example. As I came to understand, the increasing complexity and stability encountered in moving away from the water is a consequence of each zone representing a range of interacting conditions that, through longer aging, have evolved to become more hospitable to life, such as producing greater soil fertility. Thus, the increasingly favorable environment inland provides for an increasingly more complex biotic community.

I am still amazed, nevertheless, that however more "favorable" the overall environment becomes as I move inland, the supporting growing medium is still deep sand. There is no top soil of humus or other organic material, not until one gets into the forest anyway, and there it is but a normally very thin mantle on the dunal ground. That plants can grow on the pure mineral sand of beach and new foredunes, especially, I find remarkable.

Each zone has a rather special range of those biological possibilities, a particular selection of species—for the moment, that is, as there is nothing static about the environment. For as one community

In delineating the changing landforms and habitat zones within our coastal location, I was merely following somewhat in the footsteps of Henry Chandler Cowles of a century earlier. For it was in the dune system along the Lake Michigan shoreline of northern Indiana that Cowles, a youthful biology professor from the University of Chicago, had done pioneering work in the study of ecological succession. Expanding upon ideas of other Midwestern scientists and the results of his own meticulous studies in the natural laboratory of what later became the Indiana Dunes State Park, Cowles published, in 1899, "The Ecological Relationships of the Vegetation of the Sand Dunes of Lake Michigan." This thoroughly developed explanation of the process of succession, in the eyes of many, earned him the title, "Father of Ecology."

Finding myself in such good company made me eager to investigate more fully the forested duneland that extended inland beyond the cottage and the borders of our small property. Our beginning years beside the inland sea had found us focusing our time, energy, and learning upon the lakescape scene and the needs of the cottage, placing far less attention upon the larger setting. But it came to be time for further and more thorough explorations, so we acquired some new guidebooks and a U. S. Geological Survey topographic map of our area. And, when possible, Doug traded tools for hiking boots, and I, paintbrush and cooking and cleaning items for notebook and pencil, and we joined up in heading out the door for the dunal world behind the cottage and lakeshore setting—ventures now being taken with a growing recognition of the interrelationships of living things to this fascinating, multi-faceted terrain.

of life emerges in a newer landscape, usually it will gradually set up the conditions for the more diverse life forms of the older landscape to take hold—to succeed the previous pioneering biota. Each earlier stage normally prepares the way for a different stage, and while each zone's biota will likely overlap and meld into the adjacent one, in time, a preceding community can be greatly or entirely displaced.

As our cottage years went by, we came to see this natural process of ecological succession taking place: the emergence of the Marram grass, followed by other plants on the new foredunes; the increasing vegetative growth on the bluff slope and on top; and the advance into and the maturing of trees in the sandy swale. Atop the bluff, surrounding the small open area associated with the deck, trees were invading beyond the swale, right up to the bluff edge, and the opening between the forested high dunes and the bluff drop-off was closing. Given enough time, it seems very likely woody plants will descend the bluff and also emerge in the foredunes as this new landform ages—that is, if the sea stays at bay.

If, indeed, a general stability of sea and landscape remains in place long enough, the low levels of diversity in the foredunes will gradually become a condition of the past, and I can foresee the possibility, decades hence, of the edge of the forest itself invading the foredunes. This maturing scenario will have the forest community replacing, or succeeding, several of the intermediate habitat zones. Now knowing how dynamic is the coastal environment, I would make no prediction that this will definitely happen. But we have visited Lake Michigan shorelines where trees have come down to the beach edge and stand only dozens of feet from the water.

Doug and I had been enticed to this coastal world by a sense of drama—the action of wind and water, the changing beauty of compelling sky and landscape. As with so much else, we had no clue that there was a slower ecological drama playing out, not as readily observable but constant and relentless just the same, in the ebb and flow of life upon the land beside the sea.

In a single view, exist the close-in habitat zones beside the inland sea here: the swash or wet zone, the dry beach, the grassy foredunes, the swale (behind the bluff edge), and the higher forested duneworks in the background. (The last grouping, to the center left, of forward trees overlooking the foredunes is our bluff-edge Balsam Poplar stand.) As can be seen, the coast line will vary in its configuration and zonal areas.

93

The rise of the sand dunes gracing the eastern coastline of Lake Michigan is most commonly viewed from the lakeside. But coming from inland, traveling lakeward across ancient beach terraces shorn of their natural arboreal covering, one can sometimes view the "backside" of the forested duneworks rimming the lake from miles away.

DUNEWORKS

Going for a woods walk into the forested back dunes of our cottage setting is a trip back in time. If we were to head directly east from the back of our dwelling in basically a straight line, perpendicular to the lakeshore, it would be a very demanding hike as well, for almost immediately there is a steep descent down the backside of the wooded dune ridge where the cottage is nestled. That drop is as vertical as a slope of wind-piled sand is capable of attaining. And it goes down deeper than the landscape immediately in front of the cottage before the dunework quickly rises again in another slope, nearly as steep, topping out in a second ridge. In the narrow depression between these two steep inclines is where the hemmed-in, primitive access road to our cottage and the two lakeshore dwellings to our north enters from the park on the south.

The top of the second backdune ridge is higher than the first—both running parallel to the shoreline—and then it abruptly drops down on its backside a little more deeply than the access road depression. From there the rise and fall of the forested duneworks is somewhat less rugged, until one-third of a mile from the lake, the tall dunes, having risen some one hundred feet above the water level, end abruptly, and the landscape at the bottom flattens out. Further inland still, through woods and wetlands, and eventually through farmland and scattered country residences, the irregularly flat terrain gradually rises until one and one-half miles from

the lake the ground has sloped up to a slight ridge whose elevation is some twelve feet higher than the tops of the backdunes. The terrain then dips slightly before gradually ascending again where it peaks, 3.3 miles inland, at an elevation some sixty feet higher than the backdunes, and nearly one hundred and sixty feet above the lake.

If we move in any direction from this straight line in the forested dune structures, the topography quickly begins to change in a chaotic fashion, with rugged slopes, low swales, meandering ridges, and varied inclines. Of course, we never travel that straight line route. Surveyors will strenuously trek from point to point in beeline fashion in their quest for delineating human land ownership here. The simple plat map of our cottage lot shows a series of straight lines (and right angles) making up a perfect rectangle, but that is an imaginary overlay on this landscape where the only aspect of the terrain that comes close to a straight line is some sections of the steep dune inclines. Everything else is curves, ins and outs, ups and downs—and that is the pattern of our backdunes exploring.

When Doug and I leave the cottage for a sojourn deeper into the wooded dunes at any time of the year, we walk down the curved, sand-gravel driveway cut into the steep dune slope to the sandy access road at the bottom, usually turn left, and follow its gradual ascent north between the two high dune ridges some 220 paces, and then turn eastward through a gap in the secondary ridge. The narrow, two-track roadway, revealing at this point decades of general non-use, meanders between high dunes on either side, continues out onto somewhat open and flat sandy land beyond the dune assemblage, angles to the northeast, and eventually connects to a very straight east-west county road. In general, every eastward advance away from the lake takes us into older terrain. How far back in time go the dunes and the stretched-out sandy terrain beyond, we do not know for sure. But geologically speaking, it's not much at all.

Once, when coming north from our Indiana home, we stopped in St. Joseph, Michigan, to attend an evening program on the history and morphology of the Michigan dunes. The lecturer identified himself as a geomorphologist, a new breed of scientist as far as we knew. But not so new really, for he was a professor of physical geography specifically researching the evolution and configuration of landforms—most recently, that of Great Lakes sand dunes. We knew that these extraordinary lakes were the result of the gouging and dredging out of older river valleys by huge, southward-advancing ice sheets many millennia ago. But the lecturer went on to explain that, although Lake Michigan came as the residue of the melting and retreat of the last great northern glacier, accomplished some 10,500 years ago, the onset of the earliest dunes existing today along the eastern shore of the lake likely did not begin until less than 5,500 years ago. And that the dunes in our general area are even younger, with the initial sand deposition perhaps as recent as 3,000 years ago. All of this dune building commenced after a sustained high water stage of post-glacial Lake Michigan, known as the Nipissing Period, when lake levels were at least twenty-five feet higher than modern-era levels. And it was not until after the major dune growth was accomplished that the familiar configuration of today's lake shoreline came into being, about 2,000 years ago.

That there can be dunes at all, either here or elsewhere around the earth, is a most unusual phenomenon. It is greatly dependant upon that common but marvelous entity, sand, being of a particular size. The late geologist Philip Kuenen once made the observation that "if the particles were much bigger they could not be moved by the wind and there would be no coastal dunes or sand deserts...." And if the particles were much smaller, they "would be carried more easily by rivers and marine currents and also suspended in the air," being transported into the deep sea and spread more extensively and evenly over the land, as is loess and other finer substances that form our wind-delivered soil materials.

Although our specific area has not been studied by geomorphologists, it is possible that the two upward sloping land elevations stretching east of the dune formations are former beach terraces left from a sequence of lowering lake levels during the retreat of the high water levels of the Nipissing Period—or, more likely, of even higher levels longer ago. The higher beach terrace and ridge is the furthest from the lake and the oldest. The lower and closer beach terrace and ridge is newer, and younger still are the most inland back dunes. Moving closer to the lake, the higher dunes are of even more recent vintage. And there is a possibility that the cottage and the surrounding trees rest on a dune ridge—the most shoreward—completed only centuries ago. Our discovery of the large, squared timber sticking out from our bluff indicates that the most forward section of the frontal dune structure there cannot date from before the 1830s, when Euro-American settlements and shipping along Lake Michigan shores first began. That the oldest vegetation above where the timber is encased is still rather young further supports a recent dating for the establishment of our dunal front.

It is a sobering thought that Lake Michigan as we know it and the unique dunescape along its eastern shore are geologic infants. So young, in fact, that Indian societies had already been established in North America thousands of years prior to the existence of both grand geological features. There is archaeological evidence that early Paleo-Indians were entering southern Michigan following the retreat of the last glacial ice sheet and the subsequent emergence of a web of life soon after, for the unglaciated landscape remained barren but briefly. These early, stone-age human occupiers were hunting Wooly Mammoths, Mastodonts, and Caribou in the bleak primordial marshes and scrub forests that had come forth in the deglaciated, and still cold, areas of southern Michigan, even before the forming of ancestral Lake Michigan had ended. And it's likely that these big-game hunters were unknowingly playing a part in bringing about the extinction of that prehistoric cold-climate megafauna of large meaty creatures.

It is also thought provoking to realize that the annual migration patterns of birds that seasonally spread into Michigan and much further north are only thousands of years old. Like the strictly land and water connected species of fauna, the highly mobile avian ones advanced northward with the retreat of the most recent great glacier, perhaps some leading the way. But unlike those winter-adaptive creatures that could remain year-around, the less adaptive of the flying species needed to return southward to non-winter conditions as the northern climate annually transformed the environment into a frigid world—and with the forming of extensive shore ice, something of a semi-glacial state.

But why did some tropical and semi-tropical birds become seasonal long-distance migrants, I wondered, going through the rigors and dangers of traveling thousands of miles north to remain for less than half the year in the now glacier-free and newly vegetated landscapes of Michigan and beyond? While not fully understood, ornithological researchers suggest that as environmental conditions northward gradually warmed and changed with the glacial retreat, starting roughly 10,000 years ago, new and more beneficial feeding (particularly abundant insect food) and breeding grounds became seasonally available for many bird species and won out over those in the more crowded southern regions, and the longer summer days northward also provided for extended daily foraging and the feeding of young. There also were fewer nest predators in the new landscapes.

Many avian species took advantage of these northern seasonal benefits for breeding, but found it necessary to return south when the multiple benefits faded with the cyclical coming of winter. Some birds

only needed to retreat hundreds of miles south from their summering habitats to find tolerable living conditions. But Hummingbirds, for example, feed entirely upon nectar and insects and spiders, all generally abundant in the warmer months of temperate North America. But come fall, these foods are scarce north of the Gulf of Mexico, and the Hummers, along with many other species, must embark on a post-breeding dispersal and head south to Central and South America for adequate living resources—most making their long flights to and from the winter non-breeding grounds during nighttime under the coolth and protection of darkness. While we sleep, birds by the thousands stream overhead. These great, two-way seasonal flights of migration have been characterized as "simply organized periodic food hunts." They are more than that, but still, an immense expenditure of energy for those difficult and hazardous annual roundtrips, journeys that result in many casualties along the way.

The likely inland beach terraces and the later, younger dunes were successive creations following a series of retreats of long-ago higher lake levels—and a slow rebounding of the earth's surface that had been compressed under the weight of the build up of the gigantic, moving continental ice sheets. As water levels decreased, accumulated sand along the lake's rim, now exposed, became available for eolian transport further inland—just as our new foredunes were now being fashioned on a much smaller scale. Aeolus is the Greek god and ruler of the winds, and since the emergence of the post-glacial lake, has always had plenty of room to roam powerfully and unimpeded across the open expanse of the waters and onto the land beyond, sweeping up and spreading inland from the beaches the smaller granular detritus of the past glacial grinding.

For centuries the windswept terraces east of the shoreline-dunes-to-be were without trees. But in short time, as some semblance of top soils evolved, varied plants soon emerged, and an ecological succession gradually took place, resulting in a young forest cover. Why, in a much later period, the eolian sand came to have the dramatic vertical accumulations on the lakeward edge of the lower terrace deposits, becoming the coastal dunes, is not known—at least, I've never found an explanation. Perhaps at some point, the forest edge became a sand catcher at its most westward front, much like our beach-placed, slatted snow fencing and the Marram grass.

Initially the forward trees would have been buried as they began retaining the drifting sand. As water levels fluctuated, so did sand accumulations, allowing periods, primarily during lower water levels, for the early, smaller dunes to be inhabited by a succession of plants—probably very much like what we have seen on our beach and frontal dune system, although climatic conditions would have been somewhat different. The process would have been repeated multiple times, creating new sand accumulations on top, and in front, of the earlier dune structures—and new periods of vegetated surfaces—as dune

Rising beyond and above the flat beach—the immediate sandy supplier of coastline duneworks—are the forested dunes of our area.

building advanced lakeward over the sweep of several millennia. When digging deep into dunes, sand mining and research projects have often encountered several layers of buried trees, one group on top of another.

humped rim along this Great Lake's shoreline—came to be extensively covered by a primeval forest and to be populated by the native animal species we find there today, migrating from the older interior forests.

As new forward dunes emerged, the oldest wind-created sand deposits would have semi-stabilized as they became vegetated; and with the diminishment of the large extremes in lake fluctuations, the major dune construction slowed and ceased. Sometime afterwards, nearly all of this irregular terrain of huge heaps of sand—this very narrow, golden,

Thus, while our dunescape is quite young, the climax vegetation of a forest cover, anchored in sand, is even more recent—both being formed within the framework of early human occupation of the region. Together, the two natural features present a magnificent backdrop to the "modern" lake and beach.

What we see as attractive and alluring, however, was not always viewed as such. For the high wall of sand dunes along the lengthy Lake Michigan east coast, usually crowned by a dark forest top, appeared to be a desolate and inhospitable, if not a foreboding, landscape to many of the first Euro-American lake travelers and early arrivals to the Western Michigan coastal world. To these early nineteenth century adventurers (and anyone who then or earlier traveled on this inland sea had to be considered an "adventurer"), this was unfamiliar terrain, distant and very different from the settled world they came from, even different from the other lake shores back east and across this lake on the Wisconsin side, which came to be settled earlier. Michigan's dunal world and the wilderness beyond—"barren scenery" one called it—seemed generally hopeless for inhabitation and agrarian possibilities.

Nowhere else in the world has there come into existence such an extensive accumulation of freshwater dune formations as along "our" Lake Michigan's long eastern and much shorter southern coastline. While there are many stretches of sand dunes along shorelines of every one of the other Great Lakes, none match the variety and extent of Lake Michigan's eastern/southern shoreline dunal assemblages. That fact is quite tellingly illustrated, though not directly, by an outstanding publication entitled *Sand Dunes of the Great Lakes*. This 1997 photographic essay is described within as the "first major portrait of Great Lakes sand dunes." Of the approximately sixty-five pictures of dunescapes, there are, however, none from lakes Huron, Erie, or Ontario, and only fifteen from two areas along the southern shores of Lake Superior. The other fifty photographs are of Lake Michigan dunefields: two of very modest dunal areas along the western shore of the lake, and the rest portray the varied and exceptional dune formations rimming most of the lake's long eastern and southern coast.

I have found no explanation as to why this one coastline is so endowed. All of the Great Lakes are glacial creations, but only Lake Michigan's eastern edge emerges, belatedly, from the ice ages with such a unique geologic phenomenon occurring. The answer must lie with regions having had different legacies of glacial behavior, differing underlying bedrock over which the glaciers worked, differing drainages of glacial meltwater, and, later, differing systems of watercourses that sorted and carried inland sand to coastal waters for wave transport along and onto shorelines. Does it count, for example, that the lake's eastern shore receives the emptying waters and sediments of Michigan's two longest rivers, the Grand and the Muskegan, waterways that reach deep into the interior of the sandy state? Then, there is the singular long north-south orientation of this Great Lake that receives the broad sweep of Aeolus. And, then, there is that which cannot be guessed at at all.

It is rather astounding that so much physical, climatic, and biological change has taken place so quickly, geologically speaking, in the wake of the 2,000,000-year-long period of the multiple advancing and retreat of enormous glaciers. From out of possibly the greatest cold spell the planet has ever known, our familiar Lake Michigan world with its dramatic duneworks emerged in a mere 10,000 years or so.

The tops of the highest trees that poke up all along the edges of the shoreline forest are all Eastern White Pines.

The rich green of Eastern Hemlocks contrasts with the autumn colors of the broad-leaf trees and will carry on to brighten the winter landscape.

WOODS

Our cottage lies in the southwest section of approximately seventy-five acres of a dune and forest assemblage that spreads north and south between two modest streams which empty into the lake. Little Flower Creek, on the south and flowing through the county park, is the smaller and drains only the lower and closer beach terrace to the east of the lake and the duneworks. Big Flower Creek, emptying into the lake less than a mile to the north, reaches further inland to the higher terrace, has a much greater watershed, and is the older watercourse.

Of that stretch of complex forested dune field between the two streams, slightly less than half belonged to widow Erna when we came upon the scene in 1986. Even though Erna had sold the Chalet to the professor and his wife in 1968 and then moved to Florida, she retained ownership of the wooded acreage behind it, the remaining part of the ninety-eight acres that she and William had acquired in the late 1930s. By the time we purchased the lakeshore lot from the professor, Erna had been absent from the Michigan setting for almost two decades, and her land was known to us simply as "the woods." The primitive access road of more than one-half mile was an easement that allowed us legal passage through the center of the woods' dunescape. A granddaughter of Erna's who lived at the east end of the passageway had early on granted us permission to roam beyond the roadway easement onto her grandparent's parcel.

With our developing understanding of plant succession and dune evolution, we were increasingly able to explore the surrounding forested dunes with a greater appreciation of their uniqueness and importance— and of the solitude they offered. Moreover, we could also bring a greater concentration to this special inland environment, for the lakeshore drama had become much less intense. Now into the early 1990s, seasonal lake levels had been consistently following the historic averages for four years, even dropping slightly below during 1989 and 1990. Aeolus continued his work of beach building and foredune forming, and our concerns about a return of high water levels and dune erosion were pushed into the far recesses of our minds—nearly shuttered, but not quite.

Our winter trips into the woods were usually retreats from the harsher, sometimes even violent, conditions associated with the lake front, as were our warmer weather excursions—particularly on those sometimes blustery summer afternoons that swept the beach of most sunbathers. A stroll amidst the sheltered dunes under a broad, green, sun-blocking canopy certainly has its special appeal at such times—although some pesky insect swatting is sometimes required. Walking northward in dappled shade on the access two-track behind our cottage during one of those mid-summer times, Doug and I noticed that we were not the first to use the dirt lane that day. The dainty prints of a fawn also headed north. And we certainly were not the first to note that black raspberries had ripened in the half-sun of the lane's edge. The ripest of those remaining dropped gently into our palms with the slightest pull. A small handful sweetened the walk, even though we stirred up ten mosquitoes for each berry plucked.

This encouragement to move along left some of the low fruit for the Gray Squirrel of omnivorous tastes that took our place. Rising on hind legs to full height, it grasped the branch with outstretched arm, the dominant coloring prior to the heavy cutting of the dense forests with the coming of Euro-Americans. The theory is that the blacks thus became more visible in the opened, lighter treescape and more easily hunted than the neutral Grays. In reverse fashion, the heftier Fox Squirrel, lacking the agility of the Grays and preferring an open understory woodland, was uncommon in the Great Lakes region until that human wrought deforestation occurred, beginning some two centuries ago.

Continuing our hike and turning eastward and inland on the access roadway brought us immediately to a metal farm gate at the gap in the secondary dune ridge, beyond which the sandy, leaf-littered two-track diminishes into simply a wide woodland path that bisects Erna's parcel of duneland before continuing on. This quiet trail was very likely a logging road originally, before becoming a long and difficult access route to the shoreline area properties for a brief period in the 1950s and early 1960s.

Doug's feet followed the stile around the closed gate, but I hesitated, my attention drawn to the view. Several tall Eastern Hemlocks, though a tree-stand minority, stood out to establish the character and mood of the wide shaded dip in the duneworks before us. Their gracefully drooping branches, a rich dark green in any season, extended welcoming gestures, and I soon followed Doug's lead.

Contoured with the help of human labor, the pathway before us dipped, rose slightly, sloped down again, and turned with gentle ease. On each side we were surrounded by huge, elongated hills of sand, the largest rising almost one hundred feet above the level of the lake, which we could still barely hear from beyond the dune ridges to our backs. No expanses of exposed golden sand here. Virtually all surfaces were darkened with the accumulating, but still very thin, organic matter of a forest floor.

We were now centered in a land of varied perennials; a mosaic of long-lived life forms that I've found encompasses a continuum from

pulling the prize within reach of the other paw. Releasing the stem, this arboreal rodent sat to savor the small purplish morsel before repeating the process. The larger Fox Squirrel and the smaller, feisty Red Squirrel also inhabit this wooded landscape with its combination of edges and deeper forest environment. I am aware of no other animals that move so freely, so adeptly, between ground and tree, branch to branch, and tree to tree, as these tree squirrels.

It has been fascinating to observe, particularly in the more open setting of the cottage, a variation of the Grays which is entirely black—so totally black that its dark eyes are lost in the creature's face—the only animal of this solid hue of which we are familiar. I'm a little confounded that this gray-colored species with a white underbelly, like that of a White-tailed Deer, and a white bordered tail can produce an all-black variant. As we only occasionally see the blacks here and never in our Indiana location, I was surprised to learn that in Michigan and most other northern areas, it's likely that the black variation of the Gray Squirrel was the microscopic to the huge, from the invisible underfoot to those forms that require me to tilt my head back and upward to take in their full expanse. In this end stage of ecological succession, the most dominant and expansive perennials, of course, are trees—with over a dozen species of mixed ages sprinkling the hollows, climbing the slopes, and riding the ridges, the taller ones stretching up to seventy-five feet or so.

This is terrain traversed daily by White-tailed Deer. Their distinct cutting trails, many following the rugged contours purposefully to ridge-tops, show us routes away from the beaten path. Turning northward from the old roadway, we followed a line of split hoof prints, winding our way toward a ridge. It was somewhat a steep climb, nonetheless, and we paused for breath and surveyed the scene. Despite the presence of two conifer species among these dunes, we were immersed in the most southern range in Michigan of what has been classified as a Northern Hardwood Forest community.

Further on, near the ridge line, several American Beech trees, already huge, extended their smooth angular branches, some low enough to lure passing boys of all ages to forbidden heights. Doug was no exception, and his antics made me chuckle. The Beech, with its rather distinctive, smooth pale gray bark, is one of the dominant tree species of this most northern deciduous forest community. The other prominent deciduous species that define this woodland community, Sugar Maple, Northern Red Oak, and the Yellow Birch, grow generally straighter and taller than the Beech. And straight and tall is the prime characteristic of this forest's larger trees, all reaching upward and competing for sunlight, their leafy spreads high up, most trunks having shed most side branches. Rare is there a tree here, like the enticingly climbable Beech, that had enough open space and light to emerge and prosper while retaining a wide stretch of large lower branches.

While Sugar Maples, with their beautiful fall foliage of rich oranges, are abundant in this dune field, Yellow Birches are sparse. This later species offers its special color to the woods palette with a light- and expansive perennials, of course, are trees—with over a dozen species golden sheen and scaly bark. Sprinkled only here and there in the forest, the rather few Yellow Birches that we do find are not large trees, and the species appears to be dying out, as we have not come across any young descendants. The Yellow Birches will be missed, as they are quite distinctive, for one doesn't think of tree bark as having a shiny, golden-like hue.

Northern Red Oak, a member of the Beech Family, is the most northern of the great many, widely-adapted species within the Oak Genus, Quercus. In an apparent adaptation to colder climates, Red Oaks take two growing seasons to fertilize and mature their acorn seeds. I have also read that another adaptation for this species, as well as a number

105

of other oaks, was to change from being evergreen to being deciduous, losing their leaves with the coming of cold weather.

Along with the Beech trees, Red Oaks are the most numerous species in terms of mature specimens in this dunal forest, with the Oaks coming out a little ahead, as best our observations can determine. This is not surprising, as oaks are the most common hardwoods, and the most important genus, of the vast deciduous forest across the temperate climate region of the northern hemisphere. As both Red Oaks and Beeches produce nut seeds, this is good news for many forms of wildlife in this intriguing woodland. Acorns and beechnuts are a basic, nutritious food source for the diminutive Deer Mouse to the largest creature to roam this woodland, the White-tailed Deer.

Nuts are one of the fruits of flowering trees, trees that are conventionally called "hardwoods," or "deciduous." All flowering trees in northern climates are deciduous, meaning their leaves are not persistent on the branches—they grow, mature, fall off, and re-grow on an annual cycle.

On the other hand, conifers, usually called "softwoods," or "evergreens," are trees without either flowers or fruits, their reproductive processes for producing seeds being evolutionarily older and involve male and female cones. These reproductive organs are not visited by bees and butterflies, as with flowering plants. The uncovered seeds of conifers have no protective casing and are known as "naked seeds," while flowering trees produce more highly evolved *angiosperm* seeds, Greek for "seeds in a container." Of all seed-reproducing plants, conifers are the earliest to survive into modern times.

Conifer leaves are simpler also, and smaller, taking the form of narrow needles or scales. As the needles/leaves of most conifers stay on the branches for longer than a year, and are shed gradually—a few each fall—as new ones grow, these descendants of the planet's earliest

trees remain green year around—"evergreen." The bark and wood of conifers is also simpler compared to those elements of the "newer" hardwood species. While the wood of conifers is usually less dense, and thus "softer," than that of deciduous trees, Doug has laboriously hand sawn some coniferous "softwood" that was harder than some deciduous "hardwood." It all depends upon the particular species, the conditions under which the tree grew, and the age of the wood. But whether a "soft" or a "hard" wood, for its weight, this structural component of trees is an immensely strong material, more so than even iron.

Since hardness of wood is not a clear distinguishing factor between flowering trees and conifers, nor is "deciduousness"—in warmer climates, all trees retain their leaves for periods longer than a few seasons—and some conifers (or "evergreens")—such, as Larches (or Tamaracks), which grow in Michigan—annually lose their needles/leaves in colder climates, then, difference in foliage is a way of more precisely distinguishing between the two tree categories. Needles and scales of conifers are not only composed differently than the leaves of flowering trees, they are smaller, narrower. So the term, "broadleaf," is sometimes used to designate flowering trees with their substantially larger leaves.

Higher locations in these duneworks often provide vantage points that reveal the most prominent of the two coniferous species here—the graceful Eastern Hemlocks of lacy foliage—with many gathered below in small stands in the cooler, deep shade, growing with patient slowness in the low light. Well-adapted to a paucity of sunlight resulting from an extensive hardwood canopy, the short, deep-green Hemlock needles spread close together along branches in a non-overlapping pattern that allows little light to escape their use. Shade beneath groups of smaller, evergreen conifers is deeper still. Undergrowth surrounding them is sparse, for the thin acidic nutrient layer of discarded Hemlock needles along with the lack of light discourages a luxuriant near floor. This species is long-lived, and the largest Hemlocks we've found here, some approaching eighty feet in height, are among the tallest trees in these woods.

Far lesser in number than the Hemlocks is the other conifer, the Eastern White Pine, which we come across in more spread out, higher locations of this dunal forest. Although somewhat shade tolerant, these trees require substantial light for germination and growth, indicating that their immediate local environs earlier had been more open to the sun. Conifers grow taller than broadleaf trees here, and the White Pine, with its long lifespan, was once the supreme giant of this and many other forest regions of the Great Lake states and New England—"the Sequoia of the East." Larger specimens once soared well over 200 feet into the air with diameters of more than six feet across at the base, and the very largest were the tallest trees on the continent east of the Rocky Mountains (just as other conifer species are the tallest trees west of the mountains). But those straight and tall marvels are long gone, having been rapaciously and thoroughly harvested for lumber many decades ago wherever they grew. With the extensive extraction of the splendid White Pines and various other tree species in our region, newly arrived Euro-Americans of not that long ago wrought a major landscape transformation.

It has been stated that the continent's largest White Pines were found in the sandy Michigan landscape. One of the last truly mammoth pines to be converted to sticks of lumber was cut some sixty miles north of here in Lake County, Michigan, in1893. Measuring over eight feet across at the stump, it had stood as a landmark for many years, and its size was remarkable enough to have been noted in newspapers of the time. Today, a few, rare large White Pines, sprinkled in the central region of the state and in the Upper Peninsula, have survived, but none of these centuries-old remnants measure up to the magnificent ones of the past.

And this is regrettable, that none of the largest ones were set aside, as the Eastern White Pine (Pinus strobes) is the official state tree of Michigan (as well as that of Maine, where this pine species, too, was heavily relied upon for lumber beginning early on in the nation's colonial period).

In our locale, White Pines are actually most prominent along the higher dunescape fronting the lake, where they have had more sunlight to grow. There, strung out along the frontal dune ridges, these trees tower above the rest of the coastal vegetation—their verdant caps particularly prominent during the half-year of colder weather as they punctuate the meeting line between sky and land. None of the taller pine conifers of our general landscape, however, are aged, having survived the great exploitation of the original forests of Michigan and the other Great Lakes states. Our guess is that the largest are only a century or so old.

It's apparent to the eye that the conifers are rather more symmetrical than their deciduous neighbors, whether in the woods here or on a Christmas tree lot. I'd never really given any thought early on as to why, just accepted that the generally straighter and neater coniferous appearance was simply a difference. But the explanation, I now know, is that a defining distinction between the two types of trees is that the more ancient conifers have a single terminal bud at the top of their trunks responsible for the main upward growth, adding annually to the trees' height. A broadleaf tree, on the other hand, has no singular terminal bud, but many branches that come to split up the trunk and grow upward simultaneously. This division may occur lower down on a deciduous tree or not exist until near the tree's crown, which is usually the case in a forest where trees have to competitively "reach" upward for sunlight, as here.

The single leading terminal bud of conifers and the more concentrated growth of a straight central trunk would seem to greatly explain why a variety of conifer species have become the tallest and largest pillars of wood in the entire world, the monarchs of the planet's living landscape. This distinction between conifers and hardwoods is hardly perfect, however, for I have seen that odd pine tree with two or more trunks and Red Cedars that are multi-stemmed. And then there are low-growing forms of conifers that spread out multi-branched and shrub-like.

A broken leader on a pine can sometimes cause its top to branch out and no longer have a central stem, although I have seen specimens of a more southerly pine species that seem to do forking of top branches other than for this explanation, as well as sporting large side branches further down the trunk. Recently, I discovered that the young Arbor Vitae (really a "domesticated" Northern White Cedar) that Doug and I bought and put in as a landscape planting at our Indiana home has two main trunks. Growing so close together and in such perfect composition, the two trunks and their side companions have always formed a singular conical shape that has deceptively insinuated a central trunk within its dense scale-like foliage. However, as the shrub-sized tree has gotten taller, I've noticed two leaders at the top, one a little lower than the other, but together retaining the consummate conical shape. Enough exceptions here that this "defining distinction" between the two categories of trees is something of a generalization.

The existence of conifer species among the broadleaf species makes this dune forest a special type of association within the extensive Northern Hardwood Forest community. Red Pines are sometimes found in combination with this mixed softwood/hardwood forest type, but we know of none here except some small stands that were planted adjacent to the inland side of the dunes some decades back. It's possible that this native species will eventually become naturalized into the edge of the dunal landscape here, as there are a few young, or "second growth," trees coming up on their own. And we have found a few scraggly-looking Jack

Pines, a species of generally more northern distribution, very close by in the same sandy flatlands just eastward of the dunes.

Trees are the largest and the longest-living life forms ever to inhabit the earth, an imposing presence upon the land. In fact, trees are the only upright plant of any great height, being also the most complex of any in the plant world. And while the architecture of bulky woody denizens of this dune field instills a compelling richness of interest to the landscape, a forest is more than an arboretum, a collection of tall, massive, vertical structures with outstretched solar-collecting greenery. As I stood nearby to the enticingly climbable Beech, I was more drawn at the moment to the fascinating growth at my feet—the very skinny, foot-tall, branched stems of Beech-drops. Along with the more attractive, whitish and translucent Indian Pipe growing occasionally here, the light purplish-brown Beech-drops secure their rations not like the surrounding green, leafy vegetation, but parasitically, from the roots of trees. For these two unusual plant species of shady woods lack the true leaves and green chlorophyll needed for the photosynthesis for their own food production.

In the case of the very particular Beech-drops, seedlings will only develop if the new plants can soon attach to the shallow upper roots of a Beech tree, and only a Beech, sucking nourishment from its host like a vampire of the forest. (One entertaining botanist has called them "sons of Beeches.") The whitish, waxy Indian Pipe, on the other hand, relies upon an underground fungal connection between it and the roots of various other plants for its water and nutrients.

Similarly, underneath the surface layer of the dead debris of tree parts and other plants, and at root level, soil-inhabiting fungi, themselves lacking chlorophyll, must depend upon extensive below ground networks of white, threadlike filaments, some microscopic, to take in nutrients and water. Called mycelium, these fungal networks, or fungal "bodies," inconspicuous because of their hidden lifestyles, but some species are somewhat commonly seen as yeasts and molds, as well as the more familiar mushroom fruiting bodies. Secreting powerful enzymes and acids into their immediate environs, that break down dead or living materials outside the fungal body into a solution of molecules, the fungal filaments absorb this carbon-based food through their cell walls, rather than ingesting, or eating, it. It is a form of "absorptive nutrition" by way of externally digesting food. And the filament tips of some fungi also can exert enough pressure to break through a variety of rock materials, dissolving and consuming the minerals. In time, these minerals get pumped into the surrounding ecosystem.

Interestingly, I've learned that various fungus species, called mycorrhizal fungi, form beneficial associations with many species of trees. Particularly among the dunal forest's evergreens, spread-out mycelial filaments of mycorrhizal fungi penetrate or surround the tree rootlets, greatly increasing their absorptive surface with this substantial extending of the root systems. In a symbiotic or mutualistic relationship benefiting both life forms—the very large and the extremely small—these chlorophyll-less organisms take in vital minerals and water from the soil that the trees need for growth, extracting in exchange some of the sugary compounds from the trees' energy-capturing photosynthetic processes. An exchange transpiring between the hidden forms of the dark below and those exposed to the brilliance of the world high up. Such a symbiotical relationship with soil fungi is crucial for a vast number of the world's plant species for establishing healthy environments for their roots.

This vital fungal alliance is especially true regarding the strange case of the woods' translucent Indian-pipes that pop up in early summer through the leaf litter on the forest floor. The plant's root ball below is penetrated by filaments of a fungus that has its mycelium network in association with roots of a nearby tree. The fungal link transfers organic

penetrate the dead organic matter of the forest floor and below, including animal and bird carcasses, secreting digestive enzymes to extract the food molecules needed by the fungi. We sometimes see the short-lived, reproductive fruiting bodies of some of the fungi in the form of sprouted mushrooms and toadstools that are sent up through the forest floor's refuse carpet after a warm rain. These visible reproductive

Indian-pipes, members of the Wintergreen Family, are also known as Ghost Flower or Corpse Plant because of the colorless, waxy appearance.

structures produce and disperse microscopic spores for making new fungus filaments. And that's usually it: a fungal fabric of interconnected filaments, short-term fruiting bodies, and spores—no permanent or elaborate aboveground structures to build, or roots.

Abundant worldwide, fungi are a "kingdom" of organisms separate from plants, animals, and bacteria. Tenacious and resilient, they grow in every ecosystem from bodies of water and frigid Antarctica to, as I am personally well acquainted with, human skin. Fungi are usually food molecules produced by the tree's photosynthesis to the roots of the chlorophyll-less Indian-pipe. The mystery is why this association occurs at all, as it is unknown how the fungus and tree may benefit from this tripartite relationship.

But not all is well between certain fungi and trees. For we pass a few trees, some living, that have fan-shaped "shelf fungus" fungi." Also called "bracket fungi," these spore producing structures usually of greater longevity than ground based mushrooms, tell of invisible filaments having invaded the heart of the tree, feeding away. And if the tree is still alive, it is dieing, for there is decaying within from the thin fungus threads secreting enzymes that are breaking down the structural heartwood for the invader's nutritional purposes. Doug and I have occasionally come across shelf fungi that are brightly colorful combinations of yellow and orange, known as "Sulfur Shelf," some extending out from the tree, or a log, for six inches and more and reaching a foot across. Although found mostly on decaying logs or stumps, feeding on dead wood, and perhaps for many years, Sulfur Shelf fungi can also live parasitically on live trees already damaged, to the detriment of the hosts. Other fungus species can wipe out acres of mature trees, sometimes very quickly. In rare cases, some fungi can grow into massive membranes, living for thousands of years as they expand to cover thousands of acres.

While the rather soft, fleshy spore factories of the Sulfur Shelf loose their attractiveness after maturing and deteriorating, they, along with a variety of other, shelf and ground fungi, some brilliantly red, outshine the wildflowers and even the birds in bringing, surprisingly, the most exciting colors to the woods—although that's a tough call in comparing fungi colors with certain avian ones.

One fungal item from a tree we have collected is a fruiting structure that is tough and woody—and very resilient.

Brought home, this shelf fungus body has been displayed on an outside window sill, from which it has fallen several times onto cement, proceeded to bounce, and once was slightly broken. Glued back together, the dark brown, semi-

The most colorful organism of the dunal woods, the layered Sulfur Shelf is also known as Chicken-of-the-Woods. Many say the brilliantly orange and yellow fruiting body tastes like chicken when cooked, making it the most popular edible shelf fungus.

circular solid object, ten inches across and nearly four inches thick where it attached to the dead tree and having stuck out six inches, carries on, year after year, as an unusual shelf (pun intended) *object de art* at our home.

Like the tree upon which it grew, this shelf fungus reproductive body was a perennial and added annual growth rings in concentric horizontal bands around its sloping perimeter. We are not knowledgeable enough to determine the number of existing rings, but are sure this "conk," as such forms are called, was at least six years old before dying. Strangely, the host tree might have been nourished below by one species of fungi and then succumbed to another type aboveground. The small spore pores of some shelf fungi become habitat for tiny spiders, mites, and insects; and tree-abiding squirrels will feed on the fungal bodies feeding on a tree. Multiple types of very different life all tied together.

The woods is packed full of fungal types, from those of creeping tentacles feeding on the dead plant material at the covered surface and in the underground darkness of the forest floor to those subsisting on woody substances many feet above the ground. While there are species that are parasitic and pathogenic, weakening or killing other life forms, most fungi are what we would consider beneficial, many forming mutualistic associations with varied organisms.

But most importantly, perhaps, fungi perform an indispensable role as decomposers and nutrient recyclers of plant and animal materials, especially in forests. Thousands of pounds of matter descend to the woods' floor each year--leaves; dead limbs and bark; deceased birds, mammals, insects, bacteria; an occasional entire tree; and other materials from the vertical world above—most to be consumed, converted, and downsized by fungi.

As one mycologist has stated it, "A forest ecosystem cannot be defined without its fungi because they govern the transition between life and death...." Simply put, without fungi, there would be no dunal woods for Doug and me to explore.

Fungi marched onto land, it appears, more than a billion years ago and came to carry on vital ecological functions, such as building soils and providing for biodiversity. And with this ancient kingdom of life being so widespread and diverse, it's been stated that without fungi, *all* ecosystems would simply fail. Remove only a small category of certain fungi and many human industries would fail with the loss of the fungal yeasts necessary for such as bread, ale, and wine making.

Hemlock Varnish Shelf fungi, with their shiny, lacquered appearance, grow on dead or dying conifers, with these acquiring their nutrients from a dead Eastern Hemlock. During the summer, many millions of tiny spores are released into the woods from the undersides of shelf fungi, such as from this grouping.

the encapsulated nutrients would not be recycled back into food available for the trees and other plants. At the ground's surface and extending well below stretches a habitat of plant and animal life we rarely consider, an arena of immense biological diversity in miniature of which we are mostly ignorant. The imaginary underworld of a Hell of the dead stands in stark contrast to the real, living, evolved cooperation of a forest community's complex subterranean realm.

Because of those complexly interconnected lives and processes, Doug and I can walk upon a woodland floor of but a thin layer of humus and leafy and woody litter, despite thousands of years of many thousands of tons of vegetative and other matter having been deposited there. While dead branches are scattered everywhere, there is no accumulation piled high impeding our walking progress. Many thousands of trees have fallen in this dunal forest over the millennia, but we come upon just the occasional prostrated tree carcass (sometimes several together), most in a state of decay and diminishment, not huge sprawling heaps of the large wooden forms from the distant past. It should be a matter of wonderment that this vanishing act is so. And a bell-ringing reminder that a landscape of plants and animals cannot function and exist without the decomposers-recyclers, especially the amazing fungi, processing the remains of the ubiquitous dead and sustaining the recovery of energy and nutrients through a forest or other ecosystem. And we humans would do well to better emulate this efficient woodland economy where there is no waste.

There is still more to this hidden mass of underground living material and activity. It has become common knowledge as part of our understanding of the build-up of greenhouse gases in the atmosphere that forests play a highly important role in regulating atmospheric carbon dioxide concentrations (a greenhouse gas) and associated climate change. Through their leafy components, trees take in great quantities of carbon dioxide (CO_2) from the atmosphere, retaining the carbon in their structures and sending the residual oxygen back into the skies by the tons.

Passing a blown-down tree, with its large circular root-ball now sticking up vertically like a dirty, broken spoked wheel with its long, huge axle sprawled out along the ground, we realized that a very substantial proportion of this woods' biomass is ensconced underground and out of sight. Below the surface, the wind-slain giant had left severed likely miles of root branches and tiny root hairs, along with extensive mycorrhizal fungal strands, tightly encased in the packed sand. Mature oak trees, particularly, have extensive root systems (some up to hundreds of miles) that radiate out many yards beyond their solid trunks, much farther out than the spreading branches overhead

During the growing season, new root tips fronted with hard cells are constantly pushing through the underground in a corkscrew motion, advancing in minute increments by the addition of new hard cells at the front of the tips. The roots themselves once formed do not move, but progress by lengthening and expanding in diameter and branching and re-branching in all directions possible. Behind the extensive advancing root tips emerge minute root hair projections that absorb water and dissolved minerals, living for a few days before new ones take over the collecting job back of the growing, extending root tips. Requiring much of the food that trees make, the growth of new roots extends in a maze everywhere we step, a subterranean, creeping, expanding motion throughout the forest, another vast network of life so very close, but its activity totally undetected by us.

And interspersed with the expansive root systems of the forest flora are not only the underground fungi, but also myriad microbes, insects, worms, and other hidden organisms—a vast, complex, and efficient network of decomposers-recyclers of organic matter and nutrients providing vital support to the above-ground life functions. Without these unseen billions of organisms at work, the refuse on the forest floor would just keep accumulating, piling higher and higher, and

Consequently, they provide the enormous benefit of "sequestering" carbon from the atmosphere.

What is only recently becoming more widely recognized is that the subterranean processes of a mature forest also provide that carbon sequestering benefit in substantial measure—with the estimated amount of carbon stored in the forest soil being three to four times as high as that bound in the vegetation. Remove the trees, and not only does that extract these major consumers of carbon dioxide from the environment, but the evolved, belowground exchanging of carbon between plants and soil, and the carbon sequestering there, is also greatly diminished. Consider the vast amount of land area that humans have transformed from dense perennial forests and grasslands to bare-soil growing of small-scale annuals for food and have built and paved over, choking off the dark life of the soil.

Doug and I get to see merely a portion of the throbbing, living forest as we make our way amidst it. And the energetic forest floor and subsurface activity, unseen and unheard by our human senses, is matched by the daily flow of tens of thousands of gallons of groundwater and nutrients ascending and descending in the many tree structures we walk among. This enormous pumping process, constantly at work in all but the coldest weather, goes on through vertically oriented cells tightly packed together in parallel rows beginning just inside the protective bark of living trees—in a zone of cell production and circulatory active that sheathes each tree from its base and roots up to the tips of the smallest branches.

Immediately inside the dead, shielding bark, there exists a thin layer of phloem tubes that transports carbohydrates produced by the energy capturing and converting leaves in a downward direction. The amazing paper-thin cambium layer is next, providing by prolific division the billions of new cells of the tree's vascular system and its outward growth—generating the phloem cells of the inner bark on its exterior side and, to its inside, simultaneously producing the xylem tube cells that convey water and minerals upward—the "sapwood." (It is the rising, carbohydrate-filled xylem sap in late winter of maple trees that provides sweet maple syrup.)

On into the leaves through the stems continue the cellular tubes of xylem (Greek for "wood") and phloem (Greek for "bark") conducting water and dissolved mineral nutrients from the soil into the extensive networks of leaf veins and the photosynthesized glucose out from the leaves and downward to the very ends of the roots. And somewhat magically, the delicate, cell-producing cambium tissue that wraps the whole tree and generates all woody growth must reproduce itself. For as the tree expands in circumference,

Although deeply riddled by large holes made by one or more Pileated Woodpeckers, this slender White Pine carries on. Most of the excavations are into the inactive heartwood, while the tree's living outer ring of phloem, cambium, and xylem tissues remain mostly undamaged, allowing for continued growth of the Pine.

that thin layer, too, increases, and migrating outward, stays just inside the bark. Our enveloping skin expands as we grow bigger, but unlike the mother cambium, it does not produce the vascular and structural components of our bodies. Astoundingly, the thin cambium provides for all of the tree's massive development which can go on for century after century.

One wood scientist has stated that "the wood in a tree trunk is the most complex, beautifully structured water transporting system in the world." We move among hundreds of these magnificent systems in this dunal forest with thousands of gallons of liquid in motion. Yet, when we put our ears to one of these natural pumping stations, we can detect nothing, although the action begins just a fraction of an inch away. With the conducting of water through all plants there is silence, for they exert no energy themselves, but have their processes powered by the sun—that same distant fiery orb that sets so many other earthly processes in motion. It's an incredible, intricate world at work close by, but beyond our senses.

But how does it work? We humans would need a noisy mechanical pump to raise a liquid straight up a tube as high as a tree, some of which, such as the giant Sequoias, are over 300 feet tall. Scientific sources provide various aspects of an answer. The main element at work apparently is transpiration of water from the leaves. Unlike with the heart pumping blood through the body of an animal, a plant's flow of life liquids is not a completely closed system. Transpiration "runs the show" by releasing water vapor (as in evaporation) into the air through millions of tiny controlled openings in a tree's leaves, the stomate pores. That flow of moisture out of the tree results in a decrease in hydrostatic (water) pressure in the very small diameter xylem tubes and that brings about ("pulls") the massive flow of mineral-laden water all the way from the roots to the leaves. This process has almost all of the water entering a tree's roots rising up the structure to be sent into the atmosphere. (In a

real sense, here is previous precipitation water now "raining" upward.) Only approximately ten percent remains in the tree to provide for photosynthesis and the downward flow of leaf-solar generated food.

I have found no discussion of how that downward flow is "powered". But, then, this life functioning of trees is a complicated process with many variables and is not completely understood. It is known that gravity will not force a liquid down tiny cellular tubes. Perhaps, the production of cells that is occurring throughout the tree's perimeter (where the food-carrying phloem tubes exist) "draws" the food-laden liquid down from the leaves. As this cell multiplication occurs all the way to the far reaches of the extensive root system underground, maybe the extraction of the molecules of water and carbohydrates from the phloem liquid in the cambium's creation of new cells "sucks" the liquid along downward. Whatever the process, it appears some of the groundwater drawn into the roots ascends all the way to the top of the tree to leaves in the canopy and, then, (now carrying glucose/food), descends all the way back to the farthest, deepest root tips for growth—in some trees, traveling a fifth of a mile.

Interestingly, the moisture content of deciduous trees is generally highest in early winter, for transpiration greatly dwindles with descending temperatures and the trees fill with water. There is a gradual decline in the trees' water content as the winter progresses and new growth processes begin to get underway. Arboreal species of northern climates have evolved several strategies to keep their water-filled cells from freezing and bursting when temperatures dip below 32 degrees. Boreal forest conifers and hardwoods are particularly adept at dealing with extreme cold, some able to cope with temperatures well below minus 40 degrees. It has been discovered that these far northern species can tolerate freezing solid by dramatically drawing down their internal water, accumulating antifreeze sugars in their cells, and, probably most importantly, drawing the remaining water in the living cells into the spaces between the cells where the water freezes without cell damage.

We can look out at trees and they seem so commonplace and simple. Yet they are breathing, transpiring, liquid circulating, energy converting entities—and habitats for multiple life forms. As with our blood pressure, the internal water pressure of a tree can be measured in its needles and leaves by instruments. A dying tree will have reduced water pressure, a dead tree, none.

Commonplace, yes, anything but simple.

It is not necessary to dig among the roots of trees to find the most charming of forest ground dwellers. For scattered in mostly semi-shady areas throughout the dunal woods are rich green patches of Clubmosses, low-growing, primitive vegetation with scale-like leaves that produces neither flowers nor seeds, and thus evolutionarily preceded even the conifers. They are not mosses at all, but, like the Horsetails, the unusual Clubmosses belong to the very old fern family. It has been determined that these ground-level plants

we find in usually thick patches are diminutive descendants of giant, tree-sized plants that lived in huge numbers 300 million years ago in the Carboniferous Era and left us seams of coal (sequestered carbon of the ancient past that we humans are increasingly releasing). I was carrying a new guide book to help identify these perennial, magical-looking "fern allies," and some were nearby poking through the mossy pads of an otherwise sparsely carpeted forest floor.

temperate forests still thrive in this corner of our Michigan world, and they never fail to delight me.

We descended from the ridge which curved around to partly loop us back southward toward the roadway trail. Once below, we made our way through a north-south hollow enclosed on the lakeside by a high slope so steep I would need to scramble on all fours, like the regular inhabitants, to scale it. I never even tried. A friend of ours whom we introduced to our cottage setting several years later would name this deep interdunal space "the Sanctuary" for the feeling of being totally set apart from the outer day-to-day world. Effectively hidden from view, it is a rarely visited site. Some of the most attractive non-tree inhabitants of a forest such as this are the gracefully rising woodland ferns, and the Sanctuary floor was blessed with a wealth of them.

It was here, in a future spring, passing through the upward arching ferns, that the Sanctuary-namer and her husband and Doug and I almost stepped upon a recently born fawn—so perfectly matching the leaf litter on which it lay hidden, its earth-tone exterior sprinkled with spots to look like dappled light coming through the tree canopy. At the very last moment it leaped up out of seemingly nowhere and trotted off on wobbly legs, with us backing off in surprise, gaping at this delightful wonder of nature as it disappeared upslope and deeper into the woods. The mother White-tail was probably away feeding or had heard us and left the fawn hidden, as she herself went for cover not wanting to flag the location of her defenseless offspring—who was *not* supposed to move. Evidently in our approach, we four must have seemed like a horror to the fawn, giants about to crash down upon it, and it could not be controlled by its normal stay-hidden instinct.

A fawn spends its first weeks as a rather solitary creature, hidden and quietly waiting for its mother to return from her woodland browsing

Comparing the erect six-inch evergreen shoots sprouting off a creeping horizontal stem in the closest patch to the drawings and descriptions in the book, I grinned with success. "This group is called Shining Clubmoss."

"Come over here," Doug urged, having joined me again on *terra firma*. "These are half again as tall, and they look like miniature evergreen trees."

"*Lycopodium obscurum*," I repeated aloud, grappling with the pronunciation, after locating the correct identifying page in the book. "Commonly called Ground Pine." Later, we were to find patches of this densely ground-covering species up to sixty feet across.

Once more on our hike, we discovered another variety of these unique plants of ancient lineage. All of the species have tiny leaves that resemble Hemlock or Cedar needles/scales and even have the general appearance of diminutive conifers. Some authorities believe that each Clubmoss patch, or colony, is a single clone, spread slowly outward, perhaps over centuries, from an individual plant, as its rootstock gets longer and branched. Aged as well as ancient. The Clubmosses have a history of human use, too. They produce great numbers of reproductive, dust-like spores, so fine and high in oil content that they explode when lit—giving off a burst of light, burning rapidly and brightly, but with little heat. The spores thus were once commercially gathered for flame effects in Victorian theater, and the flash powder needed for old-time cameras. Among other past uses for the spores was the coating of pills.

The evergreen Clubmosses were also harvested for Christmas decorating, and their range was much depleted as a result. Doug, some years back, once came upon a large patch of Clubmosses in a wooded area of a Tennessee state park, but we've not found any in our Indiana location or elsewhere in our travels. However, these little beauties of so it can nurse, as our little surprise was very likely doing. The doe must renew its own nourishment from pregnancy and in producing milk for the newborn. Within three to four weeks, the developing fawn is running along with its mother, learning the ways of its habitat. If all goes well, the adorable (is that too anthropomorphic a description?) youngster will make it through the coming year and possibly stay with its mother as a yearling for a few more seasons—or longer, if it is a female.

It was here, too, in this protected ravine—and designated sacred as well—that a future wind would reach down and tear through, uprooting and sending to an abrupt death several tall, sun-seeking trees with heavenward-lifted tops. Aeolus has no reputation for reverence. Indeed, here and elsewhere throughout the forest, it appears to us that windthrow, or "blowdown," is far more responsible for the demise of "adult" living trees than the ravages of insects, diseases, and old age.

Several modest rises and turns took us out of the south end of the Sanctuary, and we were soon reconnected with the main trail. Forays through this dunal forest are not difficult passages to make. If Doug doesn't insist on tackling the truly steep and longer dune slopes, exploratory hikes here allow fairly easy negotiating of the intriguing contours to observe and investigate this land of diverse perennials. And we don't have to force our way through a crowded landscape of lush growth, thick vegetative stands, or entangling vines. The more mature hardwoods and conifers are spread out with a relatively sparse understory of smaller trees and shrubs, an understory held back by a poorer soil and the reduced sunlight coming from a generally closed canopy—and, we're discovered, the surreptitious White-tail browsing of the lower young growth from deer-head-height on down to the forest floor growth. Although this is a little less true for Doug, I, therefore, seldom have to duck under lower branches while walking as they are mostly gone.

There is seldom any dense growth of herbaceous plants to be careful of stepping on either. With no woody stems, these plants generally die back to the ground at the end of the growing season. By summer the delightfully flowering spring ephemerals are gone—having already done their "whole thing"—and there is little to take their place at foot level. In a few locations, our footsteps tread upon the nicest of carpets, thick, rootless pads of rich green mosses. At times we must wind our way around small patches of ferns and colonies of the evergreen Clubmosses. There is certainly no need to bring a machete or handsaw to clear a route anywhere—certainly not a roaring chainsaw. All and all, it's nice going in this varied dunal forest, even without trails.

In their dead, decaying, horizontal state, it's not easy to imagine that those larger downed trees we encounter while hiking were once conduits for the transfer of huge amounts of water skyward. One source has stated that a large oak can transpire some 40,000 gallons of water annually. Not unusual for an oak to live 200 years, and if only one hundred of those years are considered well-functioning mature ones, then, that translates into well over four million gallons of water having been conducted from the tree's roots up and out into the air during the fallen stalwart's lifetime. And hundreds of thousands gallons more conducted for cell growth. It just doesn't compute that those long, dark wooden carcasses we step over and maneuver around were once elaborate, prodigious plumbing systems.

If this were an old growth forest, the ground would be messier with woody debris and a few more dead, leaning trees would be hung up among a more crowded living. As is, only an occasional wind-toppled tree or a decaying log slowly dissolving into the ground and the atmosphere must be gotten over or gone around. There also would be a significant number of really large standing trees, but the lack of such specimens and the moderate number of medium sized ones, along with the other conditions we find here, says that this forest underwent a "life-changing experience" sometime in the past few centuries. Was it a large fire, a violent windstorm toppling the bigger, older trees, or an extensive insect infestation? If any of these, the forest floor would likely have more debris and a thicker build up of organic matter, for none of these events would have removed the trees and their many embodied constituents from the landscape. Even a fire would have left burnt carcasses and the mineral content of the consumed portions. No, there seems to have been something that took away the old growth trees in the past, that extracted life from this dunal world on a substantial scale—a human infestation?

After a number of observing woods walks through this multistoried community, it dawned on us that there are no streams in, or emanating from, these dunes—or in other dunescapes we have visited. No above-ground watercourses, not even little rivulets during heavy rains, flow toward either of the bordering Flower Creeks. In other terrain types of our experience, moving water has created canyons, ravines, gullies, and the like, gathering surface water from far and wide and then funneling it downhill to ever larger watercourses and collecting bodies. The creeks and rivers that cut through the shoreline dunes and empty into the lake, such as the two Flowers, were gathering water and flowing to the lake long before the forming of the coastal dunefields. But in the dune formation process, the pre-existing watercourses acquired no dunal tributaries as the sand built up around their channels to the lake. Here, within these sand assemblages, the valleys, swales, and other low areas have not been formed by flowing water, but are the product of that ever shaping element, wind.

The old adage, if lost in a wilderness follow a stream or ravine downhill and it will eventually lead you to somebody, doesn't work here, or in any dunal world. For there are no streams, and generally there isn't

any downhill for long either, as the dune form will rise up again, leading nowhere in particular. Precipitation that does fall in the dunes doesn't run off, but soaks into the sand, with the duneworks becoming huge sponges, retaining water with remarkable efficiency. Substantial water is thereby readily available to the roots of trees and other plants, supplying their growth needs and returning millions of gallons to the atmosphere. And that life-giving liquid not taken up and embodied into cellular constructions of the forest's diverse and bountiful life, or sent skyward slowly, percolates further downward, some remaining in the interstices of the tightly packed subterranean sand, the rest gradually finding its way underground to the streams that make their way through the dunes (but are not of the dunes), or directly to the lake.

In view of our growing acquaintance with this dunal woods, it was slightly embarrassing to find that it was not our powers of observation that called to our attention the prevalence of one of the most interesting forms of visible life here, but simply reading about that ubiquitous presence that opened our eyes and forced our seeing. Everywhere Doug and I now looked with this new awareness, there it was. In fact, we didn't even have to go into the heart of the woods to observe samples of this life form, for when sitting on the cottage deck, it was but feet away. With enlightened minds, we now could see that on seemingly every living woody structure, near and far, grew a composite organism of fungus and alga. Without fail, for every tree and shrub now checked, around the cottage and into the woods, this primeval biological partnership called lichen, somewhere on it, had found a bark habitat.

Of course, we had previously noticed irregular circular patches of light grayish green on the trunks of many trees, mostly on the smoother, grayish bark of Beeches, but the rather nondescript mottled splotches were just passed off as an inconsequential abnormality and not given any further thought. These common, drab-colored lichen forms, being

118

Covering most of the lower portion of this Oak tree are at least 2 species of lichen (the light gray-green and brown patches) and dark-green moss.

Beeches and a variety of other tree species, it could be imagined that canisters of a soupy slop had exploded throughout the woods, splattering many trees here and there with thin splotches or crusts. In some cases, the lichen growths appeared as faded paint having run down the trunk in long patches before it had dried.

Some shrub stems and branches, I now found, were so encrusted with lichen growth that the bark color barely showed through. Many trees appeared to be lichen-less, but that was not so. Face up close to the trunk, I could see revealed individual growths on each little raised area of the fissured bark, adding a slight greenish tinge to the dark brown surface. All this overlooked life that now I could detect throughout the woody landscape existed without soil and generally took nothing from the host bark. The partnered fungal and algal components soak up water and minerals from the atmosphere like little sponges, with the tiny green algal cells, like leaves, capturing energizing sunlight and absorbing carbon dioxide gas and moisture to manufacture carbon sugars to feed itself and the surrounding, protective, tough-skinned fungus. As with certain fungi elsewhere in the forest environment, the lichen fungi have entered into a symbiotic relationship with another life form, the embedded algae in this case, as fungi are incapable of making their own food. Some lichens take a small amount of minerals from the dead bark, but otherwise are benign appendages to their hosts.

Algae are members of an early kingdom of life, one that is evolutionarily precedent to fungi, plants, and animals, and are a large and diverse group of organisms ranging enormously in size from small single-celled forms to complex multicellular ones, such as giant sea kelp. Usually found in association with aquatic environments, such as the lake and the nearby streams, algae here in this terrestrial setting on the forest's trees exist in a watery environment provided by the enveloping fungal tissues. Alone or in symbiotic association with other forms of life, generally only inches across and rising but a sixteenth of an inch or so up from the bark surface, don't call much attention to themselves. When finally I came to notice they were nearly everywhere on the numerous photosynthesizing algae "fix" more carbon dioxide and release more oxygen into the atmosphere than all plants in the world, put together.

In an immense variety of forms, sizes, and colors, the union of varied fungi and algae, in over ten thousand combinations or species, grow on a myriad of usually stable and long-lasting surfaces around the planet, both natural and human-made. Able to survive extreme heat, cold, and drought by temporarily shutting down metabolic activity, lichens most often colonize marginal habitats too harsh or limited for other life forms. The outer surfaces of trees are solid and semi-permanent, exposed continually to the extremes of weather, and normally eschewed as habitat by other life—perfect for us, say the lichen partners. There is not a single rock (bigger than a sand grain, that is) in this landscape, but if there were, islands of lichens would likely be tightly attached, with colors of many possibilities. The symbiotic lichens are perennials, slow growing and long-lived, and reproduce by a form of division or by dispersing spores. Wind-driven, spores can land high up in a tree to regenerate new lichens, with the companion life advancing up the structure as the tree extends higher.

Awakened to this widespread, but overlooked, life form in the dunal woods, I wondered if lichens were abundant in our Indiana urban landscape. Tree after tree, specie after specie, I found that lichens had found them, in ours and neighbors' yards, along streets, in tree-lined parking lots. As in the forest, sometimes only a glance was necessary to now see what had been passed by thousands of unseeing times. For some trees, diligent inspection was necessary, for there were only minuscule lichen specks. Like in the woods, variation in color and form was found: a neighbor's Sugar Maple was adorned with a modest splattering of bright orange bumps along with the dominant and common light gray green hues, and our short Dogwood yard specimen became the first tree found to sport curly, leaf-like protrusions sticking out from the bark in tiny gray-green swirls up to a half-inch high. In forest and town, life within life, life upon life. Now that we could "see", it was evident to us that lichens, those abundant and complex partnerships of early organisms, were a major component of the earth's biological diversity. It is an encrusted world.

The lichen connection to trees revealed how multifaceted are arboreal habitats. Remarkably, five kingdoms of life are commonly found in association with trees. Fungi is one kingdom and algae is a member of another; birds, squirrels, and insects are representatives of

The red fungal component of this lichen produces the spores, and the "red caps" suggested the specie's name: "British Soldiers".

the animal kingdom; mosses sometimes grow on tree bark and along with the tree itself are of the plant kingdom; and lastly there are bacteria, the oldest and most abundant organisms, that are everywhere. A tree is a veritable Kingdom of Life Zoo.[1]

A study of anything is a series of revelations. And my learning about lichens was an excellent case in point. It also brought home to me in new understanding that not only can observing bring knowledge and insight, acquiring a little knowledge and understanding can, in turn, greatly magnify perception.

Back at the cottage, as evening settled in after a consumed dinner, I swept the cottage entry and walkway of the day's collected sand and pine needles. Part way through, I quickly raised my head to the woods from which we had earlier returned. "The Veery is calling!" I announced over my shoulder to Doug, as I stopped to aurally savor this Neotropical bird's hauntingly beautiful song. Like a descending spiral of flute notes being played through a long metal pipe, the off-repeated vocalization adds an element of magic to the dimming light of the early evening forest.

Weeks earlier I had taken great delight in knowing that this softly cinnamon-colored thrush had made the marathon journey back to its general birthplace from its threatened winter home in a particular area of Brazil. Now, in its northern breeding grounds of shady woods, this male Veery was on high stage for another series of summer dusk renderings of its distinct serenade, offered after most other birds have quieted down.

It was enchanting the first time I heard that somewhat eerie serenade coming from somewhere out in the dunal forest, the most wonderful wildlife sound I have known. Hopefully, there was a female Veery traveler who had made the long, difficult passage to these woods to be as readily seduced by the singing as I was.

Curious as to how this species could produce such delightful music, I finally came across a reference stating that the intriguing distinctiveness of the Veery's song comes from the ability of this bird to sing more than one note at a time—described as singing in harmony with itself, a self-sung "duet." But how does it do that? Only more recently did I learn that birds do not have a larynx with vocal chords, located in the upper part of the trachea, as we do, but a syrinx at the base of their trachea, which straddles the tops of the two large bronchial tubes coming from the lungs. Each tube top is equipped with sound-producing connective tissue and elastic membranes, muscles, and neural connections. And there is a far more complex respiratory system than ours, as well.

This elaborate and highly efficient sound-producing organ is unique to birds, enabling many species to produce two separate sounds at once, with modulations or harmonics, as each side of the syrinx functions independently. "True" songbirds, or oscines, have the most complex syrinx, with up to nine pairs of muscles operating their musical sound box. Generally, the more syrinx muscles a species has the greater is the complexity and quality of its singing.

The oscines is a large category of birds, with many species existing throughout the world. And each individual (essentially young males) of most songbird species has to be a song-learner—going through a developmental stage of learning from others, with much practicing, until vocalizing perfection is achieved. Memorization is then necessary, often of elaborate sequences of notes (tunes), with changes in note

1 _In recent decades, a sixth category of life, named Archaea, has been designated with the discovery of microscopic organisms that commonly exist in extremely hot, acidic, or alkaline environments. These single-celled organisms are like bacteria in some ways, but different enough from any of the other life kingdoms to be classified separately. While none exist in conjunction with trees, some forms are very close by, in the dark digestive tracts of various animals, helping to break down what these creatures have eaten.

As with the timing of migration, the amazing reproductive behavior of songbirds is set on its course by hormonal releases triggered by seasonal lengthening of daylight. Migration, courtship, mating, nesting-building, raising of young, molting of feathers, migrating again—all set in motion by variation in sunlight levels, an external cue or stimulus, although it has been determined that there is also an "internal clock" at work in birds, as well. The timing must be right for all to be accomplished successfully in the limited portion of the year available "up north."

Syrinx is the Greek designation for panpipes, a connected row of small flutes that produce a haunting sound when blown across. According to mythology, an amorous Greek god, Pan, fashioned the first panpipes from hollow water reeds that were the transformed body of a maiden he had been pursuing and who had thereby hidden from him. Her name was Syrinx.

A number of thrush species have the ability to utilize their syrinx in highly melodious ways, emitting pretty flute-like songs during the breeding season; however, none compares to the complexity and beauty of that of the Veery, in my estimation. And I have heard recordings of the delightfully sounding human-devised syrinx, the panpipes. But it is still the Veery's syrinx that brings forth the most enchanting music.

While this migrant's ethereal strain comes from on high, it is another of those songbirds of mature forests that nest at ground level. Sightings, however, are rare. I had seen it but once, along the woodland floor, Doug, not ever. The Veery is a shy bird, but its secretive habits don't bother me—if I am simply entitled to savor its wonderful song. But I am concerned that the time is coming when that will not be possible, for the Veery is one of those many species that has experienced a steep population decline in more recent decades.

122

frequency, pattern, or lengths of song phrases. And males of many species learn and memorize quite large repertoires of vocalizations. Certain core features of birdsong are innate, or instinctual, but as one ornithologist has succinctly put it: "Before songbirds become musicians, they have to be music students."

Some extraordinary "students" have the cognitive (learning) ability to widely mimic—even to incorporate the human voice and whistling into their songs—and to rearrange their library of acquired vocalizations in endless variety. The Brown Thrasher, a mimic, can sing a staggering 2000 songs, or more, according to ornithologists. Although the summer range of this migratory species includes Michigan, we have not heard it here (it's not a forest bird), but are well familiar with the long-tailed Brown Thrasher in Indiana. The male produces a song sequence of rich musical phrases, each usually repeated two times, with the vocalizing lasting up to half a minute. Then another long series of different phrases ensue. This melodious variation goes on and on. It doesn't seem like these are memorized songs so much, as it appears the phrase series are made up along the way by the Thrasher—delightfully improvising like a jazz reed player.

That most songbirds acquire their tunes by learning rather than by instinct has long been known, but I have found that but rarely mentioned, which surprises me. And while the differences between the human larynx and the avian syrinx have also been known about for over two centuries by ornithologists, it has just been in the past century that researchers have discovered how a bird's voice box works. And it has only been decades since it has been conclusively determined why male songbirds sing: to attract a mate and defend territory—"an expression of love and male rivalry." Before and after that avian drama takes the stage, the arias are quieted. Operas and birdsongs—it's all about the same thing. But for the winged actors, the arias are a little more important than entertainment; they're an essential of life.

Some of the bare, high dunes that rise elsewhere along this West Michigan coast present the aura of a desert and are beautiful and compelling in their grand, extensive, curving mounds of light tan. But here, "our" dunes, capped by a rather young forest regime, provide a grand richness that brings an added sense of wonder. These and similar vegetated landforms along the eastern Lake Michigan coast are, so we've read, the most fertile and complex dunes in the world.

And to hear the beauty of a Veery's strain from out in the woods makes decidedly clear that "our" forest, any forest, in any season, is so much more than an arboretum, a collection of trees—it is a most valuable community of immensely varied and interrelated life, visible and invisible, known and unknown, one to be treasured and protected. While the magnificent lake and beachscapes appeal to the eye, I think it is the multifaceted dunal woods that engages my heart the most.

The fruiting bodies of this shelf fungus inhabiting a Beech log are layered and multi-formed.

Little Flower Creek leaving the duneworks to flow onto the beach and to the lake

FLOWERS

Approximately one mile apart, and to either side of our short stretch of shoreline, two modest streams empty their gathering waters into Lake Michigan. Both have been named "Flower Creek," going back at least to the 1870s, but the reason for that designation remains a mystery to us in spite of repeated research in local sources. To compound the puzzlement, several early references and maps have the spelling as "Flour."

Each Flower creek and its tributaries is a post-glacial drainage system beginning on the sandy uplands stretching eastward beyond the dunes, those likely beach terraces from millennia ago. And each cuts through rural territory, draining a watershed of small farms, woodlots, and modest home sites, gradually dropping in elevation almost a hundred feet before spreading out lethargically into marshy richness on the flat lands immediately behind the dunes. Then, the waters of each Flower finally gather together to squeeze their way through gaps in the duneworks to make their narrow channel runs to reach the beach and lake.

As with many other watercourses that have to complete their routes through the extensive coastal dunes to help fill Lake Michigan, both Flower Creeks have "drowned" mouths. Over our years of visiting the Michigan west coast, we noticed that many rivers had lakes just

upstream from their outlets into the larger lake. Our learning about the evolution of coastal dune morphology provided an explanation: With the forming of substantial dunes along the eastern rim of the lake, previously existing streams came to have their outlets to the lake partially blocked and dammed up, resulting in the spreading out of their waters into wetlands and lakes of various sizes behind the shoreline's sandy barriers.

As there is a semi-continuous band of dunes along Lake Michigan's eastern coast, nearly all rivers and lesser streams of Western Michigan emptying into the lake have restricted outflows producing impoundments behind the duneworks, or "drowned" river-mouth systems. Along with the extensive dune assemblages, the many associated drowned river mouths are another rather unique feature of this inland sea's eastern coast.

In the case of the two Flowers, we have on occasion seen the channel mouth of the larger stream, the one to our north, totally dammed up for a short time at the very point it empties into Lake Michigan. With a period of strong winds, waves off the lake collide with the less powerful flow of the narrow channel and can force the stream waters to move backward, raising the upstream wetland level noticeably. Sand is deposited across the channel mouth in the process, and when the waves subside, a low, weak dam can remain.

The blockage becomes a temporary bridge for lakeside walkers, but be careful, the newly deposited sand is water-saturated, not compacted, and can be very much like quicksand, letting one sink further down with each struggling step. The quiet backwater behind the choked mouth of Big Flower Creek and the dunes grows in volume until reaching the critical mass and pressure necessary to force a break through the sand dam to the big lake. The rushing wave of the breakthrough flow provides for a few minutes an exhilarating ride to young and adventurous rafters who know when to be ready. It's about the fastest any water flows in this region.

The Little Flower Creek outlet just to our south is too puny to provide such excitement, which is somewhat unfortunate as it bisects the sizeable public beach of Meinert Park. Its final path across that expanse is usually a lazy wandering as the water seeks to meet the big lake. And with strong waves often forcing the shoreline sand around, the outlet of the poor little stream gets pushed all over the place. The final location of the actual emptying of its waters is so variable that it can be more than a hundred feet away from where it was six months before—and then, later, back again. One summer, the very narrow, searching stream channel traveled north several hundred feet along the park beach, parallel to the lake, before finding release at the edge of our property line.

While the width of Little Flower is generally about eight feet across before it advances onto the beach, once there, it is as highly variable as the course of the water flow. Becoming less than a foot in depth as it proceeds on to the lake, the stream can spread out to four or

five yards wide and narrow in to only three feet or so across. Though no provider of excitement, Little Flower does invite the toddler to discover the gentle caress of lazy current and the young army corpsman to divert and dam its course. The outlet at some point is usually jumpable for the long-of-limb. Doug's tall, athletic frame can usually clear the water with effortless stretch, while I must approach as in a field event, and continue my walk on the far side with one wet shoe.

After a great many beach strolls during our first half-decade beside the inland sea that took us to both Flower outlets, and usually past them, and after a fair number of woods forays, we felt both streams begged to be explored inland. Our topographical map revealed that there were upstream wetlands just behind the dune formations, and like the young dunal forest, these impoundments would be newly evolved ecosystems, only a few thousands of years old.

On a mid-spring day, Doug and I decided to follow Little Flower Creek upstream from the park beach. We advanced alongside the shallow waterway into the forward dunes that came down to the back-beach which had little yet in the way of new foredunes. The stream on the south side was tucked tight against a steep slope, with Hemlock, Beech, and Yellow Birch along the upper edges. We were afforded a low, narrow bank on the north side for passage along the watercourse, overseen by Northern White-cedar trees on the higher adjacent ground. Scattered clumps of Buttercup, orange Columbine, and wild Blue Flag Iris provided enticing color amidst crowded shrubby Willow trees.

As Little Flower Creek soon curved sharply northeastward, the opening to the beach receded out of sight. Some ninety yards further upstream, the forested dune slopes backed away, and on both sides of the watercourse the ground gradually widened into a flood plain of fifty feet and more across—indicating that this creek had once been a much

126

broader watercourse than its current upstream width of five to eight feet. This was likely the beginning of an earlier impoundment, when Little Flower was a fuller stream.

The partially sun-lit flood plain floor was covered with tuffed grass and clumps of the alien Dame's Rocket, its beautiful and sweetly fragrant white and lavender blossoms still in bud, not yet ready to aromatically overwhelm the swale. Interspersed in the semi-shade of scattered trees were Horsetails, the short, lacy-leafed Rattlesnake Fern, the Cut-leaved Grape Fern, and occasional swatches of low Trout Lily. The last, with its nodding yellow flower poking up above a pair of broad mottled leaves, is another spring ephemeral, soon to be gone above ground—to have done its "whole thing" for the year. The mottling of brown on this small lily's green leaves suggested to early Americans the skin of the Brown Trout, providing one of the plant's several common names.

Now overseen by a high dune slope on the north side, the quiet little creek gently curved its way eastward through the open back side of the small park campground for some eight hundred feet before fanning out behind the end of the duneworks into its three tributaries. Beyond the confluence and between the two northern stream fingers lay a water-saturated landscape. Here began the currently existing, low-level impoundment of Little Flower Creek. The shallow backed-up water we encountered at the confluence supports, first, an untamed, swampy thicket of spindly hardwoods, and beyond, a semi-forest of mostly evergreens—a secluded and not very accessible area stretching further inland for nearly a third of a mile.

We curved around the edge of the wetland to the northeast, away from the campground and the dunes, into the shade of where the larger trees of the slightly higher, adjacent landscape meet the evergreens and thickets of the lower waterlogged ground. Interested as I was to know the

127

The solitary flowers of the Trout Lily hang from leafless 8-inch stems, with the reflexed petals closing at night. The flowers of this spring ephemeral are pollinated by ants, but here, each flower has a small beetle on it, possibly doing that job—or dining on the flowers. The plants' tiny bulbs were eaten by Native Americans.

character of this natural inner sanctum, where water table and soil surfaces are essentially the same height, I did not venture within that day.

"Go ahead," I said, as Doug tentatively moved from the more solid, drier land into the messy wetland, across the remains of a decaying fallen tree. It was nearly impossible to know for sure where the Little Flower tributary was, as water existed more in puddles everywhere.

The closest to a detectable stream course was along the northerly edge of the impoundment where there existed a somewhat continuous and narrow ribbon of very shallow water forcing its way around, over, or under logs. With the slightest appearance of movement, the clear liquid struggled lakeward over a totally black, mucky bottom.

Less reluctant to traverse spongy, uncertain earth, Doug gradually disappeared into the rather dense environs of both decay and life, cautiously maneuvering from one raised mossy mound to another and skirting the impenetrable entanglements. I lingered behind, taking notes and careful steps along a few hundred feet of the impoundment's wooded perimeter while he explored the unknown terrain inside Little Flower's spread out backwater.

On moist, squishy little overflows

along the northwest edge of this wet land, I noticed the brown remains of last year's artistic fronds of Sensitive and Cinnamon Ferns lying matted atop the decaying tree leaves of last fall and this spring's emergence of new plants. During a later visit in the summer, which provided slightly drier terrain, I would be delighted to find the fern patch luxuriously dominated by the tropical-like Cinnamon Ferns, grown to nearly five feet in height. Parting a way through the giant fronds then, I briefly disappeared from sight in bending to examine the feathery whorls of Meadow Horsetails growing just beyond in erect patches like foot-tall displays of flimsy, spring-green bottlebrushes.

Horsetails are rather close relatives of the ferns, and, along with the Clubmosses, the three are primitive plants of ancient lineage that reproduce by dust-like spores, having preceded seed-bearing species in the evolutionary chain. In varied ways, much of the reproductive life cycle of spore plants, including fertilization, occurs after the spores have left the home plant and found suitable moist places. Flowering plants consolidate this process within the flower, producing an embryo plant with its first leaves and even its own initial food supply. Dispersed from the home plant, seeds are already "children," ready to grow into "adults," without needing the more exacting environmental conditions spores require to germinate and develop. This reproductive innovation allowed flowering plants to expand into a broader range of environments than plants with water-needing spores.

The ancestors of today's spore-producing plants had been prevalent even before the development of insects (which came to do so much pollinating of flowering plants), and these early plants have persisted with few alterations, other than their great reduction in size

from tree proportions, for hundreds of millions of years. Although many species of ferns and their "allies" have endured over that very lengthy period, the "younger" and more adaptive seed-bearing plants have come to outnumber the older plant organisms by roughly thirty to one. And that greater number and diversity of flowering plants is what we came to find within this watery world, although not by such a wide ratio.

Continuing on my exploratory walk along the shaded perimeter of this newly found environment led me to further encounters with plants not associated with the shoreline zones or the forested dunes. I came upon multiple groupings of two tall shrubs of northern distribution, Speckled Alder and Cranberry Viburnum (Highbush-Cranberry) which waded the sluggish shallows. My steps in the soft, moist, blackish ground sometimes pushed away enough soil to reveal the brilliant orange-gold underground runners of a low evergreen ground cover of lustrous leaves. I was later able to identify it as Goldthread, a member of the Buttercup family and

short Alders. A pair of tilted and bent Hemlocks, sliding imperceptibly from the inland slope toward the water-dominated ground while their tops turned upward still reaching for the sky, grew in graceful curves with a horizontal section of one just right for sitting on. I placed myself upon

In a somewhat drier location of the Little Flower swamp, the delightful fall hues of the ground-based Cinnamon Ferns more than match the trees' aerial autumn finery.

a dainty plant of northern bogs and swamp forests. A bitter extract from its network of pretty rhizomes was once widely used, beginning with Woodland Indians, as a natural remedy for a variety of ailments—and some still rely upon it for treating mouth sores and digestive disorders..

While Beech, Oak, and Maple dominated the containing forested slopes of the impoundment, aged Paper Birches, a scattering of Northern White-cedars, and numerous Hemlock trees graced the lowland ground. These species melted into the wetland to join inside Red Maples and the

this convenient seat to await Doug's return.

The report from "the interior" was of such interest that, weeks later and nearly into summer, when the water table proved less extreme, I joined him for his second escapade into the waterlogged world.

An uprooted White-cedar, shoots now growing upward from its fallen trunk clad with fibrous bark, afforded passage across the water's edge, moving us from a small Cedar grouping to a scrubby section of raised, mossy ground on the opposite end of the tree. At our entry, a patch of large Marsh-Marigolds brightened the edgewaters with their intense yellow sepal-petals and rich, glossy-green, kidney-shaped leaves. The foot-tall plants are another member of the Buttercup Family, and Native Americans called them "the flower that opens the swamp."

We searched for footholds of drier ground among the shallow watery pools and slippery muck of organic matter, making our way southeastward around clumps of Alder and extensive circular clusters of tall Cinnamon Ferns whose ornate curled heads were finishing the new season's unfurling in the partial shade. Come autumn's cold killing touch, the tall, arching leaves will be transformed from light green into a stunning lacy spread of dull gold. Although the graceful Cinnamons were the dominant ferns of the wetland interior, Royal Ferns with their delicately veined leaflets were also encountered—which meant the Little Flower streambanks and wetland provided habitat for at least five species of ferns.

A variety of trees had some years ago placed their bets on leaner-watered years. Half of them were now in various stages of decline and decay, listing or lying upon the spongy surface. Further in, toppled trees raised their surface-spreading root masses dramatically out of the soggy morass as their bodies stretched out horizontally to block our advance. We climbed over the larger casualties and picked our way through the crisscross of older fallen carcasses that laid like swollen veins of green, so thickly were they covered with mosses, soft, spongy plants of more ancient lineage than even the ferns and horsetails.

The lowly, diminutive mosses thrive in moist environments throughout the world and were in their element in this wetland. Not having true roots that take in water and nutrients, these plants need no soil for growing and cling to many types of surfaces without taking in anything from them. The simple leaves of mosses simply absorb moisture, carbon dioxide, and nutrients from the rain and air. Rootless, mosses are also "non-vascular" plants, that is, they have no internal liquid-bearing vessels or veins, as in "higher" plants, to carry water through the carpet-like mass of leaves, thin wiry stems, and the root-like rhizoids that do the anchoring of the plants.

The wooded terrain rose slightly as we headed eastward and the extent of the water-saturated ground diminished accordingly. After a hundred yards or so of difficult travel, we turned north, gradually rising out of the damper landscape to enter a semi-open, sandy upland of trees and Bracken Ferns. Heading northwest, we began circling back, which brought us to the familiar walking trail that came through the dunes from the cottage.

Although Doug and I had scouted the banks of varied wetlands around the Midwest in our camping days, we had never truly penetrated into one as with our exploration of the Little Flower impoundment. While not a large wetlands by any means, this bog-like area nevertheless proved to be quite intriguing. The chaotic and messy nature of the dense interior, the abundance of greenery at the floor level mixed with water, and the decaying and decayed matter were quite a contrast with the dunal woodland—and unlike any other landscape I had experienced.

I was surprised at the apparent absence of wildlife. Our labored movements may have warned any away and perhaps the bogginess of the environment was not supportive of the variety that we could readily detect, at least during the daytime. Here and there, though, were the sloppy tracks of the White-tails that travel everywhere.

It took the use by me of four field guides to really become acquainted with this out-of-the-ordinary setting. The indicator plants I identified pointed to this backwater landscape as being a small version of a Northern Swamp Forest. More specifically, it appears to be a White-cedar Swamp Forest. Not only are Northern White-cedars (actually cypresses) scattered throughout the waterlogged area, but we came across stump remnants encased in molded green which seemed to have been cut off—and were the modest size of Cedars.

By this time in our cottage residency, we had begun seeking out the human history associated with the larger coastal landscape and knew that the rot and termite-resistant White-cedars, with their easily split wood, were harvested beginning in pioneer times to make shingles by the tens of millions. Early on, groups of shingles and cut lengths of trees to make them served as a medium of exchange on the Great Lakes frontier. This species of durable wood was also important for making fence posts, log homes, and, later, railroad ties. The remnant stumps we came across were obviously quite old and the tree sizes not really large enough for normal lumber, so it fit that the moss-encased stumps had been White-cedars. The apparent prevalence of this tree species in the pre-settlement past, as well as its current existence, strongly suggests the Little Flower impoundment tended to be a White-cedar Swamp Forest community—

although the probable past harvest of Cedars has since left Hemlocks to become the more dominant tree species. And, in more current times, deer browsing of young Cedars has very likely held back their regeneration, for we found no young Cedars.

Swamps are defined as wetland areas having some surface water flow, at least part of the time, dominated by trees and other vegetation that can tolerate standing in water or very wet ground. Bogs, on the other hand, are fed only by precipitation, with no water flowing in or out of the holding basin. Since the Little Flower Creek wetland has much of its visible water in stagnant puddles and not flowing on the surface, it has the characteristics of a still-water bog as well as a swamp. Nature seldom fits human attempts at establishing precise categories. While Little Flower's very modest stream channels carry inland drainage water to the lake, there is an invisible underground flow making its way lakeward, as well.

Although I at first had found the Little Flower swamp a little forbidding, it was rather exciting to have encountered a very different environment within such a short distance from lake and dunescape. And Doug and I found it intriguing that nearly all of the vegetation I could identify here were plants that are also found much farther to the north, while only a minority are found substantially further south. The range of Meadow Horsetail even extends to the Arctic Circle.

Having explored Little Flower Creek's unique environment at our backdoor, Big Flower Creek now beckoned, for we were interested in seeing what additional wetland features we would find nearby.

The larger Flower Creek is a brisk, stretching beach walk to the north of us. It is a wadable stream only if an arching underwater sandbar can be found a little out in the lake just beyond the mouth and the meeting of the two waters. Even then, those of us with less than lengthy legs cannot always count on shorts remaining completely dry if there are any waves at all. The crossing is a treat reserved for summer walks—or when there is a substantial winter ice shelf for a bridge.

This stream and its tributaries collect their fluids from a watershed of roughly twenty-three square miles. Heedless of arbitrary human boundaries, the main branch crosses back and forth between the two counties of Muskegon and Oceana on a twisted and multi-fingered path through rolling farmland, abandoned pastures and orchards, fragmented woodlands, and scattered country home sites. Some 1000 feet back from its entry into Lake Michigan, the southwestward-flowing Big Flower Creek runs into the coastal duneworks—and "drowns."

The gathered water from behind the barrier of sand squeezes through to the lake in a channel with low dune on the north side and on the south, by the end of the high, forested forward dune line that runs north from the park and our cottage. A half century ago, the north bank of that channel was straightened and stabilized by a solid, wooden retaining wall so that several vacation homes could be built there amidst the dune trees. The width of the constricted, emptying passageway varies depending on water level of the lake but averages roughly twenty-five feet, and the channel depth can be over six feet before rising to meet the lake's sand bars at the stream's mouth. As with Little Flower Creek, the outlet course of the big sister can be forced sometimes to wander along the beach for well over a hundred feet before being allowed to mate with the lake.

The ever-shaping force of wind and wave pushing the shoreline sand around seldom allows the Big Flower Creek wa-tercourse to enter straight ahead into the lake.

Hidden from shoreline sight, the impoundment behind the forested dune barrier spreads out into a wetland that runs north and south in a fluctuating size that at its wettest and largest encompasses more than one hundred acres. Several times we had walked in from the beach along the top of the steep south bank of the lower stream channel to get a peek from the edge of the watery world within, but that is not the way to really experience a stream-based wetland.

133

Twenty years earlier, Doug had built a kayak-like Folbot in the basement of our Indiana home. Besides paying a visit to a hospital emergency room from sawing a short gash into his left hand while constructing the eleven-foot-long boat, he found himself in that classic situation of not being able at first to get the elongated finished product out of the basement work area. After a great deal of struggling, varied maneuvering, certain male-type exclamations (by him), and a slight bending of the rigid craft, we were finally able to squeeze it up the constricted stairway to higher ground. The low, sleek boat with two floor seats had been brought north a few years after our acquisition of the cottage, and now on an early summer morning, he and I were paddling up the calm lake to enter the Big Flower Creek inlet.

Passing several small ducks that were floating downstream, hugging one bank, as we glided upstream along the other, Doug and I traversed the outlet channel's course between the dune slopes, turned a short bend to our left, and silently advanced into the wetland. The open expanse before us provided a long view north of over a half mile and eastward a stretch of about one-third that distance. From our topographical map, we knew that the long, north-south wetland area continued well beyond our line of sight as it gradually diminished and curved to the northeast. Bordered by low dunal woods on the long western side paralleling the lake, the greater portion of the wetland perimeter, in the distance, was ringed by shrubs and small trees at the damp edges with an upland forest regime just behind. But very unlike the

Only after winter's snow packs have flattened the wet meadow vegetation, can the winding course of Big Flower, coming out of the northeast, be partially discerned from ground level.

134

Little Flower Creek swamp, the wetland, itself was completely treeless, with wide open sky above.

We quietly paddled forward upon a winding path of somewhat murky water and submerged vegetation, a route that snaked its way through moist land thickly covered with perennial long-stemmed grasses, reeds, sedges, and Cat-tails reaching up four feet and more. The shallow stream, varying in width from twelve to seventy-five feet as we wound our way left and back again every fifty to seventy-five feet, never gave us much of a clue of where we were going, as the course turned right and then northward amidst the tall, concealing vegetation of a wet meadow. While the connecting channel water had a definite current to it, here, the flow we leisurely paddled against was negligible.

The term "wetland" is a broad one, referring to any area where water is the dominant factor determining the nature of the soil condition and the types of plants and animals that range within that environment. In our case here, Doug and I were now exploring a waterlogged area more specifically defined as a "marsh"—a wetland ecosystem with permanent or nearly permanent shallow or deep water, dominated by grass-like, semi-aquatic vegetation and absent trees within. And, in this case, a drowned river-mouth marsh of modest size. Here was a wetland complex very different from the Little Flower swamp, which is a decidedly wooded wetland ecosystem—no boat needed or possible there!

Our low, water-level profile allowed us to maneuver unobtrusively upstream, and for a while we were gently gliding through floating islands of Bullhead-Lily leaves and flowers festooning the sluggish waters. Reaching overboard, I touched the globe-like fleshy yellow sepals that cupped and all but hid the interior slender petals and circular stamen. An aquatic perennial, the Lilies' wide floating leaves and showy bulbous flowers were anchored by underwater stems to rhizomes rooted in the bottom mud several feet below

If the two of us communicated at all, it was in hushed tones, as explorers of rare new worlds should. The slim-winged, long-tailed Marsh Hawk soaring above was silent, too, but for differing purpose. Such quiet behavior allowed her, and us, to witness some of the numerous inhabitants of the wetland; but her sightings sometimes became a meal.

Red-winged Blackbirds, songbird residents of both marshes and dry meadows, sat atop erect Bur-reeds and tall Cat-tails seeming to proclaim the glories of blossoming Blue and Yellow Flag Irises. In actuality, the males were sending forth their song of liquid notes, followed by a strange burbling trill, as a territorial statement, while hunching up their backs and spreading out their shoulders to boldly display red patches. Each black macho male with his red epaulets was possibly making a claim on a harem of as many as three brownish females. (Promiscuity is not at all uncommon among songbird species, but some males are more possessive than others.)

It was our guess that very few human ears ever listened to the Red-wing's rich musical offerings here, or to that of the more rare Marsh Wren with its gurgling song repertoire. While all of the wetland and the surrounding area beyond is in private ownership, with one exception, only on the upland southern curve of the marshy area are there any residences. And all but two of the half-dozen homes are seldom-visited vacation cottages. The two primary residences are set back amidst the surrounding mixed forest of the deciduous hardwoods, Hemlocks, Pines, and some White-cedars.

We were pleased that we saw or heard no one else to disturb the setting, which we ourselves were careful to respect. Our slow advance along the winding waterway, however, did occasionally disturb a small flotilla of ducks. Rounding a bend, we sometimes were greeted with an explosion of flapping wings rising from the water as the birds took to the sky and settled down well out of sight further upstream. And then there were the prolific, foot-long Muskrats who would swim away upon our coming into sight, showing only the tops of their little heads, noses leading the way, and leaving slight wakes fanning out behind the gliding, disembodied head tops.

Other Muskrats came and went from mounded lodges of woven vegetation and mud in the shallows of the stream and burrows along the steeper vegetated banks. Like Beavers, Muskrats have underwater entrance tunnels to their cone-shaped, chambered living quarters which rise several feet out of the water. These dark-brown, aquatic rodents gather roots, stems, and nutlets of Bur-reed for munching, their appetites coincidentally helping to maintain areas of open water conducive to the landing of waterfowl. Well evolved to their aquatic lifestyle with specially adapted eye, nostril, and respiratory systems, Muskrats can remain underwater for as long as fifteen minutes.

This water mammal will build floating mats from shredded vegetation for eating on, rearing young, and leisurely sunny siestas. They'll be wise to keep one eye open, though, to watch for hungry hawks or two-foot-long Mink which prowl the fluctuating edges of the marsh unseen or take to the water, looking for a favored meal of Muskrat or a ready-made Muskrat den for its own.

Humans also find this widespread water denizen of value. Its thick underfur makes an excellent pelt, and was once a very major item in the fur trade. Even today, trapping for the pelts is a multi-million dollar business, with the Muskrats' lustrous hides producing more fur coats than those of any other animal. There is also a past usage of the animal that relates to its name. I had half-wondered about that designation of "Muskrat." I never thought of them looking that much like rats, but I now find they are indeed related to certain wood rats and mice. It was the "musk" part, though, that was strange. As it turns out, these large "rats" have a pair of musk-exuding glands in their abdomens, and the inoffensive musk from these lowly creatures was once dried and used in the "classy" perfume industry.

Humans have long eaten Muskrats, with particularly the French-Americans in southeastern Michigan having a tradition since the dire circumstances of the War of 1812 of consuming the "swamp rabbit." And it is those musk glands that determines the time of year that allows the meat to be palatable, for only in the winter is the musk not so strong as to adversely affect the taste of the animal's flesh.

Occasionally, turtles, those reptiles with the unique arrangement of the vertebrae being incorporated into a protective carapace, or shell, would slip into the greenish-brown water from their shoreline dozing as we floated into view. So quickly did this happen that we were not able to identify the species, but they were probably Blanding's Turtles which are very timid and, when surprised basking, will dive to the stream bottom and stay there for hours. We have found an 8-inch-long Blanding's Turtle shell, with the backbone and an attached set of ribs and the neckbones fused to the underside of the carapace, which is composed of layers of keratin—that same proteinous material of which feathers are made (as well as the outer layer of human skin). By adding new layers of the tough, plastic-like keratin under the old ones, a turtle shell grows and expands. Counting the lined layers on the found carapace indicated that this Blanding's Turtle was only a dozen years old when it died. But in the order of turtles there is unusual longevity, and members of this species may live as many as eight decades.

On a beach walk in the spring of another year, we had the fortunate timing to see highly aquatic Snapping Turtles mate for a protracted period in the deep current of the Big Flower outlet where the murkier water of the creek mixes with the clear lake liquid. Evidently the submerged creek couple didn't mind us watching their slow-motion love ballet. Each of the gently tumbling, engaged lovers was thick-bodied and over a foot long. The massive-headed, powerful-jawed Snapper, the largest turtle species in our area, hibernates through the winter beneath a blanket of mud or sometimes in a Muskrat bank burrow. Having evolved in North America, this species lives nowhere else but in the Western Hemisphere. Turtles are toothless carnivores and will eat any animal it can readily capture and is able to swallow whole, with the large Snappers gulping down even baby turtles and small mammals.

Frequently during the first part of our float trip, in the lower reaches of the stream, there occurred light thudding noises against the submerged sides of our boat. It took us a while to see in the less-than-clear water what we were hitting—or what was hitting us. We determined that large fish were bumping into the boat, perhaps in some aspect of procreation, because occasionally we'd see disturbance of the water's surface caused by the flopping of fish forms just below. We later learned that the large, broad fish, up to thirty inches long, are Eurasian Common Carp introduced into American freshwaters by government agencies, beginning in the 1870s. They spawn in early summer in warm, shallow water such as we were negotiating.

Promoted at first as an excellent food and game fish, the Common Carp as a culinary delicacy failed to catch on with the public, and within decades, problems were emerging where the highly adaptable species became established—which in time became very widespread. Their spawning activity and the digging for snails, crustaceans, and roots of aquatic vegetation stirs the stream bottom's organic sediments into a muddy stew. Not only are these alien fish competing directly with diving waterfowl for similar food sources, but the resulting turbidity of the water interferes with the feeding and spawning of native fish, decreasing the numbers of those desirable lake species which require streams such as Big Flower to spawn, seeking to bring forth the next generation.

The Carp's bottom-feeding also destroys submerged plants. We had the answer to both the thudding noises and some of the cloudiness of the water.

Coastal marsh habitats are critically important as feeding, mating, and nursery grounds for a broad range of wildlife. They are especially valuable for the itinerant clientele of migratory waterfowl that require stopovers to rest, feed, and sometimes find refuge during high winds and storm events on their way to Canada. Even though the Big Flower marsh is not a large wetland, over forty avian species were observed and recorded by a Michigan Department of Natural Resources staff biologist in a mid-1990s survey of the marsh and its woodland perimeter. A far more capable and knowledgeable observer than Doug and I, he further found that approximately half of the species were seasonal breeding residents. The others were either short-term "stopovers" or permanent residents.

Among the variety of summer ducks seen here in the Big Flower wetland by the biologist or ourselves have been Mallards, Blue-winged Teals, Black Ducks, Ring-necked Ducks, Goldeneyes, and Wood Ducks—the last two species being nesters in cavities of trees on the perimeter of ponds, lakes, and marshes. I had long wondered why a wild duck would be named "Wood," when it is a bird associated with aquatic environments. That Wood Ducks are tree cavity nesters wasn't enough of a reason since a range of other ducks are, as well. But when I learned that the multi-colored Wood Duck is the only native perching duck species (even having well-developed claws for gripping tree limbs) and that these fowl wander well beyond the water's edge into adjacent woodlands to augment their aquatic and shoreline diet with berries and a variety of nuts and other seeds, I took that to be the explanation for their name designation.

Waterfowl young spend a long developmental time in their eggs and are hatched covered with down, with eyes open, and are ready to leave the nest quickly, often the first day after hatching. They are immediately able to feed themselves and swim. Like the deer fawns, able to function and walk very soon after birth, waterfowl hatchlings are designated "precocial," as in "precocious"—having an unusually early development or maturity. To accommodate the more completely developed embryo, the calcium carbonate and protein encased eggs of precocial birds are larger than those of altricial species that hatch as helpless nestlings. I was surprised to learn that waterfowl imprinting of young upon their parents begins even before hatching, with the incubating female initiating low calls, and the chicks, still in the egg, calling back.

Being predominantly ground nesters in the shoreline vegetation, ducklings and goslings being able to walk and take to water promptly likely enhances their survival chances—although Wood Duck young, born in the height of a tree cavity, also leave their nest soon after hatching. Within a day or two, these ducklings, at the soft calling of their mother from ground level, leap from their elevated nest and, attempting a glide, land on the ground usually unhurt, then follow their mother to nearby water to feed. As with the males of other duck species, the Wood Duck drake would have departed the scene soon after the hen had started laying.

With its shallow water, Big Flower's wetland attracts mostly migratory waterfowl species that are classified as "dabblers," such as the Mallard, the ancestor of the common white domestic ducks. These dabbling species forage from the water's surface and often tip up while floating ("bottoms-up") to reach aquatic plants, such as Duckweed, in the water not far below. The vegetable matter and insects are strained through tooth-like edges of their bills as the bird's head comes out of the water. Dabblers are walkers and can also feed on land, eating seeds, foliage, and insects. Mallards are the largest dabbling ducks—far-ranging and easily the most numerous duck species on the continent—and we have even observed a mating pair on the very modest and confined waters of Little Flower Creek's outlet channel.

Diving species, on the other hand, have evolved to descend into the water to exploit different food resources: vegetation, fish, and other organisms further down. The divers generally are heavier and ride lower in the water than the more buoyant dabblers and most require deeper bodies of water, such as the lake. The diving ducks mostly eschew smaller waters, such as ponds and Big Flower's stream, because they also tend to migrate in large flocks. Divers, including non-duck species such as Loons, have shorter legs placed further to the back of their bodies than dabblers, making them more powerful swimmers. But with their legs and feet off-center, divers are poor walkers and spend little time on land.

Categories are rarely ever fully precise, and as it turns out divers will also do some dabbling and some dabblers do a little diving. Divers generally need a short run across the water's surface to take to flight, while dabblers can take off immediately, the Mallard only requiring a single wing beat to go aloft. All in all, there is no other animal group that is as adept at both swimming and flying as ducks.

Among the marsh's largest birds are groups of Canada Geese (once almost extinct, but now the most common and widespread of geese), Great Blue Herons, which are among the most ancient of birds, and a nesting pair of misplaced Mute Swans. The Mute Swan is another example of a non-native species being deliberately introduced into North America. Brought from Europe in the 1800s to stock estates and parks, escapes developed into a wild population that now outnumbers native swans in the eastern United States. It has been referred to by birders as the "Great White Starling," for it is aggressively competing with native waterfowl species for breeding and food sites, similar to the European

Starling's competition with native birds for nesting cavities and food. A breeding pair of large Mutes will brook no other waterfowl nesting in its defended area of up to ten acres.

Some of the flying residents, like the gaggles of gregarious Geese, sometime ascend from or land on the marsh's open waters with fanfared announcements, while others, like the "Great Blues," up to nearly a dozen at a time, arise on silent wing in the shadowy hours of dawn and dusk to stalk the shallow shoreline of the big lake, spear fishing for their meals. Spending the day in the more secluded marsh, the Herons retire at night to rookeries of large platform nests of sticks high in the taller trees ringing the wetland. As this is done away from human intrusion, we've not been able to locate the elevated stick nests.

On a later float trip, we rounded a stream bend and were fortunate to notice in the short distance ahead a Green Heron crouching on a large log along the water's outside edge where the watercourse swung in close to the tree line. As we hugged the inside bank, with just Doug slowly, gently paddling us smoothly along, it stayed hunkered low in place and motionless, delighting us with a close-up view of our only ever sighting of this rather reclusive species. While the Great Blues are the largest of North America's herons, the Greens, at large crow size, with long, sharply pointed bills, are nearly the smallest. It also differs with its larger relative in that its nesting is lower, in a bush or thicket near water. Along with several other heron species, this dark green-gray bird's foraging behavior includes "bait-fishing" — attracting small fish by dropping insects, seeds, flowers, and other available items on the water's surface.

The Green Heron was not recorded by the DNR biologist, and very likely there were other species not observed by him, so the avian tally here probably goes up to a notable fifty different bird species during the summer and migratory periods. And the range of species types and behaviors in this wetland complex is a remarkably broad one, from aquatic to land based, from quite large to the very small. Wading, swimming, and perching birds make this their summer nursery grounds. There are raptors and songbirds; and shorebirds, such as Gulls and Sandpipers, will make visits in from their normal shoreline habitat. The swimming waterfowl include both surface feeders and divers into the marsh's waters. Other feeding types include insectivores and scavengers, again with the Gulls, along with Crows and Turkey Vultures. The thickset perching Belted Kingfisher is a "plunge-diver," hovering briefly above the creek before plunging head-first into the water to snag its small fish prey. Ground nesters are matched by cavity nesters, both in trees and in dirt banks, where Kingfishers spend up to a week or more tunneling three most common otter social activity. Growing more than three feet long, the streamlined North American River Otters are larger, semi-aquatic relatives of the solitary, vigorous, and lethal Weasels and Minks, as well as the nonchalant Skunks, of the adjacent dunal woods. The gregarious Otters are fast, powerful, and extremely graceful in water, swimming with an undulating movement of their bodies and tails, up and down, rather than with the in and out sideways movements of fish. Their water locomotion also differs from that of the much slower Muskrats, which use their partially webbed hind feet to push them forward. Otter dens are dug into the creek's banks, tunnels about ten inches in diameter and three to five feet deep.

Seldom still except when sleeping, these restless mammals widely roam the marsh environs feeding on its many offerings, such as crayfish, frogs, and insects, although they are preeminently fish eaters. The carnivorous Otters and the Muskrats can co-exist as aquatic mammals in the same limited environment, as the latter are essentially vegetarians. Throughout areas of the Midwestern region, otter populations are considered vulnerable or imperiled, although their range has been expanded by stocking. It was very satisfying to know that Big Flower Creek was home to this playboy/playgirl species.

The clientele of the Big Flower wetland locale turns out to be a large and interesting one. Yet, in feeding, nesting, and locating, each group or type of bird, animal, reptile, amphibian, or smaller organisms finds its own functioning niche within the offerings of the marsh and its adjacent surrounding area. Gradually, we were learning that the varied physical and vegetative features of this wetland combined with the fauna richness presents a complex ecological community of interdependence.

Unlike the Little Flower swamp wetland, Big Flower's marsh is hydrologically connected to Lake Michigan. That is, the wetland water

to ten feet into a bank to create a nest chamber to lay their eggs. The constructed reproductive structures in trees range from tiny cup nests to the large, messy-looking stick conglomerations of the Great Blues. In an area of open water, wet meadow, and surrounding upland of some 120 acres, no bigger than a small farm, the breadth of avian diversity and activity is somewhat astounding.

As with the forest's songbirds, virtually all of the wetland's bird species migrate back south in autumn, but a few are reluctant to relinquish resort-like amenities at season's end and stay year-round. But all of the fauna thrives on the wetland's varied smorgasbord and revels in the relative seclusion that Big Flower's marshy mini-world provides. When the migratory birds have vacated the premises and many of the permanent resident species of the marsh have gone into a cold dormancy or the torpidity of hibernation, there still remain some hardy creatures that are active during the winter. And the most interesting activity is undoubtedly that of the Northern River Otter, the "playboy of the wild."

In the 1990s we became friends with one of the two human families who had come to reside year around on the upland edges of the southern portion of the marsh. They told of a family of fun-loving Otters they had seen during one winter, sliding from the creek banks and playing their own version of hockey upon the stream's frozen surface—exuberantly chasing and batting an object back and forth across the ice with their wide, webbed feet. In the angled light of that season, the team's tan throats and chests were highlighted against the lustrous background of chocolate fur, warm and waterproof—and also valued by trappers. So dense is the undercoat that it can hardly be parted down to the skin.

A most group-oriented animal, in late winter and early spring, Otter families will be intact with the previous year's pups in tow, and males often join females with older young. Both juveniles and adults will tussle about in vigorous fun, with such play wrestling being the rises and falls with the fluctuating level of the bigger body of water via the connecting channel of the lower stream course. In times of higher lake levels, strong storm surges can even send lake water flowing back into the marsh, presenting temporarily the appearance of a large pond. With this direct and substantial lake influence, the Big Flower wetland is thereby considered a Great Lakes Coastal Marsh, a rather unique environment. In the process of learning about the functioning of this type of lake-influenced wetland, I was surprised to read that such coastal marshes occur only near the shores of the Great Lakes and are considered globally rare.

The great variety of plant and animal biota, aquatic and terrestrial, found in this and other Great Lakes coastal marshes is greatly dependant upon the fluctuation in the water level of the lakes—the very fluctuation that was of so much deep interest to us. The range of historic extremes of Lake Michigan's water levels has been 6.25 feet, which brings drastic changes to the wetland complex. The higher levels restrict the advance of woody plants into the wet meadow component of the marsh and keep aggressive species in check, while the extensive beds of submersed aquatic flora are kept in check by periodic lows that allow the wet-tolerant meadow plants to expand. Water-level changes in the wetland provide opportunities for different species to re-emerge. Some seeds, like those of sedges and Boneset, remain dormant for years, awaiting the needed conditions for growth. Wetlands with connections to the lakes generally have a more diverse and abundant flora and fauna than those with no connections.

I could clearly see that difference in comparing the Big Flower marsh with the "land-locked" Little Flower swamp. While much of the flora I identified in the Little Flower wetland can be found in the perimeter plant communities of the Big Flower marsh, virtually none of the marsh's extensive aquatic and wet meadow flora exists in the swamp. And then there is the wealth of the marsh's wildlife.

But there is one substantial similarity, of sorts, between the two wetlands, and even with the forested dunes. And that is, all three ecosystems are built upon perennials, hundreds of them, and though there is little overlap in the species, the collective wild flora (whether spore- or seed-producing) is composed one hundred percent of perennials, as best I can determine. The only native annual in this varied area of which I am aware is the little Sea Rocket out on the dry beach just inland from the swash zone. Come late fall, this tenacious plant, already surviving in the harshest of all environments here, succumbs to the fatal stress of frigid temperatures. Much further south, along warmer seashores, Sea Rockets may live through the wintertime, but here there must be a new generation each year to continue the species.

The times of extreme high or low lake levels may cause concern and problems for us humans, but the wetland fluctuations are an essential element for the broad biodiversity of the marsh. We've come to understand that the Big Flower coastal marsh is a very active system, biologically and physically complex. However, we've wondered whether the water level extremes can go too far from an ecological standpoint.

Our earliest explorations of the Big Flower marsh took place when the lake water level was still somewhat high, followed by a period generally in the "average" range. That seemed to us to be providing the "normal" appearance and status for the wetland. In terms of marsh biodiversity, we thought it could hardly get any better than what we had been observing and were learning about. As the decade of the 1990s progressed, the lake levels rose again to somewhat above the long-term average, providing for a modestly fluctuating wet marsh. Our beach and foredunes continued to gradually expand despite the lake level increase, and it appeared that with the close of our first decade beside the inland sea things were going quite well for our coastal world.

Then we got something of a fright as lake levels zoomed up from mid-1996 to mid-1998, coming close to the historic high levels of a decade earlier for a matter of months. Doug and I watched the beach retract, and concerns emerged that we needed to brace ourselves for a repeat of the extensive beach and foredunes loss of the 1980s. But near the end of the 1990s, precipitation in the Lake Michigan basin diminished greatly, and along with high temperatures increasing lake evaporation, water levels began dropping as quickly as they had risen. Beginning in December 1998, Lake Michigan descended below the monthly average level and proceeded on downward. For the next decade, water levels continued to remain below their historic monthly averages, dropping in both 2001 and 2003 close to the lake's historic low point. We now had seen the magnitude of Lake Michigan's water level vary by almost six feet in a decade and a half.

From the late 1990s on, as a regional arid period set in and lake levels diminished, the beach and foredunes area went back to expanding lakeward and continued broadening in depth almost exponentially. Dry land came to extend over 200 feet in front of our bluff. The lower steps of our stairway were buried by drifting sand, and foredunes kept building upward and lakeward, in concert with the advancement of extensive Marram grass growth. By early 2001, there were over 300 feet of beach and foredunes stretched out before us. As it expanded even further, Doug came to joke that we now needed to pack a picnic lunch to travel from the cottage to the water's edge. Of course, with its hydrological connection to the lake, the marsh's water levels were diminishing substantially as well, and the amazing extension of dry land along the lakeshore was being mirrored in the wetland.

By this period, it generally wasn't necessary to use a boat to enter and explore the Big Flower marsh any more. Where there had been a twelve- to twenty-foot wide stream course meandering through soggy wetland meadows spread out hundreds of feet in most directions, there was now a somewhat narrower and much shallower stream clearly defined by land that was only damp. We noticed that the vegetation had changed as well. Across most of the northern portion of the drought-stricken wetland grew rampant a plant we identified as Reed Canary-Grass—another alien. The spread of this species almost certainly came from carry-over growth from earlier farming days, when Eurasian seed was brought for pasturage plantings, and this tall-stemmed, many-branched grass thereafter became naturalized far beyond its original agricultural locations.

In our historical research, we read in the local newspaper of the 1890s that during droughty times when regular pasturage failed, marsh grasses were harvested for livestock. An August 1891 news item noted that the Big Flower marsh grasses that "heretofore have been too wet to mow [for hay] are this season dry enough to drive on to with team and wagon." During the drought of that year, another report declared, "All of the marsh grass is being cut, as without it there will not be fodder enough for the winter." Whether that hay was from native species or the introduced Reed Canary-Grass there is no way of knowing. But it may have been at this time that the newcomer grass began its invasion into the dried-out wetland.

This alien species is a modestly high, aggressively-growing perennial, forming extensive and persistent monocultures that choke out native plants, reducing diversity. Worse, it has little value for local wildlife as it is not a food source (although Bison would relish it), and the plants generally grow too dense to provide adequate cover for waterfowl. In winter, snowpack easily flattens the dead, straw-colored stalks, leaving them lying close to the ground and useless for much wildlife protection.

As I have read, the Lake Michigan coastal habitats of dunes, forests, and wetlands support a significantly greater native biota than regions inland, with a variety of life that's hard to match anywhere else in the country, for complexity of habitat equals species diversity. The marsh wetlands, particularly, are among the most productive ecosystems known. The region's native biodiversity was once greater, of course, but humans have in record time substantially reduced that magnificent range of biota, here and elsewhere. Some reduction has come deliberately, such as the outright extirpation of Cougars and Gray Wolves by Euro-American newcomers. But numerous other actions, meant to be additive rather than eliminative, have also had a serious impact.

As Doug and I explored and learned about the Big Flower marsh over more than a decade, it became apparent to us that the introduction of alien species into the coastal environment—the Carp in the water, the Reed Canary-Grass on the marshland surface, and the Mute Swans amidst the native waterfowl—has converted a naturally very diverse and complex wetlands system to a lesser grade system, particularly as a wildlife refuge. Ironically, while the alien species were introduced into the American landscape by humans for worthy (human) purposes, they have done much ecological damage.

We also now can understand that our (human) desire for consistently lower lake levels in order to have a suitable beach and foredune area as part of our particular little environment is not best in the broader world of the lake-associated environments. We're hoping there will be an end to the below-average precipitation levels that have continued in the region now into and throughout the first decade of the twenty-first century. There needs to be a return of a higher water level of the lake that will inundate the dried marsh adequately enough to drive the Reed Canary-Grass back and allow the "seed bank" of the more desirable native species to bring forth a more natural vegetative cover. Perhaps, though, it is simply too late for that hoped for recovery.

In coming to this lakeshore location, we had but a limited antici-pation and understanding of the wealth of experiences and enrichment that we would garner from the immediate shoreline and cottage environments. That we also would have the opportunity to experience the nearby richness of two secluded Flowers' wetlands, there had not been the slightest inkling. Sort of like winning the lottery without even knowing we had entered. And the fortuitous winnings in this varied coastal arena kept coming.

As the standout yellow of the Hairy Puccoon makes that flower the showy species along the shoreline, so the bright, shiny color of the Marsh Marigolds makes them the show-stoppers in the Little Flower swamp. The umbrella forms in the lower left and upper right are emerging Mayapples.

CLUES

A chase scene suddenly interrupted an otherwise quiet summer afternoon. I dropped my garden trowel to run after Doug, who had called to me as he abandoned hammer and drill to hurry down the cottage driveway. A series of strange cries had come from the duneworks not far to the north, and his first thought was that of a child crying out, but no human came down the access lane from that direction. Then came an insistent bleating—a mysterious, unfamiliar sound, perhaps an animal in great distress, a doe having a difficult birthing (although it was late in the year for that). Just as I nearly caught up with Doug as we hurried up the two-track, a large fawn frantically raced across the roadway fifty feet in front of us, followed, in hot pursuit, by an exuberant Red Fox—fluffy white-tipped brush flying fully extended behind. In an instant, the pair left the lane behind and disappeared east into the woods, the bleating cry fading.

Perhaps instinctively seeking to give the fawn assistance, Doug jumped into the chase, as I trailed behind. Our ability to maneuver the forested hills was clearly no match for Fox or Deer, and quickly even the sound of them had vanished. Still drawn to discover the outcome of the episode, we searched the rolling wooded dunes unsuccessfully for nearly a half-hour more. We wondered aloud why such an event had even occurred. Not much heavier when full grown than a husky, overfed housecat, Fox will eat carrion Deer, but healthy White-tails (even well-grown fawns) are not suitable prey for such a singular small predator, one that happens to have the largest geographical range of any living carnivore. At times, the intelligent and highly evolved Red Foxes will playfully agitate large grazing animals to move about, thereby stirring small rodent prey from beneath matted vegetation, but this escapade seemed merely sheer sport on the part of the little rascal.

While Fox, fawn, and definitive answers eluded us, the entertaining enigma led us to the chance discovery of an enchanting place and an historical mystery. Doug, always ahead of me, spied it first and turned to stop my approach.

"Close your eyes," he teased, returning and grasping my hand and leading me carefully forward from a Hemlock-dominated dip onto a light-filled dune-top graced by a small grove of Paper Birches, the one white tree species in a landscape of grayish and brownish trunks..

We develop an immediate affinity for certain spaces or views, and this was one such place. For over 200 feet along the dune ridge, there was an airy openness, with reaching views of the surrounding undulating dunescape through the several dozen white-barked columns, and a dappled light coming down through the green leaf canopy to the ridge floor carpeted here and there with verdant cushions of soft moss.

"Oh, wouldn't it be neat to…," I began, fantasizing designs for the human occupation of the spot, all the while knowing it was a ridiculously impractical location, and one that should not be invaded by such a presence, in any case. Fashioning an imaginary dwelling within a striking landscape was just our automatic response to a scene that pleasured us. We briefly played with ideas tossed back and forth as we rested on moss cushions before heading downslope to return home.

This previously unexplored area of Erna's wooded duneland behind our lakeshore home brought more than new delight; it also aroused intriguing questions. The attractive, medium-sized Paper Birch species grew scattered in the semi-moist lowlands near Little Flower Creek, we had found, roots close to the water table. Yet, here was a grove on a high and dry section of a dune ridge. And, as we searched about in the dunal woods, this also was the only such collection of Paper Birches we could find. Why was this singular grouping here? Clearly, we still had much to learn about the woods and its denizens.

Consulting references, I found that Paper Birches, also known as White Birch with its peeling, coiling, clear-white bark, and a species of small size and northern distribution, were tolerant of a variety of conditions. In addition, like the tall Black Cherry trees scattered throughout the woods, a Birch stand is evidence of once-logged land. Paper Birch is specifically characteristic of burned-over areas, its small seeds quickly finding germinating opportunity in the mineral-rich ash of fire and then flourishing in the sunshine provided by the fire-created opening. The two tree types, being early colonizers of disturbed sites, are known as "pioneer" species. When we found the Birches, had we also found clues as to what had happened on this sandy ridge many years ago?

We returned to the inviting spot in early winter when the first powdery snow had filled the woods with softness and light and contrast. Vestiges of faded gold hung from the Birch branches and shivered in the slight breeze. In their scantily-clothed starkness, many of the distinctive white-trunked trees stretched out along the dune ridge showed signs of stress we had not noticed in summer's fuller green leafy dress. Some had broken, dead branches. Others were standing corpses—a condition well noted by excavating woodpeckers. None of the living Birches were young. Here and there among the aging pioneers, a few young White Pines, offspring of several nearby, tall stalwarts, and a scattering of spindly hardwoods stretched upward toward the sun. In due time, they would join the surrounding large trees of the forest in overshadowing and totally displacing the sun-loving species with the white, paper-like bark. A case of ecological succession.

Sunlight, meanwhile, danced upon the snow, calling our attention to some low dark forms now highlighted—odd, aged tree stumps lingering mostly on the outskirts of the stand of white trunks. We had missed these amid the summer greenery and our

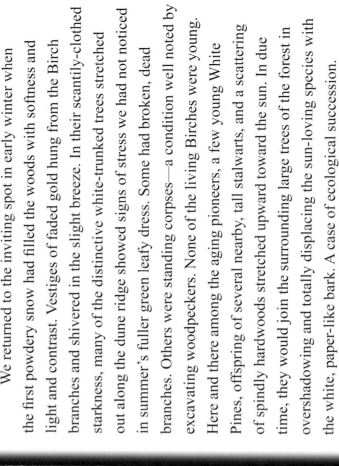

146

delight in finding the unexpected alabaster columns. There were seven stump forms altogether, none whole, but all similar and obviously of the same species. The centers of these tree remnants had long ago disappeared, but the barkless, gray vertical sections of the outer sapwood, the final growth area, rose from the ground in fluted woody spires roughly three feet in height, some sections collapsing inward across their fully hollowed centers.

Perhaps, we thought, these aged remnants could be remains of the first timber harvest here—and the earliest human impact upon this dunal forest. How long ago had that occurred? While in the process of uncovering the basal perimeters, I also noticed that particularly the inward surfaces of the hollow forms were checkered with telltale black charring. There had been fire here, as well. Again, just like the Birches had suggested.

This new discovery confirmed what the Birches had hinted to us. This was indeed a cut-over area, one with intriguing evidence of past events—and of a human intervention in these woods. In our walks in another section of the woods, we had become aware of stumps left from a relatively recent timber harvest, a scattered dozen of valuable Black Cherry trees that had been cut low to the ground. Why had the trees of the far older stumps been cut so high—not much below waist height? Also, what species were they? The specimens were far too old and desiccated for woodworker Doug to determine the species by aroma or texture. The decaying fluted forms seemed to be pine, but he couldn't tell for certain. Taking a broken piece, we'd see if we could get it identified.

I knelt down to brush the snow away from one of the protruding hollowed stumps, exposing the full outline of the flared base in the moss-covered ground. These trees had been larger than we had first realized. The basal diameters of some, it turned out, ranged from three to four and one-half feet across. I stepped backward, eyes uplifted, and tried to reconstruct an image of their once-living structures in my mind. Still, I could not really imagine it. No tree near that size now stood in this forested duneland to lend me perspective. If the species were indeed White Pine, diameters of that size occur in very tall trees that survive as many as two hundred winters, even three, reaching well over a hundred feet.

147

We had never seen stump forms of this nature before, with their dark gray, ragged-topped outer shell encircling a totally vacant center area, and it required some studying about tree growth and decay to help understand how these unusual formations came to be. As the aboveground structure of a tree grows from the center outward, the inner wood increasingly becomes the oldest. With annual new woody growth—the sapwood (the xylem cells)—occurring around the perimeter, life ceases progressively outward from the center in this older, interior wood as the tree lives on. Although now dead (or biologically inactive), this gradually expanding central core of former sapwood is called "heartwood," but, unlike an animal's heart, it is no longer participating in circulating the tree's water and sap-blood of life skyward, as its conducting cells have become clogged. This means that only a very, very small percentage of a mature tree trunk is fully alive. Actually, the only living, cell-producing/dividing portion of the entire visible wooden structure is that very thin, remarkable cambium layer just beneath the bark of the trunk and branches, along with the leaves or needles and the flowers or cones—perhaps as little as one percent of its entire bulk. While the heartwood of formerly water and mineral-conducting cells is nonfunctioning biologically, it, of course, serves to provide the strong structural framework and the rigidity to the tree as it extends upward and outward.

Once cut down or broken off, the remaining stumps of many tree species deteriorate faster in the center where the older dead wood is, particularly as this area becomes spongier material holding water. In the case of pine stumps, resins in the outer sapwood area can become hardened by the heat of fire, leaving most of the stump's perimeter to survive while the decayed interior burns away. This process of deterioration from the inside out also explains the existence of certain standing trees becoming hollow (even many while still living) and of hollow logs lying on the forest floor—a boon to cavity- and den-needing wildlife.

With the discovery of the Birch grove and the fire-damaged stumps, our further exploratory walks across this land between the two Flowers would always include the search for further clues to help us understand the current landscape and any transformation from what it had been. We suspected the setting held interesting stories, and our investigations into the natural and human histories of the area were enlarged as our curiosity was heightened.

While this dunal treescape is today part of the Northern Hardwood Forest—North America's northernmost deciduous forest community—our reading revealed that it had not begun as such. The earliest forest cover and community that eventually emerged in Michigan in the cooler millennia following the last glacial retreat was a Boreal Forest. This is overwhelmingly a forest community of cold-climate conifers, one that today persists in North America across Canada and Alaska, and into several small regions of the far northern United States and upper elevations of mountains to the south. And with Boreal Forests also sweeping across northern Eurasia, it is the largest forest type in the world. Though spruces and firs predominate in this circumpolar evergreen forest, Eastern Hemlock, White Pines, and White-cedars are components of a Boreal Forest, as well, in the more southerly regions. Among the far fewer deciduous trees, Paper Birch, Balsam Poplar, and Bigtooth Aspen are the primary species. Today, the Boreal Forest of North America is the biggest migratory bird nursery in the world.

For thousands of years after the disappearance of the great North American ice sheet, this boreal-style forest prevailed throughout the Great Lakes region. But with the gradual warming of climate, broadleaf trees came to "move" northward, displacing much of the cold-climate conifer regime, as disturbances such as fire, blowdowns, diseases, insect epidemics, and even old age of trees brought death and openings

148

in the forest cover—opportunities for seeds of new tree species from the south to take hold under the changing conditions. This large-scale ecological succession—of varied plant and animal species "on the move" in response to climate change—was gradual and has been estimated to have brought a mixed hardwood-conifer forest to most of the Michigan Lower Peninsula by about 3,500 years ago. Post-glacial Boreal Forest succeeding to a Northern Hardwood Forest—a forest community of transition, however, for the succession remained incomplete.

Except for the general absence of native spruce and fir, substantial southern Boreal Forest components persisted in the northern two-thirds or so of the Lower Michigan peninsula down to the modern era. In fact, from the Grand River valley north, considerable stands of several pine species, along with Eastern Hemlock and lesser numbers of White-cedars, continued to co-exist with the now dominant hardwoods until those conifers were voraciously harvested for lumber, other wood products, and bark tannin (from Hemlocks, used for leather tanning), beginning in the second third of the nineteenth century. With the arrival of Euro-Americans, faster than any climate change or glacial retreat could accomplish, the entire Lower Michigan peninsula was further transformed into a hardwood landscape—where trees remained, that is, or where new (or "second") growth occurred.

In the second half of the 1800s, Michigan became the nation's top supplier of the highly desirable pine lumber for much of the eastern half of the country, with the demand for cheap lumber never ending. Growing straight and tall, White Pine especially met building needs. This species gradually loses its lower branches in a forest setting, providing long, clean logs, relatively free of knots, a lumberman's dream. Less dense than most hardwoods, conifer logs from distant forested areas could be floated down stream courses and lakes to saw mills.

Sliced into lumber, White Pine is relatively light, strong, durable, and resistant to warping, shrinking, and splintering—in all, the species became the most valuable tree of the northeast quadrant of the nation. And its functional qualities are matched by a measure of beauty, for the creamy-white to light tan wood, with the spring growth rings a slightly darker color, is most attractive left unpainted. Doug has trimmed out several rooms of our Indiana home with simple White Pine boards coated with only a clear finishing oil. With the passing of the years, the wood has aged to a rich honey brown.

The pioneer settlement of Muskegon on the drowned-river mouth of Muskegon Lake, sixteen miles to the south of our cottage, became such a prodigious producer and exporter of pine lumber that it rapidly grew to city size, becoming known as the "Lumber Queen of the West." It took only decades—by the early years of the twentieth century—for the extensive stands of the magnificent pines, and most of the Hemlock, to be thoroughly stripped from the Lower Michigan peninsula.

In our driving through the West Michigan region, Doug and I have found little evidence of that grand transitional forest of the not-so-distant past. Actually, there is no longer any true forest, as such, so great was the harvesting of both conifers and hardwoods in the nineteenth century and into the twentieth. While trees are sprinkled everywhere, the terrain coverage is a highly fragmented one, divided up by human occupation and devisements. And none of the patchwork of tree stands are "old growth," left from pre-settlement times. Typically, areas of re-growth are stands of early successional, small to medium-sized trees, densely packed together, competing for sunlight and space. Such naturally occurring stands are invariably hardwoods.

In leaving the dunes, the woods trail first threads its way eastward through closely spaced, planted Red Pines. With the little, corn-row stand never having been thinned, the trees have remained skinny and their lower branches have died from the paucity of sunlight reaching them.

Amidst the landscape's highly dominant deciduous trees there are many evergreens here and there, but any stands of conifers are human-planted, mostly attempts at "reforestation," with closely spaced, regimented rows of tall, skinny Red Pines, begun in the late 1920s.

Under governmental auspices, Red Pines became the most widely planted tree species in the Great Lakes region after the original stands of pines and most larger hardwoods were extracted from the landscape. Supplied from government tree nurseries at little or no cost, this conifer was considered highly suited for poorer sandy soils of cutover lands, growing faster initially than White Pines, and less susceptible to windthrow. But these extensive, even-aged monoculture plantings were not for re-establishing the forests of old; the primary goal was to put post-logging, degraded land into a commercially-viable state, able to produce a variety of wood products, easily harvestable, within decades—tree crops.

Sometime in the late 1940s or early 1950s, even William and Erna planted three small strips of closely spaced Red Pines on their barren flatland property behind the dunes. With the relatively few, modest-sized White Pines in the dunescape and the new stock of hundreds of the young Reds, they proceeded to call their summer offering of four little cottages, "The Pines Resort." (There were, of course, a scattered number of Eastern Hemlocks that outnumbered the few White Pines, but they were evergreen, too, so who would really notice the difference and quibble.)

And, then, in addition to the unnatural grid stands of Red Pines, there are the non-native Norway Spruce and the out-of-place Colorado Blue Spruce installed as decorative screening or specimen trees in many residential landscapes. Field plantations of Scotch Pines, a species imported from Europe, supply many with their Christmas trees. Western Yellow Pine was another government-supplied species for replanting cut-over lands. And in many residential settings are Austrian Pines and various nursery-bred Junipers.

Naturally established native conifers are "second" (or even "third") growth, and they are mostly pines, in rather sparse numbers. For outside the coastal dunes and wetland areas, White-cedars (except those that have been planted, often in straight lines as windbreaks) are rare, and Hemlocks hardly exist—occurring naturally only in cooler, moist, lowland areas, such as along wooded stream courses. From along roadways, conical-shaped Red Cedars of small to medium size can be seen invading unattended fence rows and neglected fields. But this native and naturally-occurring conifer is a sun-loving pioneer species of human-disturbed, open areas—an early successional tree, not a forest denizen. In fact, Red Cedars (actually not Cedars at all, but Junipers) will die when an enveloping group of other tree species overshadows them. Thanks greatly to human clearing activities, the highly aromatic Red Cedar (of cedar chests and closets) is the most widely distributed conifer in the Eastern United States. All in all, the treed landscape of Michigan bears little resemblance to that magnificent forest mosaic that the Euro-American lumbermen and settlers relentlessly engaged and exploited.

While the broader landscape is highly transformed from the past, when we enter "our" duneworks and look about, we've become fairly certain that this sylvan landscape has a semblance of that pre-pioneer transition forest in composition—a mix of northern hardwoods and varied southern boreal species. And while its current structure and density is most certainly diminished from that of the past, those specie and community characteristics must still be closer to the historical forest

of the much larger region than any of the treed landscape of today beyond this, and likely other similar, forested dune assemblages.

As the coastal sand dunes were coming into existence during the later transition of boreal to mixed conifer-hardwood forests in Lower Michigan, it's clear that the dune fields never entertained a full boreal tree cover. But it appears that a large host of lingering boreal species came to find refuge in the geologically new landforms. Even today, these dunes along the lakeshore, with their moist and slightly cooler climate, are a logical habitat to find any remaining grouping of remnant boreal species. And, except for spruces and firs, the most cold-adapted conifers, we have found the other major southern boreal tree species in "our" dunes or along the adjacent inland edge. Besides the evergreen pines and Hemlock, our dunes boreal inventory even includes the deciduous Paper Birch, Bigtooth Aspen, and our bluff-edge Balsam Poplars, North America's northernmost hardwoods, with their true homes being in the Boreal Forest—where such trees can freeze solid without damage.

The Northern White-cedar of the Little Flower swamp is also a prominent resident of a Boreal Bog—and one lonely White-cedar has been found nearby, up in the dune forest. Then there are the many lower-level plants of both the woods and the adjacent Little Flower Creek swamp that are found on into Canada, such as: Mountain-ash shrub, Goldthread, Canada Mayflower, Bearberry, Northern Starflower (*Trientalis borealis*), and Meadow Horsetail. More recently, we were pleasantly surprised to discover a small Balsam Fir tree on the edge of the Little Flower swamp, and the DNR biologist noted specimens of this same boreal species in conjunction with the shrub edge of Big Flower's marsh.

It was a revelation to me how extensive is the connection of the biota of the dune forest and the adjacent swamp to that of a boreal landscape, particularly after noting that almost all of the avian species

Without fail, Paper Birches are always in association with the remnant pine stumps we have found—sometimes exceedingly close. And, in reverse, the successor Birches in the woods are almost non-existent outside their association with the fire-scorched relics.

152

that breed here are either year-round or summer residents in the more northern forests, as well. All of "our" Neotropical species breed in the immense Canadian boreal landscape, although a few, such as the Wood-Pewee, migrate only into the southern edge. Interestingly, far more Neotropical birds follow summer on into the northern boreal forests than decide to stop here to breed. There must be a deep and advantageous avian connection to that particular coniferous community.

A visit to a Purdue University forestry professor who has had students do summer field work in Michigan provided the answer to the species of the old stumps. They were indeed pine, and almost certainly White Pine, for these remnants flared where they entered the ground. (Red Pines don't really flare at the base of their trunk, we learned.) Such stumps are generally long-lasting, and the fire charring had helped preserve the outer wood of the ones we had discovered by hardening encased resins. As they were also in a sunnier, drier upland location, enhancing preservation, the stumps could, indeed, be a century or so old. Moreover, the height of the fluted forms meant that the trees were laboriously cut by hand, either by men standing swinging an ax or bending over at the waist, working a cross cut saw. The somewhat-recently harvested Black Cherry stumps, severed very close to the ground, were cut by a modern chain saw that allowed a single man to sever the tree from a low position. We could, therefore, now assume a solid historic presence for pine here in the dunes, and clearly an existence more prevalent than today. Then came further evidence that conifers were historically much more abundant in this landscape.

Clues to flushing out a story of the past can come from many directions. Our early visits to the woods gave us an acquaintance with the terrain and the vegetation, followed by attempts at understanding the physical and ecological setting. With both growing knowledge and appreciation of its uniqueness, Doug and I began trying to "read" the landscape, to learn its story from within. The Birches and the old charred stumps were parts of the landscape text, and finding them spurred us on. But just as learning more fully about the formation of the dunes was only possible by acquiring information from sources beyond the duneworks itself, the same would hold true for the story of the forest cover.

With our purchase of the cottage came a copy of an "Abstract of Title," a listing, or "chain," of previous ownership and related financial documents, such as deeds and mortgages, going back to the first conveyance of land (usually a tract of forty acres or more) from the federal government to private hands. Early on, we had read that title

abstract with much interest and had made notice of an item new to us—a "timber deed"—associated with the earlier, much larger land parcel from which the cottage property had come. Later, looking for clues outside the woods to help tell its story, we recalled the existence of the timber deed. This dealt with trees in the past; what could it reveal?

Most of the many abstract listings were simply very brief synopses of the documents: type of document, cursory survey description, parties involved in the transaction, its date, and the document's public location. The only useful information from the abstract's timber deed entry was its execution date, December 15, 1890. But that in itself was *very* interesting. The next woods' clues were hidden in the vault of the Muskegon County Register of Deeds Office, in Liber (Book) 78, page 123. And they were an eye-opener.

153

DU... FARMERS PICNIC DINNER

STORIES

"In consideration of the sum of one hundred and five dollars lawful money to them in hand paid," two parties of the city of Muskegon conveyed to "Charles Huston, of Clay Banks, Oceana County, Michigan...the following described property, to wit: all of the hemlock logs and timber lying upon the ground; and all of the standing hemlock timber over twelve inches in diameter at the base; and all standing pine timber upon" more than a quarter of a square mile of land that included "our" forested dunes, the cottage area, the main portion of the Little Flower Creek wetlands, and more.

The December 1890 contract, hand-copied into a huge, century-old, cloth-covered entry book, further stipulated that Huston "shall remove said timber before May first 1892...and shall have the right to use the shanties upon the said premises...[and] what stove wood there is piled near the shanties upon said land. In the cutting and removing the said timber[,] care shall be used[,] and no waste or other damage shall be done to said premises."

Well, we were amazed at what this copy of the contract document revealed. There had been a major timber harvesting in our area, and we even knew its timing—some nine and one-half decades before we appeared on the scene. Actually the timber deed disclosed that substantial logging had been going on slightly earlier, for there were workmen's shanties on the land as well as cut and fallen timber on the ground when

the 1890 contract was executed. The greatest revelation was that there was enough Hemlock and Pine on the dunal and adjacent terrain to make harvesting such trees a commercial activity—by two different parties.

Probably the first harvest was a bigger operation that took the larger conifers, and the timber deed was conveying the right to remove the financially less-valuable trees to a smaller-scale operator. Here, then, in this original forest had been a considerable number of evergreens, clearly far greater than their representation in today's landscape—perhaps they had even been the dominant species. And here had been a substantial vestige of the earlier Boreal Forest of post-glacial Michigan, a forest type now moved north 200 miles, having become the greatest forest type on the planet. We had missed the main portion of that local cast by less than a century!

A door had been opened wide in our search for the story of the dunal forest, and our desire to know its history was now matched by the need to flush out an accompanying and intertwined human story. And in that dual search for the natural and human history stories of our cottage area—and the larger coastal and inland region—Doug and I have read or scanned thousands of pages of deeds, mortgages, and other public documents recorded in four west Michigan county offices. In all of those old, nineteenth-century volumes dealing with varied land transactions across decades, we have never come across another recorded timber deed, although such arrangements must have been numerous during the half century of the logging-lumbering era. To have had the one associated with this woods area publicly recorded, thus preserved for posterity, and for us to have been made aware of it, turned out to be the most fortuitous serendipity. It told so much we couldn't have otherwise known.

Just as remarkable was our locating in the local newspaper of the times several brief accounts telling of the implementation of the timber

Later in the year, the newspaper announced that "Mr. Charles Huston will lumber again this winter" at Little Flower Creek, "and the logs will be hauled to the lake shore." And that was followed by a report at the beginning of 1892, that Charles "will move his family into the woods for the winter." Thus, in a very short time period in the early 1890s, the wholesale removal of marketable conifers from the landscape would be accomplished in the larger area surrounding our lakeshore property. With major evergreen components of a Boreal Forest gone, the transition of the dune and adjacent inland forest to principally a hardwood community would be completed. In a geologic instant, an ecological transformation.

The paper trail we were upon brought more revelations. For the sequestered records buried in the heavy, old books in the county's Register of Deeds vault held other helpful clues to the story of the duneland environment and its new human engagement. Shortly before the deadline of the timber deed expired, Charles Huston and a younger cousin signed a three-year land contract, in March 1892, to buy for $550 the 186 acres of land upon which the timber was growing—a price of $3 per acre, no money down. Like timber deeds, land contracts are not always recorded, as there is no deed transfer until payment is completed, so once again we were extremely fortunate for there to exist a telling copy of the document in the Register's valuable public keeping.

Sometime after the contract's inauguration, a 2-story, 14 by 22 foot log cabin was constructed on the south side of Little Flower Creek where the stream backed up to the dunes on the north. There, in semi-frontier mode, Charles and Mary Huston, and now seven children, took up permanent residence, becoming the first to settle on the land.

The parents, both slender and handsome, and their still-growing family had been living only two miles to the north, just inside Oceana

deed provisions: "Mr. C. F. Huston is soon to move his entire family to a point near the mouth of Little Flower Creek, where he will engage in the lumbering business for the remainder of the winter. The logs, both pine and hemlock, will be hauled to the shore of the big lake," reported the January 1, 1891, issue of the *Montague Observer*, the newspaper published at the small lumbering village of Montague on White Lake, six miles to the southeast. Seven weeks later there was an update that "C. Huston, who is putting in logs at Little Flower Creek[,] has been good constantly at work with sleighs…and that the sleighing has been good since he commenced work at that point." (Though Huston was not forest to produce lumber at a sawmill was often included under the term sawing logs into lumber, the initial process of harvesting logs from the "lumbering" during this period.)

No mention was made that 28-year-old wife and mother, Mary, came to the primitive duneland logging camp from their farm two miles to the north with a 6-month-old infant boy and five other children to take care of, along with making a household out of a crude shanty, and feeding the logging work crew. Several months later, the paper did report that "Mrs. Chas. Huston has been quite sick with measles," and that the rest of the family, except for Charles, had been stricken as well—although the family may have been back to their farm by this time as it was then early spring.

The harvested logs "hauled to the shore of the big lake" were either placed on small boats or rafted together to be floated on a calm Lake Michigan day south six miles to the sawmills along White Lake, the drowned-river mouth of White River. Soon, the beach area at the mouth of Little Flower Creek, there on the south edge of our cottage property, came to be known locally as "Huston's landing"—"landing" being a common term of the times for places along the shoreline where boats stopped to pick up logs or firewood, and sometimes to drop off supplies.

County in Claybanks Township, where thirty-four-year-old Charles, upon the death of his father in 1886, had taken over his parents' "sand farm" on which he had grown up. In late November of that year, it was here, "at Charles Huston's place," that the body of the crew member of the wrecked *L. J. Conway* was taken, according to the *Montague Observer*, after the sailor was found washed up into the mouth of Big Flower Creek.

Heavily mortgaged, the Huston family farm was let go after six years of financial struggling. Timely payments not being made, the farm was put up for sale at a foreclosure auction. Moving south two miles

across the county line and starting afresh, the Huston couple, Charles now into his early forties and Mary thirty years old, set about the hardscrabble work of fashioning a new homestead. Charles' cousin eventually ended up receiving the east fifty acres of the property, but never lived upon it, as best we can tell.

To have given up on the established family farm must have been difficult, particularly for Charles. However, we've visited the terrain of the old Huston homestead in

157

In addition to the very low cost of the new land being purchased, Charles and Mary must have found something quite appealing about the landscape beside the inland sea that the family had now engaged during two winters of logging. After enduring several summers of heat and severe drought and diminished crops on the old farm at the close of the 1880s and into the 1890s, it is no wonder that Charles and Mary could be attracted to the lazy waters of Little Flower Creek flowing into the big lake, a half mile of their own sandy beach to offer respite for the family from the heat and the day's work, and sheltered land and home site immediately behind the forested duneworks (and close by to today's county park entrance). And there were prospects for continued income from "lumbering," this time from their own, large woodland, and from the establishment of new farmable acreage once clearing of the flatland inland from the dunes was accomplished.

It's quite likely the two looked forward to a much better future as they labored at pioneer farm-making to create their new home during the later part of 1892 and into 1893—not able to know that the Panic (depression) of 1893 lay just ahead, with more hard times to be gotten through. It didn't help in the family's new endeavor that "Mrs. Chas. Huston has been very sick. Is improving slowly," reported the *Montague Observer* during the Huston's first summer along Little Flower Creek. It

Claybanks Township and can understand why Charles and Mary might have been prone to part with it. The land is generally higher ground and flat and, mostly cleared of trees, somewhat windswept, being slightly less than a mile inland of the lake. After more than thirty years of farming, the loamy sand soil undoubtedly wasn't very productive, if it had ever been. In this area, shoreline dunes give way to a high sandy bluff overlooking the lake. That high, steep bluff is underlain with clay, exposed at points, and hence the name of the township. No access to the lake and beach was easily available here.

would be a handful of difficult years before the family could really get their heads above water, but they made it. And it was no small feat, for by the early1900s, the Huston household numbered ten children in addition to Charles and Mary.

The success of the Hustons by the end of their first decade beside the inland sea is illustrated in the bucolic scene on page 154, at their homestead on a summer's day, sometime about 1902. "Our Farmers' Picnic Dinner" is a gathering of the extended families of Charles and Mary, with three generations present. Charles is the mustached man in the foreground, and Mary is barely visible behind the handsome daughter on the far right. Mary's aged parents, the Bogues, are in center background. (Charles was eleven years older than Mary, and his parents were both dead.) This picnic assemblage was in the vicinity of the Huston cabin home, and there were most certainly other families at tables nearby. For the farm residents in the area would annually have a "Farmers' Day" when the local families would come together for eating, socializing, and varied games. The Huston farmstead location next to Little Flower Creek and the big lake and its beach--"Huston's Landing"--was a popular place for such events for many years. (Note the general consumption of bottled soda pop, a relatively new item in American culture--and the Paper Birch trees that had come up in the two decades since the first timber harvesting in the area.)

Human occupation of the land parcel which stretched more than a half mile inland from the lakeshore and a half mile north and south was to bring further ecological change. By the time the Hustons had begun harvesting conifers at the start of the 1890s, the "Pine Era" in Western Michigan was fading fast as such trees were becoming scarce after more than fifty years of relentless extraction. Increasingly, as the nineteenth century was coming to a close, lumbermen and farmers were turning to

harvesting broadleaf trees, particularly to feed a growing Western Michigan furniture manufacturing industry. (The early decades of the twentieth century saw the city of Grand Rapids, sixty miles to our east, become the nation's leading furniture-making center.) Already, certain hardwoods such as oaks had come into great demand as the railroads expanded into upper west Michigan from the 1870s on. The laying of tracks took several thousand wooden railroad ties for each mile and thousands more in years to come to replace older decaying ties.

The use of hardwoods for heating and the making of large amounts of charcoal consumed an enormous number of trees each year as well. The steam engines powering the locomotives, steamboats, and many of the growing manufacturing processes of the nineteenth century were first fueled by the deciduous trees of the wilderness. And there was far more varied consumption, of both hardwoods and conifers, for it was still a wood world, with this biomaterial being indispensable in nearly all aspects of life. As it had with pine in the second half of the 1800s, Michigan became one of the foremost hardwood producers in the nation by the beginning of the 1900s. And for the first decade of the century, the state (Upper and Lower Michigan combined) was North America's leading supplier of hardwood. The landscape was cleared even further.

While the 1890 timber deed made no provision for cutting any species other than Pine and Hemlock, that restriction would evaporate after the Hustons were buying and occupying the land. And the evidence is that the Hustons went on to harvest most of the larger and older broadleaf trees from the dunes and further inland after suitable evergreen trees were no longer available—and that this went on for a number of years. We know for certain that Charles did substantial tree removal in the late winter of 1899-1900, for there is a brief news item in the *Montague Observer*, March 15, 1900, that "Frank Mansfield is going to move his mill from C. Huston's place to the farm of Mr. Perrin, near Hart[, Michigan]."

By the end of the nineteenth century, small, portable steam sawmills were available that allowed individuals to cut their own lumber from their trees or to hire out to do the sawing for others on site. As the pine trees on the Huston land large enough for lumber would surely have been cut and sold by this time as a "cash crop," the Mansfield mill would have been fed hardwoods—possibly for making lumber for new buildings the Hustons were wanting to erect and maybe for fashioning railroad ties to be sold to the Western Michigan railroad company.

"Cedar posts for sale. Enquire of C. F. Huston, White River [Township]," announced an ad in the February 15, 1906, *Montague Observer*, telling of another category of trees that Charles was harvesting. The brief ad also verified to us that the Little Flower Creek wetland was indeed a White-cedar Swamp. Even as late as 1914, tree harvesting was taking place, for the Huston land "together with all logs and timber now upon said premises" was signed over by Charles and Mary to a son for three years.

For some two decades, the Hustons lived off the land, clearing several portions of the sandy flatland inland from the dunes and turning it into marginal crop and pasture areas. The several ecological communities making up the acreage that Charles and Mary owned offered them varied resources, principally trees (for wood products, maple syrup/sugar, firewood, wood ashes) and game. As for all pioneering agriculturalists, the forested areas, dwindling though they were, served as economic storehouses. But the nutrient-deficient sandy soil of the flatter landscape was not adequately suitable for any sustained form of agriculture, and once the modest income from a diminishing stock of profitably harvestable wilderness trees petered out, the couple was hard-pressed to make a comfortable living from their land—especially in the face of the growing costs and ever increasing complexity of commercialized agriculture.

159

In 1912, Charles, now sixty years old, and Mary gave up their demanding sand farming and rural life. With their youngest child, 13-year-old Doris, the aging couple moved into Muskegon Heights, twenty-two miles to the southeast, following their oldest children to a greatly different urban living. In the decade of their migration from farm to city, the country-bred Hustons joined in that continuing shift of farmers and others from the countryside to the cities that helped statistically make the United States an urban nation for the first time. For the 1920 federal census revealed that slightly more than fifty percent of the country's population now lived in urban areas.

As best we can tell, the rural lifestyle and the agrarian society that the Hustons left behind in the second decade of the twentieth century was not much changed from that semi-pioneer mode of existence that had sustained them since coming to the Little Flower Creek location in the closing decade of the 1800s. While the narrow, rough, sand-dirt county roads would have been slightly improved and extended, horses still provided the means for transportation and the pulling of farm machinery—the new-fangled automobiles were still only for the more-well-to-do few in towns and cities, and few roads were suitable for them anyway. No telephone or electricity lines extended into their rural area.

The log home Charles had built twenty years earlier still had no indoor plumbing, with an outdoor hand pump providing water and an outhouse serving for human waste disposal. (Such was the rural norm for years to come, even when William and Erna were to locate on the Huston land in the late 1930s.) Wood from the landscape still supplied fuel for heating and cooking, as it had for humankind for millennia. And it's almost certain that Mary still prepared the family's soap from saved animal fat and wood ashes, although she and her daughters may have begun, by this time, using perfumed commercial soap on their faces and for bathing.

The Hustons and other country residents had seen a big improvement take place eleven years earlier, however, when Rural Free Delivery (RFD) of mail had been established in this region of Western Michigan. Instead of the rural residents having to travel periodically to the local post office for their mail as in the past, now mail was delivered (and could be sent) by way of the daily arriving of a mailman in horse and buggy. Surprisingly, this delivery service to every outlying farm residence would pre-date home delivery in Montague and other area villages by more than a half century. And, interestingly, during our first decade at the cottage, we had the very same rural route address that Charles and Mary had beginning in 1901: Rural Route 1, Montague, Michigan. That meant that the rural mail carrier, operating out of the Montague village post office, had to know by name where every mail recipient lived on his extended country route—the official road names and house-numbering system did not exist for some decades to come.

The Hustons, both parents and offspring, were thus part of that great exodus of the times from the marginal lands of varied rural (and, often, isolated) landscapes throughout the nation that had been found to be poorly suited for human cultivation.

In the forested areas of the upper Great Lake states and elsewhere, the extensive exploitation of the tree cover had been carried on not only for the economic wealth to be acquired from manifold wood products, but also because of a prevailing outlook during much of our national history that more and more land was always needed for farming. Actually, trees were generally viewed as being in the way of the march to agriculture, the advance of "progress." The two "complementary" motivations propelled a rape and conversion of forests to an agricultural overexpansion, irrespective of the suitability of soils and other conditions for most agricultural activity. Today, none of the former Huston homestead, once entirely forestland, is in agricultural production, nor has it been since Charles and Mary left. Nor is anyone else in the area attempting to farm or raise livestock on the sandy land that comes close to backing up to the dunes.

Interestingly, the elder Hustons were able to retain ownership of their 136 acres along the shoreline after leaving for the nearby city, using the homestead and lakeshore for family retreats. After Charles' death in 1923, at age seventy-one, Mary found it necessary to sell several portions of the land over the years. A widow in very different times, she was not favored with pension, IRA, or even Social Security benefits. The first to go was the half-mile of lakeshore frontage, the three buyers wanting to subdivide the twenty-six acres and make twenty-eight vacation-home lots. The Great Depression of the 1930s intervened (fortunately, as we see it) to spoil their big speculative plans, and in 1936, the trio ended up selling to the county a parcel of sixteen acres fronting on the lake—the beginning of Meinert County Park. The last and largest parcel Mary sold was deeded to William and Erna in 1940. Ten years later, Mary succumbed to cancer at age 87, and the Huston pioneer connection to the land ended.

Mary (Bogue) Huston (1863-1950); no date for the portrait, but it certainly would have been taken after Charles' death and while she was living in Muskegon Heights.

Strangely, in the year of Charles' passing, William and Erna sailed from Hamburg, Germany, on the cross-Atlantic steamer, *Thuringia*, to arrive at Ellis Island—and, fifteen years later, take up residence in the remodeled old log home that Charles had built (and William was to further upgrade and expand). Although they were not the first, the coming of this German couple to the lake shore area represented a return of human occupants to this region, not in an attempt to eke out a living from the land, but to reside in second or retirement homes or in outlying residences to jobs in towns. And there were some like William and Erna who catered to those wanting to spend vacations at the lakeshore. Slow at first, this reverse migration grew immensely, here and elsewhere in much of rural Michigan in the post-World War II period, coming to eventually include the professor and Alice—and, later, us.

The varied evidence from the landscape and the written records suggests that the dune forest cover, while heavily harvested by the Hustons and a previous party, never underwent a "clear cutting" leaving a denuded and decimated environment. The exploitation of the wilderness forest seems to have been spread out over perhaps a quarter of a century, and the removal of trees was done rather selectively—marketable evergreens first, followed by the more useable hardwoods soon after. Trees not large enough for selling or use otherwise were left to become "mother" trees and the enhanced forest cover of later decades. No species seems to have been eliminated from the composition, although the mix was altered dramatically. But we know the structure of the duneworks forest was greatly diminished—shorn of all its giants and substantially reduced in numbers of trees. It came to be known as "the woods."

Because the removal of trees from the dunal forest left a more open environment than before, several "pioneer" species appeared, persisting to the present day, and probably were introduced from outside

the duneworks with seeds arriving in the droppings of birds. The white Paper Birch and the dark-barked Black Cherry require adequate sunlight for germination and early growth and do not regenerate in a forest setting once other species fill in and mature around and above them, producing a closed canopy. Some three quarters of a century and more after the main coming forth in the grown-back forest, we find no young Birches or Cherries harvesting of the duneland forest, we find no young Birches or Cherries Nor do these species seem to have ever been even a large minority within the forest composition, essentially proving that the tree cover had never been drastically opened.

The narrow ridge-top Birch grove is the largest congregation of pioneer trees we found, and its association with the charred pine stumps was mute testimony to a historical fire in this area. While periodic fire is a natural part of a forest's regimen, the infrequent incidence of forest fires in the upper Great Lake states greatly increased with the coming of the extensive logging of trees by Euro-Americans in the 1800s. Tops and branches trimmed on site from the trunks of the felled giants and smaller trees crushed in the felling process left a huge amount of logging debris, or "slash," strewn on the forest floor. This unnatural fuel bed could be a yard or more deep and became a breeding ground for wildfire. The extensive deadwood accumulation soon dried out, becoming easily ignitable by lightning strikes and human carelessness. The practice of settlers clearing land for agriculture by burning trees, felled and standing, and stumps, slash, and brush, sometimes led to out-of-control wildfires. All could be much more intense than natural fires, consuming more vegetation and thoroughly scorching and degrading the soil of its organic matter and subsurface life—a dual environmental loss, along with the incineration of wildlife and its habitat.

By the 1870s fires were consuming tens of thousands of acres of forests and adjacent landscapes on either side of Lake Michigan nearly every year. Some years, hundreds of thousands of acres were consumed, with several conflagrations claiming over a million acres at a time. Towns were devastated, hundreds of people died, and many thousands more made homeless. Even into the twentieth century, the more northern regions of Michigan saw villages and small towns partially or wholly destroyed by forest fires. Periodic drought combined with the ongoing build-up of forest-floor fuels from logging was a recipe for the frequent outbreak of naturally caused fire or human-set ones getting out of control.

"Give us rain, rain, rain. Forest fires are doing much damage all around us," came a report from the Huston family area printed in the *Montague Observer* in August, 1890, four months before Charles signed the timber deed. From the village of Montague itself, six miles to the southeast, the assessment was "there is so much fire in the woods surrounding Montague that if we don't get rain before long we may be smoked out." A general period of drought that had begun in 1889, accompanied by the outbreak of forest fires, continued on into1891, and in August of that year, the weekly newspaper proclaimed, "We are again surrounded by forest fires. Yesterday morning it was so smoky it was difficult to breathe [in the Montague area]." In the rural Huston locale six to eight miles to the northwest of Montague, known as the Flower Creek community, the paper reported that flowing wells and springs were failing. This was the same early period in which the news appeared in the Montague paper that the Flower Creek marshland was dry enough to enter and mow.

By the end of 1891, rains did arrive to bring relief for well over a year, but by late summer of 1893, the newspaper reports were that fires are "raging all through the county," although September rains again brought abatement. The following year drought returned in earnest, and the cry was going up in Montague that "it is very dry in this section and the air is full of smoke from woods fires." And from the Flower Creek area, the dire news at the beginning of August, 1894, was that crops were greatly suffering from the drought and "there are extensive forest fires to be seen in nearly every direction, in the evening [when the glow of the burning would be highlighted against the darkening sky]…. Some of the fires have done considerable damage already. There is no effort made to check the fires at this point, as with the high winds we have had lately, it would be of no use."

Other areas reported fire damage and smoke, and for a brief period rains did check the fires. But by the end of August, Montague reported smoke "is with us again, wonderfully thickened up with fog." "For the last week it has not been necessary to use smoked glass to look at the sun. The orb looks like a big blood orange suspended, and was easily mistaken by early risers for the moon." On into September the smoke continued, but that month finally brought the prayed-for rains—to the point that soon the Flower Creek area was reporting that constant rains were making "many fields…so wet that they cannot be worked at all."

However, come the following April, 1895, the story was much the same as in the past half decade, with menacing fires starting even earlier in the year: "Forest fires are doing much damage this Spring. Farmers are complaining already of fences, etc., being destroyed by fire and to save their houses and barns, in some localities, are compelled to fight fire night and day. …. Rain is badly needed in all parts of the county at present." While modest precipitation did bring some relief in mid-May, drought along with high temperatures returned, and by early July the newspaper was again reporting that "forest fires are becoming a source of trouble to the farmers in this vicinity." But elsewhere, a far greater problem existed, for many areas of Michigan were experiencing truly large-scale burning at the same time.

"Widespread Destruction and Suffering Caused by Forest Fires" was the news in mid-July that included the report of two small villages eighty miles to the north of our area that "have been entirely wiped out," and the residents have taken refuge at Thompsonville. "People are without clothing or food. One child is missing. Many were overcome with the heat. Already a number of farmhouses have been burned and the people are coming into the towns with tears streaming down their faces, because, as they declare between sobs, they have lost all the property they have on earth."

Trains arriving at Grand Rapids from the north were delayed because of fires at places along the rail lines. The burning was extensive enough that "from the ports along Lakes Michigan and Huron come messages that the smoke from the forest fires are [sic] proving a serious menace to navigators." As the end of July approached, "generous rains" arrived to begin the ending of the long period of summer droughts that had plagued our area and much of Michigan.

Was the burning of the pine stumps we found part of any of the local fires that widely occurred in the first half of the 1890s? The timing certainly is right—some one hundred years before Doug and I stumbled upon the first clues in the early 1990s. The stumps could be a century old it had been determined, and the Paper Birches, known to emerge in the aftermath of fire, were definitely less than that age. However, the dune-top burning area is not large and seems to have been a restricted one, as we have found no evidence that fire did damage in other areas of the duneworks.

A lighting strike might have caused a very localized fire in the dried out logging debris left along the dune ridge, as possibly happened at times in the surrounding region where the forest fires abounded during 1889-95—although lightning is a rarity in periods of drought. On the other hand, a fire on the flat inland area beginning at the base of the back dune ridge, on terrain that the Hustons would have cleared of trees for agricultural use, might have been set ablaze to eliminate the wood

debris. The burning below might have sent sparks up to land in the slash left from the harvesting of the ridge pines, causing a small-scale burning there. Initially, we had no clue as to how the dunetop fire likely started.

Although diligent search for pine stumps elsewhere in the broader duneworks has produced no findings, it turned out there were more outer shells of charred stumps to be found nearby. Spread out along the upland wooded edge of the Little Flower Creek backwater area, beginning only a few hundred feet east of the backside of the dunes, we found four similar stump specimens, unrecognized in our first explorations of that area—it certainly helps to know that one is looking for something. Then, with highly focused searching, eight more charred stumps were located at the east end of the Birch ridge along the upper forested dune slope overlooking the wetland—roughly in a line between the lower ones and the seven Birch grove stumps. Of the newly found eight stumps, all of those upland pine trees when standing would have been felled to land downslope or in that direction (to be hauled away on the flat land below), with

the cleaning of the logs leaving many needle-laden branches (as well as smaller toppled trees) along the entire slope to dry and become easily ignitable tinder.

Continuing to read the landscape more thoroughly, we noticed along that east-facing slope, stretched out for many dozens of yards, the decaying carcasses of numerous, modest-sized White Birches. This slope clearly had once been well opened to the sun—by both logging *and* fire? But the light-needy Birches had evidently succumbed while still rather young as they were not positioned to receive full-day sunshine and, in time, became shaded by a canopy of other species filling in overhead. With the accumulating field clues, a scenario of the past was developing in our minds.

Once again, it was written clues that pointed to an answer to the burning question. For at the end of the three-page Huston land contract of 1892, there is an item we had not previously paid much attention to, a short addendum that had been added in April 1894. Prior to the Hustons completing payment for the land, the seller was granting permission to the buyers to modify a large portion of the property—the lowland area extending eastward from the dunes—allowing them to "burn and seed so much thereof [of the land] as may be done without damage to the valuable timber."

It was now possible to conclude that the Hustons did indeed use fire in clearing the lower flatland area next to the backdunes. Likely already logged of its larger trees, the area would have had a significant residue of slash left strewn upon the ground, and the land would have been fire cleared of that slash and its remaining vegetation in the spring of 1894, or sometime soon after. And there is no doubt that the landscape was cleared at some point, for when we came to the lakeshore, much of that area behind the dunes was rather open with mostly bare sandy soil and only sparse vegetation—we called it "the barrens." Very likely, the

ground level fire consumed not only the cut vegetation, but also the thin mantle of humus atop the sand, virtually sterilizing the site. It's very likely that whatever was seeded by the Hustons produced little—certainly after the minerals from the ashes had leached through the sandy ground..

Fire clearing was a universal practice at the time. And Doug and I now believe that fire emanating from the flatland below, and working its way up the adjacent, slash-covered, 80-foot dune slope to the top, is the most likely explanation for the dune-ridge burn—and that it resulted from a human-started fire that got out of control. The blaze, once atop the ridge, was apparently contained there because it likely ran out of forest floor fuel, and possibly wind off the lake, riding over the dune tops, was pushing it back inland as well.

Whether a Huston fire actually occurred at the very same time as that of the widespread burning in the summers of 1894 and 1895 we cannot know, but it is certainly a very distinct possibility—and, if it so happened, was part of the reported extensive "forest fires" chronicled in the local newspapers of the times.

It is our guess that the "forest fires" in most of Michigan's Lower Peninsula during this period were primarily the consequence of fire-clearing of logged land for agricultural purposes. Interestingly, the accounts of the local fires in the 1890s newspapers during the six-year time span never included comment on the causes of so much burning and smoke. Moreover, the "damage" in the local area that was often referenced was only spelled out a few times: once as fences and orchard trees and another time as "cord wood" cut up and stacked in the previous winter. One other reference was more general: "trees, and other valuable property…." Never was there any reporting of deaths of people or animals, nor of injuries to such—or homes or farm buildings burned, although at least once there had to be vigorous effort to keep that from happening. It's clear, then, that the local fires were not large-

164

There were major fire events, however, in the northern portion of the Lower Peninsula on into the next century. In the far northeast corner, the largest such event in the twentieth century, a fire in mid-October, 1908, burned across over two million acres—and came to be known as the "Metz Fire" for its destruction of a small town by that name. Three dozen people were killed, with fifteen of them, fleeing women and children, perishing in an open railroad car that wrecked and burned in the advancing fire.

The Metz Fire has been called the worst in Michigan history—primarily because of the number of people that perished. After some five months of droughty weather, and numerous smaller fires in the area, strong westerly winds were responsible for fanning a fire, and perhaps more than one, into a fast-moving wildfire five to six miles wide that wouldn't be stopped until it had reached the Lake Huron coast. But this was not fully a wild forest fire, as it raced across large farmlands, homesteads, small settlements, and cutover areas, as well as through timber, and its destruction across a 35-mile-long path was completed in little more than a day. Most reports say the blaze was of unknown origin, but one attributes it to a brush fire started by workers clearing land.

Three years later, in the hot, dry summer of 1911, many areas of the northern portion of the Lower Peninsula experienced scattered outbreaks of fire. The worst burned tens of thousands of acres and the two small lumber towns of AuSable and Oscoda along Lake Huron. But in our region, on into the 1890s, such larger fires were very likely no longer possible, however, as spread out farming and orcharding was taking the place of large-scale lumbering with the landscape having undergone substantial deforestation, especially of the more fire-prone Pines.

(In 1980, a small prescribed burn that got out of control, fed initially by slash of harvested Jack Pines, raced across some 25,000

scale conflagrations such as had occurred in previous decades in Lower Michigan and were still occurring in regions to the north of our area and further west that were still heavily timbered.

While the Montague Observer news was periodically focusing upon the problem of smoke in the local area, it was an immensely different story in the late summer of 1894 in the most northern portions of Michigan and Wisconsin and on into eastern Minnesota. "Widespread Disaster," "Hundreds Perish" were among the headlines of articles the newspaper published throughout September about wild fires that had been raging over extensive timbered areas just south and west of Lake Superior. Conditions there were "more than terrible" with twenty towns having been destroyed and more than 400 people suffocated or burned to death. Many more were badly burned and there were thousands of refugees and those left homeless, according to the news reports.

Animals, wild and domesticated, were dead or dying from burns. A train running in the Hinckley, Minnesota, area caught fire and burns. A number of passengers were killed. A small steamer going down a Minnesota river passed through "walls of fire" and itself caught fire. The river water temperature was raised so high that millions of dead fish were seen floating along the water's surface. Across the region, property damage was in the tens of millions of dollars lost and the standing timber destroyed was in the millions of dollars.

Conflagrations like that could no longer exist in the lower half of Michigan once into the last decade of the nineteenth century, as very large tracts of timber no longer remained in the region, especially not of the more flammable Pine. Even the fire that consumed the two small villages in the northwestern area of the Lower Peninsula in July, 1895, was a small-scale event compared to those fires that had occurred the year before in the Upper Peninsula and westward.

acres of National Forest land and private property, destroying forty-four buildings and killing one firefighter in the Mack Lake area of Oscoda County, northeastern Lower Michigan.)

The Montague newspaper information suggests, then, that the "forest fires" being reported locally in the 1890s were never in the category of the large events that had been occurring, and would continue to happen, elsewhere further to the north and northwest. The local fires would have been burnings associated with many of the numerous smaller wooded tracts scattered over the landscape—a series of many blazes resulting primarily from extensive firing of logged-over areas and brush in order to further the clearing of land for crop fields, pastures, and orchards, and then getting out of control. The clearing for orchards was particularly being promoted at this time, as the coastal "fruit belt" was then rapidly expanding. Even Charles had set out fruit trees on the old Huston family farm in the late 1880s, according to a newspaper report.

Especially during droughty conditions, wind was capable of sending the set fires racing beyond the intended burn areas across dry crops and pasture land, into the patchwork of rural woodlots and the remaining, relatively small, un-logged forest tracts. Every farm had at least a small woodlot, if for nothing more than the continual firewood needs, and wooded areas were often left as windbreaks for the homesteads. With no rural fire-fighting organization and no mechanized means of movement or of pumping large amounts of water, once a rural fire got out of hand, there was little that could be done beyond watching the blaze burn itself out—and appeal for rain.

Of particular interest is that the local newspapers of the times not only failed to speak of causes for the fires or to place blame, but there was, as well, no discussion about preventing the burning and the horrible smoke. It was as if the phenomenon was simply a fact of life, something to be accepted and endured. In fact, fire was more than merely a fact of life. Fire was the natural consequence of logging forests *and* was also an essential tool for remaking the landscape for agriculture.

There evidently was a tacit understanding of this process, for a May, 1893, editorial comment in the newspaper spoke in praise of farming succeeding lumbering, as formerly untilled, cleared land was now "being worked. This is a good move. Nothing could be done to build up the country better or faster." How, then, could the editor advocate fire prevention or cast blame on those who were employing fire as a means "to build up the country?" What the Hustons did along with every other fellow farm- and orchard-maker was not in the least unusual or frowned upon—for here was a sign of "progress"—nor was there anything new about this.

In our seeking to explain the mystery of the charred stumps in the duneworks, we were also led to understanding something of the relationship of fire to the landscapes beyond the dunes, out into the watershed areas of the two Flowers, and far beyond in both distance and time. For millennia, throughout the world, humans have used the torch to remake landscapes for their own purposes. The cutting-killing of vegetation, burning it, and then seeding entirely different plants in the ashes is called "slash-and-burn agriculture," and its use continues today in many places.

It is likely that every acre of Michigan land transformed from forest into field, pasture, orchard, or other uses underwent burning at some point. For fire was the indispensable element—a rapid and effective, nature-derived, simple technology—in that wholesale ecological conversion. Seasonal fire was also used to annually incinerate post-harvest crop residues. Michigan was burned. And in certain seasons, during the years and decades of its massive landscape transformation, its occupants, humans and others, lived in smoke.

Fortunately, the duneworks did not lend themselves to being redesigned into any form of agricultural production, to having a totally different regime of alien flora and fauna imposed upon this unique

166

landscape. Consequently, the forest floor was only slightly disturbed and the diminished forest cover there was spared, left alone to continue and to be regenerated—while the inland countryside burned year after year, section by section, during the decades of logging, agricultural advance, and settlement. The dunal forest was saved by its associated geomorphology and the fact that the prevailing winds came from over the lake, laden with moisture, fanning inland fires in an eastward direction, away from the dunal trees. Very rarely, lightning might ignite dead, standing trees in the dunes, but these natural fires would not be extensive. In our more-than-two decades in the dunes, there have been no such lightning-caused fires, nor evidence of any in the years before our coming—unless the old charred stumps were actually a result of a lightning strike after all.

While we could never be fully certain about the charring of those aged pine stumps, we sought more clues that might further our knowledge of the duneworks forest story. Our initial surveys of the dune acreage suggested to us that the larger trees seemed to be not much more than one hundred years old. The taller trees, some nearly eighty feet high, offer diameters of twenty-two to thirty-two inches. These are neither exceptionally large trees, nor are they small, young specimens either. But we wondered at their ages—could any perhaps be older than our estimates and be living survivors from the original, pre-settlement dune forest? How did these existing trees possibly fit into the harvesting of that forest and the post-logging, diminished landscape?

It was several years before we got some answers, and they came with the help of the ever-active Aeolus—in the form of those gales of November. Doug was on a solo work session at the cottage when a severe windstorm, with periods of ferociousness, blew in over the lake from the southwest in mid-November, 1998. In its two-day fury, nothing of note

was damaged in the cottage scene, although electric service was disrupted for a time. However, an inspection of the woods area revealed that several tall trees had been toppled in a back dunes swale east of the cottage. Aeolus not only shapes the lakeshore and the duneworks, he works his capricious might on the forest cover as well.

That winter, Doug asked a friend who did logging as a sideline occupation to cut slices from near the base of several of the wind-thrown stalwarts. Forest clues would emerge from the counting of the trees' annual growth-rings, we theorized. For each tree, by its living processes, provides a "calendar" of its longevity (and something of the annual environmental conditions under which it grew) with the formation of its yearly, concentric growth-rings of xylem tubes—the sapwood—which increases incrementally the tree's diameter as the structure gains height.

Jim brought his chain saw, and the three of us ventured into the snow-covered back dunes where our logger friend produced large cross-sectional slabs several inches thick from three different tree species. Returning from the woods, we crunched through the snow crust and slipped unceremoniously up and down the irregular terrain hauling the rather bulky wooden disks back to the cottage.

Gathering around the kitchen table, the three of us warmed our hands on cups of hot chocolate. While we drank, Doug lifted the large wooden circles one by one, each of us in turn guessing its age. Then, taking the largest one first, the twenty-three-inch-wide White Pine slab, we carefully counted off decades and made pencil marks on each tenth dark ring that showed the end of a year's growth, the marks helping us to keep our place. The Pine tree was approximately eighty-seven years old. The smaller, seventeen-inch-diameter Red Oak weighed in at roughly ninety-eight years.

It was the Hemlock disc that narrowed our eyes as we tried to start counting from the heartwood center out, straining to see the tightly-compacted inner rings. We gave up momentarily and dug out the old magnifying glass from the desk drawer. Then our eyes widened in disbelief. No one had guessed even close on this one. The countdown deepened our respect for the Eastern Hemlock species and greatly expanded our understanding of the woodland's history.

Our Hemlock specimen had an oblong sixteen-by-eighteen-inch diameter. As best we could determine, the central core of less than four inches across held one hundred and seventeen rings, each barely discernible even with the benefit of magnification. The outer rings, more than triple the width of those in the inner core, numbered ninety-eight. Adding a conservative handful of years for germination and as a young sprout, the tree was at least 220 years old—it had started growing during the nation's Revolutionary War, in George Washington's time as a general, possibly even a little earlier.

At first thought, why hadn't a tree this old been taken during the logging of the timber deed period? Why did Charles Huston, with axe and saw in hand, walk on pass this Hemlock during those years, and even later? But counting rings back a century from when this relic was blown down, gave us a tree that was little more than three inches across in the 1890s—a great deal under the minimum diameter of twelve inches specified by the timber deed for harvesting the graceful Hemlocks—and hardly worth cutting even a decade or two later. In fact, this aged Hemlock didn't reach a foot across until about 1950.

Here, revealed in our hands, was a survivor of the early forest that the Ottawa Indians knew well before the first Euro-American lumbermen and settlers had arrived in Western Michigan. And there are many other Hemlocks in the dunes as large, and some even substantially bigger than their fallen comrade, each from that distant past—with the largest certainly more ancient. Realizing all this sent me "to the books," once again.

That the larger Hemlocks of today were passed over during the timber cutting period is due, we've learned, to the species being able to carry on in small form very slowly. Surviving almost in a state of suspended animation under a towering forest's shady canopy, such small trees can exist many decades without adding much height or mass, as obviously was the case early on with our Hemlock sample.

When the logging of the dunes forest was done a century or so before the 1998 tree blowdown, the more open treescape that resulted allowed sunlight to reach this Hemlock and its companion small trees, "releasing" them to increase their growth. Less competition for nutrients and moisture also benefited the remaining trees. The many "retarded" Hemlocks of that time could then grow at a more normal rate, resulting in some of them becoming the seventy- to eighty-foot-tall pillars of today.

Those largest specimens may be truly ancient, for I've further learned that early growth of Hemlocks can be suppressed for over 200 years, as this species is the most shade tolerant of all trees. It's likely a number of the dune's Hemlocks have had lengthy periods of slow, early growth and are therefore over 300 years old. In any case, the larger dunal Hemlocks are only recently becoming truly mature trees and have a century and more ahead of them—if they can survive Aeolus' might that long. In typical stands, Hemlock ages approach 400 years, but I was somewhat startled to read in one source that the oldest recorded specimen was "at least 554 years old" and in another that "the record age is reported to be 988 years."

Conifers are the continent's oldest living trees. In the eastern United States, there are individual trees of several conifer species that have been documented to have grown to the exceptional age of over 1600 years. These specimens, however, have matured under unusual conditions and in non-typical locations. The Eastern Hemlock follows right behind in terms of longevity, and as a "conventional" forest tree, is likely the longest-living species east of the Rocky Mountains. In our Lake Michigan area, Hemlocks are certainly the longest-lived of any species, trees or otherwise.

Other held-back species of the dunal forest besides the magnificent Hemlocks were also released, especially the semi-shade-tolerant Red Oaks, the thickest trees of today's woods with nearly a half-dozen measuring thirty- to thirty-two-inches in diameter. With our seventeen-inch-wide oak slab clocking in at ninety-eight years, clearly those oak stalwarts with nearly twice the width are many decades older—possibly as much as ninety to one hundred years older. Perhaps the biggest Maples and Beeches are also close to two centuries old. We now knew that our age estimates of the woods' larger trees were much too low—and that this dunal forest of the late twentieth century held a living history of trees that preceded the coming of the cut-happy Euro-Americans.

In the case of the mighty White Pine, however, there is no such antiquity here. Our pine slab of some eighty-seven years of age is representative in size of the largest of today's White Pines, indicating that they all emerged after the nineteenth century lumbering period. Apparently, every White Pine tree of any appreciable size was gobbled up then. If any were left from the initial large-scale harvesting, they were taken sometime afterwards, because no Pine in the landscape of today's woods—or beyond—appears to be anything but the product of the twentieth century. And, except for along the higher frontal dunes, larger White Pines are relatively scarce in the current landscape. But they do exist, and, more importantly, there are young ones, sometimes groups of them, sprinkled here and there, almost invariably in higher locations on south and east-facing slopes where sunnier conditions prevail. They are, happily, returning.

Reading the landscape further, the existence today of a considerable number of older pioneer trees scattered throughout the duneworks, such as Black Cherry and Paper Birch, says that the harvest of both conifers and hardwoods was great enough to substantially open

the canopy, allowing germination and early growth of these sun-requiring tree species to be established. The ages of the 1998 casualty trees have the two "younger" specimens, Red Oak and White Pine, coming forth as well in the openness of a substantially reduced forest in the post-timber deed period, both species preferring more sunny landscape conditions. The medium size of many other trees in these woods speaks of their emergence also in the post-harvesting period, that is, in the early part of the twentieth century. Finally, that the current forest has a generally closed canopy during the annual leafed-out period tells us that any further tree extraction since the early years of the twentieth century was minimal and selective.

But there is no true "finally" in a forest. Such a community is always in a modality of change, for it is comprised of germinating/birthing, feeding, growing, dying, and decomposing components constantly interacting with the continuingly varying elements. Here, under that spread-out canopy, the youngest trees are overwhelmingly the shade-tolerant Hemlocks and Beeches, each slowly advancing upward, on their way to taking their place in the higher elevations as openings in the canopy inevitably occur. Other forest species will continue to have their opportunities, but it looks like this will be more and more a Beech-Hemlock forest cover into the coming century. Its ancient lineage: a magnificent Pine-Hemlock-Mixed Hardwood Forest.

There was another tale our tree slabs had to tell beyond providing us the ages of their structures and revealing a measure of forest history. An inspection of their wood surfaces displayed no evidence of fire scars, indicating that there had been no extensive, large scale forest fire in the immediate vicinity of these trees. The Pine and the Hemlock had stood less than one hundred yards from the Birch grove and the closest charred pine stumps, and the Oak tree less than twice that distance. The Pine and

Oak trees were nearly a century old, and the Hemlock went back well over 200 years. This seemed to confirm that the fire that had charred the stumps had been a very localized burn in the dune woods. It also seems to point to natural wildfire as being an infrequent shaper of the dunal forest's ecology.

Why we have located no other pine stumps in the woods when we know from the 1890 timber deed that Pines had been one of the two species being harvested then in substantial numbers is something of a mystery. However, the sum of the evidence suggests very strongly that in the time of the Huston appearance on the land there was a local fire that charred and preserved the stumps that we have found. The many others, unaffected by fire, would have, years ago, deteriorated faster and disappeared.

We considered ourselves most fortunate to have stumbled across and to have uncovered so many scattered clues to the dunal forest saga—an outcome of serendipity, search, and research. We now know the woods to be a very diverse community with a history more fascinating than we could have imagined. Although the woodland overall is still a relatively young forest, it was a delight to discover that the largest Hemlocks and Oaks (and, almost certainly, some of the Beeches and Maples) are old refuges from the pre-settlement era, rare remnants from the earlier forest that go back two centuries and more.

Remarkably, with the White Pines and the Hemlocks, this forested landscape has multiple representatives of those eastern tree species that grow the tallest and live the longest. And, in addition, from the ground level up through the understory to the forest ceiling, there still remains, preserved within, an ancient touch of that long-ago, Boreal Forest of post-glacial Michigan—something of a "pocket refuge" for this association of relic species.

The woods is now more than a woodland; it has become a fully reconstituted, diverse forest in the century since the heaviest timber extraction. And even though we've learned of the magnificence of this special dunal forest, it will still be affectionately "the woods" to us.

In piecing together the multifaceted story of the woods' history, we were also led to discover the fuller story of the Huston family—and to unexpectedly find that it was so illustrative of the rapid and extensive

170

Euro-American transformation of the historical Michigan environment. Beginning with Charles' parents, the two generations of Hustons were direct, albeit very minor, participants in the immense landscape change in the region: the conversion of a vast natural forest cover to a varied patchwork of human-contrived landscapes in which most of the previous ecosystem components were significantly altered, diminished, or outright eliminated.

Most pioneer stories have been lost, but, in the case of the Huston family, we were fortunately able to uncover and reconstruct a most telling one. The account of these migrants to the Western Michigan forest wilderness began in the late fall of 1852, when Adam and Eliza Huston arrived in the White Lake area, the hub of a sparsely populated frontier community, with five children in tow and one in Eliza's arms—Charles, born earlier the same year. The family had come from southern Maine, having left behind their families, a small, rocky farm, and a hard life, to start afresh on the westward "lumbering frontier." Interestingly, there would be some similarity to the starting over of Charles and Mary and family along Little Flower Creek forty years later.

Maine, the northernmost New England region, had very early in the American colonial period become a primary lumber producing area, principally because of its abundance of White Pines and other conifer species—the very first water-powered sawmill in the American colonies is thought to have been established there in 1623. As the Euro-American population along the Atlantic seaboard grew after the Revolutionary War, and as prime timber resources began diminishing in the New England region and farm soils gave out, emigration took place into New York and then further west into the Great Lakes territories, beginning in the 1820s and 1830s.

The principal entrepreneurial drive of this Upper Midwest migration was the exploiting-harvesting of timber to sell back East, to the

villages and cities to the south, and the new towns arising in the Great Lakes basin. During the 1830s, there emerged scattered timber harvesting operations and small water-powered sawmills in the wilderness areas of the states-to-be of Michigan, Wisconsin, and Minnesota. As the century wore on, tens of thousands of people came to work in the growing number of logging-lumber operations whose prime interest was in the White (and the lesser number of Red) Pines that existed in a transitional arboreal swath across the Great Lakes region between the Boreal Forest to the north and the deciduous forests to the south.

The long-range goal for many was to come to this spread out logging/lumber frontier to earn the wages from the timber exploiting operations and then purchase land cheaply from the Federal government that they themselves could timber harvest and then turn to farming it. The general assumption was that "the plow would follow the ax." And that was the story of Adam and Eliza Huston, both into their late thirties, emigrating westward from a timber-diminishing northeastern region in mid-nineteenth century to a still young, but rapidly expanding northern logging/lumber frontier of which Western Michigan was a major component. This New England family thus came to be early participants in the immensely important "Pine Era" of the upper Great Lake states.

Adam worked for several years in the White Lake-White River watershed for one of the territory's timber barons, the Huston family of eight spending their first Michigan Christmas and winter in a snowy, up-river, wilderness logging camp. It's very likely that Eliza earned board and keep for herself and the children by providing cooking and laundry services in sparse, rough conditions for the camp work crew. The arrival of the Hustons in the White Lake area came just as the modest-sized White River was on the verge of becoming one of the most important river systems for logging/lumbering in this region of the Great Lakes.

Coming from Maine, where lumbering was the leading industry until the Civil War, Adam was valued a cut over most other working men. For he was experienced in the primitive simplicity of logging and the river drives that floated thousands at a time of the long, bulky but buoyant pine carcasses down streams to mill sites—a transportation method devastating to river ecology. In fact, Adam Huston was to claim later in life that he (as likely a logging drive foreman) put the first pine logs into the White River ever to be floated downstream to a saw mill on White Lake.

But such hard and often dangerous work was a short-term means to a more important long-range end. In 1855 Adam purchased 240 acres of public domain land on the northwest edge of the upper reaches of the Big Flower Creek marsh, in the newly established Claybanks Township, Oceana County. Nearly twenty years earlier, a government surveyor's cursory description of this wilderness terrain noted, "Land except Swamp rolling and 2d rate. Timber[:] Sugar [Maple], Pine, Hemlock, [Red] Maple and c."

There, in that mixed, transitional forest setting, Adam, Eliza, and Charles' five older siblings, adults and children alike, embarked on pioneer farm-making, harvesting much of the landscape's timber over the years and cutting and burning more to clear for crop growing—the age-old, widely used, slash and burn agriculture. In a few short years, Adam transitioned from being a hired man to that of an independent logger and farmer. Many who came to this frontier were not as successful, for there were those men and women who tried but failed to prosper, barely surviving or even dying in the effort. A large proportion moved on, for any frontier is a fluid, transitional setting.

As the forested area inland from the lake filled in with an influx of additional woodsmen and settlers, the wilderness flora and fauna community was whittled away, logging slash and standing trees burned,

and the landscape opened up with fields, buildings, and rudimentary roads. In the 1860 Federal Census for Claybanks Township, its very first, pioneer agriculturalist Adam Huston and dozens of other new occupants of the rapidly changing landscape listed themselves as "farmer."

Charles Huston was thus raised from infancy in the throes of the broad conversion of a Great Lakes forest to human-induced ecological arrangements previously unknown to the western and upper Michigan environment. There is a slight exception to that characterization of environmental transformation, for Woodland Indians of the Great Lakes region were known to have cleared small forest areas by fire or, as likely, modified natural-occurring open areas for agriculture and small settlements. In our Lake Michigan coastal area, the initial Federal government survey in 1837 of the Oceana County-to-be, noted three "Old Indian Improvements," spaced about a mile apart, along the high clay and sand bluff overlooking the lake. These small open areas in the forest cover had been summer encampments of the recently dispossessed native peoples to take advantage of the cooler lakeside environment for the season and to have access to the lake for fishing and travel.

The "Indian Improvement" closest to the Huston farm was but a mile and a half away and held a graveyard, according to an early settler. "Some of the graves were covered with bark…[and underneath were] tobacco, pipes, cranberries, and other things placed at the head for the use of the dead." The largest clearing, a mile further to the northwest along the shoreline bluff, was less than forty acres and described by the surveyor as "covered with Sumac, Briars, & grape vines"—abandoned, it was undergoing early successional growth on its way back to being forested. It never made it, as such already-opened areas became choice sites for the new Euro-American arrivals that displaced the native peoples.

172

Indian clearings and villages were very small, scattered, and usually temporary, a relatively few opened spots in the extensive forest tapestry, tiny islands in a sea of trees. And the subsistence and shifting agriculture practiced by the indigenous population used plants native to the continent. These were a forest-adapted people, ones who benignly tapped their environment for such as maple syrup and sugar, one of many Indian developments copied by invading Euro-Americans.

The new human arrivals to the wilderness, however, wrought a vast change. Now, forested areas increasingly became the spots, or islands, in a new, chopped up, open, and alien landscape. Annuals from other continents, many of them grasses, replaced the native flora of perennials, and the spread of the new, "artificial" prairie-style landscapes required constant human attention and energy inputs to keep them from returning, (succeeding back) to the natural forest ecosystems. Unlike with the self-willed biodiversity of true prairies, the labored goal of the human planters in this neoteric patchwork world was to rigorously eliminate biodiversity so as to enforce dense monoculture grasslands of wheat and corn and such. And a range of introduced animals and birds (and even fish) from "Old World" sources was inserted into this new and alien landscape where once thrived a diverse native fauna.

Charles was the youngest of four brothers in the Huston family, now settled in the Western Michigan wilderness. The two oldest brothers, in their early twenties, perished in the Civil War less than a decade later. The third, Orin, survived his Union Army enlistment to return to the Big Flower Creek neighborhood at age nineteen to follow his father in becoming a farmer, beginning in the 1870s—and to join a growing local population in further whittling away at more of the area's forest. Charles took over the family farm upon the death of father Adam in 1886, and nearly a half dozen years later moved on to become one more Huston to whittle away at the rapidly dwindling Michigan wilderness, there at Little Flower Creek and the adjacent landscape. Well before Charles' death in 1923, the once vast forest of the Lower Peninsula—west, east, south, and north—was gone.

In the years of this man's childhood, the general estimation was that the trees of the forest were inexhaustible, yet the passing of one of the world's great forest areas had occurred before this tree harvester had passed away. And only rare, diminished remnants of that arboreal community still existed in the region—as in the dunal woods.

And, so, in following the clues that unveiled the story of the dune forest and its associated landscapes, we also discovered a telling history of two generations of a specific pioneer family's interaction with that wilderness forest environment of the past—and how those two intertwined stories connected so closely with the drastic and speedy historical ecological transformation of the broader region. Not since Lower Michigan was last overwhelmed with ice has any force rivaled the multifaceted ecological impact of the coming of Euro-Americans and their exploitation and removal of the region's forest.

The same ecological processes that generated the forested world that the Hustons found and helped transform still exist today. And it is, therefore, thought provoking to realize that, if human numbers in our region (and their level of technology) would somehow diminish to match that of some period of the distant past, a vast wilderness forest would return to the Michigan landscape. It would be of a substantially different composition than that of pre-settlement times, but, even in the deserted urban areas, in time, it would once again be a grand forest. If left on its own, undoubtedly, the dunal woods would continue to exist as different from any inland forest—and to be special then, as we have found it to be now, with its greater indigenous species diversity.

CONNECTIONS

The first sighting of the Wild Turkey was in mid-May. Flushed by my sudden appearance from around the east side of the cottage, it flapped noisily to a leafy perch some twenty feet above the next-door driveway. Its movement had been at the edge of my view and its identity still a puzzle up there in the leafy cover—until a sound somewhat like gobbling issued forth. A few minutes later Doug appeared, and we watched in awe the graceful, soundless, long swooping descent of this large form to the bottom of the wooded dune slope away from us. Descending the driveway, we quietly stalked the two-foot tall bird as it strutted up the woods lane some seventy feet ahead of us before quickly and silently disappearing into the forest. This was our first up-close view of a Wild Turkey, and it appeared to be a female as it lacked the head ornamentation of a male and was of smaller size. We assumed it would be our only look at this one.

But "Momma," as she came to be called, wandered the cottage dune area a few weeks later, bringing us a special treat—five little poults, or chicks, in scattered procession. Turkey poults are precocial and able to walk upon hatching, so this family had been on the move from likely day one, vacating for security reasons the shallow depression of a ground nest and its scent-emitting broken eggshells. Pleased at the unusual opportunity to observe such cute offspring, we spread corn meal in the tiny front yard at the edge of the cottage, hoping the family would return. Indeed, they did. By the middle of June, Momma hen, as a single parent,

and her entourage of soft-feathered bundles were making daily afternoon visits, coming unannounced out of the wooded surroundings. Each time, Doug halted his deck-building on the cottage front for a few minutes and gently tossed corn or bread pieces (whole wheat) to Momma and rice for the chicks. For a bird that is one of the most wary, she became ever more accepting of our presence, even coming within a few yards of Doug's pounding hammer to secure her family's ration. Then off they would go, back into the wooded environs, Momma clucking away to keep her dallying brood in tow.

But the afternoon feeding was not enough for Momma. Turkeys normally are out foraging for food in the early morning, and then later in the day. Twice she awakened us with her gobbling outside our bedroom window around five o'clock, calling for an early breakfast feed. But our lack of response seemed understood by day three. (How did she know that's where we were?)

Over the next two weeks, as the size of the poults increased, their numbers steadily dwindled. Every few days Momma arrived with one less follower until by late June there was only one. The disappearance of the four others of her brood remained a mystery, although turkey chicks can succumb to exposure to cold rains, predation, and accidents, and we were concerned that even this last one might fail to survive. Possibly there had been chicks that had perished even earlier, as hens normally lay eight to fifteen eggs.

The rapidly growing, remaining offspring we dubbed "Buffy" in honor of the buff-colored feathers with delicate brown markings and white speckles. How cutely attractive the young one appeared in contrast to the severe, featherless, and oddly colored face and the bulky, dark brown body of Momma. In stretching, however, Momma could fluff her body and spread her tail into a fan that looked quite pretty.

We were gone for a week in early July, and neither Momma nor Buffy were around when we returned. We missed their presence. Perhaps, during our absence, they had given up on the easy meal ticket we had provided, returning fully to their natural diet of primarily seeds, insects, berries, and whatever acorns and beechnuts they could find at this time of year. By this stage of development, Buffy would now be able to fly and roost in trees along with Momma, and their range of foraging would have increased greatly. Normally the two would stay together for the rest of the year.

If Buffy happened to be a male, and survived to become full-grown, he would be a representative of one of the heaviest of bird species on the continent, have a wingspan of nearly five feet, and be a strong flyer and a fast runner. Turkeys are also the largest birds in the Western Hemisphere that are primarily ground-dwelling species. As with many other birds and animals, the Wild Turkey, a species of primarily deciduous forests with Oaks and Beeches, had disappeared in much of its former range in the eastern United States as a result of deforestation and over-hunting in the previous century. In more recent decades, however, improved habitat and the reintroduction of captured and bred Turkeys from other areas has brought back viable populations of this non-migratory bird into areas such as Michigan.

Ironically, this uniquely North American species was long ago tagged with a name coming from another part of the world. As one story goes, when the Spanish conquistadores shipped Turkeys from Mexico back to Europe in the 1500s, somehow there came to be the mistaken notion that the birds came from the Turkish Empire and were so named. And another explanation is that this species was early on confused with African Guinea fowl which came into Europe via the Turkish Empire.

In subsequent months and years, we occasionally heard and saw other Turkeys—in pairs or small flocks—foraging in the woods of the back dunes, along Little Flower Creek, and semi-open roadside areas leading to the dunal woods and the cottage, the combination being prime habitat for this species. These other Turkeys all scurried away long before we came near. Unlike Momma and her brood, they were not at all interested in connections with us.

We apparently sealed what had been its mode of ingress, and one more unwanted lodger was evicted.

Up-close encounters with dune and forest inhabitants sometimes bring humorous connections. Early one November morning, a bow-hunting neighbor, while sitting motionless up in his tree stand in the dune woods waiting for a White—tail to appear, had an all-black variant of the Gray Squirrel come down the tree and unexpectedly perch on his shoulder. Without the slightest movement of head, the man inquired softly, "What are you doing here?" The squirrel did a leaping about-face and frantically raced back up the tree. Only from much further up did it pause to peer back at the source of the strange sound below.

Another early morning, another tree, our hunter friend was confronted by a Mink of dark, chocolate-brown fur. This fearless member of the Weasel family rushed up the trunk at him, scolded loudly from about three feet away, then scurried back down to resume its early morning rounds. Most outings our hunter took no deer. No matter. Like us, he was also hunting connections.

Not one to perch in a tree, I prefer my wildlife sightings from ground level. Two quiet, early summer walks led to encounters of the limbless reptilian kind. One morning, as I proceeded down the front dune toward the bluff deck, I picked up a large twig that had fallen to the path. Tossing it aside carelessly into the grass in front of me, I startled a snake that lay hidden there, and it moved onto the sandy walkway. Feeling threatened by my approach, it raised the front of its thick, yard-long body in challenge, as the sides of its head flared wide, flat, and arched like a Cobra. Easily alarmed by any encounter with a snake, unexpected or not, I froze, momentarily frightened by the aggressive display. As reason regained control, I stepped slowly backward, studying the head of the reptile I knew could not be a Cobra. Being left alone, the heavy, tannish

body with dark splotches slithered deliberately toward cover on the opposite side of the path from whence it had been disturbed.

A race to the wildlife identification book, and I was reassured. The flattened head with a slight upturn of its "snout" and the puffing out of its upper body unmistakably identified it as an Eastern Hognose Snake—a harmless, non-poisonous serpent. This species, along with most snakes, has neither the nerve-paralyzing neurotoxins of Cobras nor the blood-destroying hemotoxins of Rattlesnakes. I had never before encountered a Hognose and had not heard of the Cobra-like defensive reaction, which can be accompanied by angry hissing and mock strikes. Because it moves rather slowly, if this peculiar threatening response to danger fails, the Hognose will do a death feign, rolling onto its back and excreting a foul smelling musk—which was not at all necessary in my case, as I had been adequately intimidated.

Although this interesting species, with all its bluffing activity, has a wide range in the eastern United States, it prefers sunny, sandy areas such as our vegetated front dune, where it prowls particularly for toads, using its turned-up snout (and hence its name) like a little shovel to root out this favorite food burrowed into the sand. Like most snakes, the Hognose has a remarkable ability to detect heat-radiation and an excellent sense of smell (via its complex tongue) for locating prey, which they swallow whole. As with their more ancient reptilian cousins, the turtles, there are no vegetarian snakes.

The Hognose's defensive behavior was decidedly different from the young Blue Racer I saw earlier in the week, sunning itself atop the compost bin at the edge of the backyard. The Racer is bluish, slender, and swift, as its name implies, and as I passed by, it preferred slipping silently to safety over the assertive confrontation it is capable of displaying if cornered. Doug once tried following one through the backyard grass for a better look, but it "raced" away effortlessly in a squiggly serpentine

Birds do no chewing of their food either before swallowing it, although raptors may tear apart their prey to make for smaller pieces to eat. An avian digestive system differs from that of reptiles or mammals, such as ourselves, and is highly efficient. There are two stomachs of sorts or two chambers, but first there is a crop at the bottom of the esophagus, an expanded portion of the throat where swallowed food can be stored temporarily while the bird is foraging. It's more or less a "doggy bag," as one commentator has described it, allowing a bird to take in more seeds and such than it can immediately begin processing.

After the crop is a stomach chamber that begins the breakdown of food with enzymes and acids. The next stomach chamber is the muscular gizzard that takes the place of teeth in grinding up the harder food substances. This is an amazing organ, a natural millstone, formed by the internal mucous lining of the gizzard secreting a keratinous fluid that hardens into horny plates or ridges. Birds take in small rocks and grit to aid the gizzard's internal hard surfaces in the grinding process.

The muscular action of the tough, rubbery gizzard is particularly essential for birds that eat seeds or shellfish which can take considerable grinding to break down. Our sons learned how hard it is to crack walnuts to get the nut meat for my making of the Black Walnut pies that the family likes so well. They used hammers and steel nut picks. Wild Turkeys, on the other hand, can grind twenty-four walnuts in the shell to get the nutrition out of the nuts. It's been reported that after being in a Turkey's gizzard, a small tube of sheet iron was found to be flattened and partly rolled up.

Understandably, it is in the older, more ecologically complex backdune forested zone that animal density and variety is highest. On a quiet morning walk on the easement path through the woods, with sun still low and hidden behind dune and trees, Doug once encountered the

route. However, a later encounter with a Racer went the other way. Same backyard, perhaps the same snake, but this time I must have come upon it too unsuspectingly and it, though only a foot and a half long and finger-thin, refused to give way and then moved straight toward me, head held high in attack mode, until I respectfully stepped aside and hurried backwards. Although there is in me an inborn fear of snakes, I also admire a creature that will challenge another many hundreds of times bigger than itself.

Because of its northern location, Michigan is not rich in snake species, and those that exist have had a hard time of it. With habitat loss, reduction in food sources such as toads, and human fear and dislike of these reptiles that often leads to their wanton, needless killing, their numbers have been reduced. Fortunately these wooded dunes provide a haven for some species, and the Blue Racer, for example, is now most common here on the state's west coast.

Neither snakes or turtles nor birds have teeth to masticate their food to aid the beginning of the digestive process. What teeth snakes do have assist in swallowing the struggling live prey, or in the case of those snakes with hypodermic needle-like, poisonous fangs, these backward curved teeth keep prey from squirming back out of the reptiles' mouths. Also, the toxin injected by venomous serpents begins to immobilize and predigest the victim from within before it is swallowed; so the poisoning is primarily a technique for getting something to eat, not a defensive measure, as we might take it to be. Once far enough inside the gullet of a snake or a turtle, potent enzymes begin the breaking down of the still whole, but by-now-dead, morsel. We've seen bulges in the middle to upper sections of snakes revealing an ingested meal before the creature within had been completed digested in its progression along the serpent's rather straight digestive tract.

cutest member by far of the Weasel family—a Stripped Skunk scratching busily in the leaf litter some twenty-five feet forward in the middle of the trail. The black, cat-sized mammal with a white "V" along its back was oblivious to him as it circled back and forth, head down, searching for beetles and such, and occasionally stopping to munch. Doug halted and waited motionless as the Skunk, still not taking notice of the unusual tall form in the pathway, gradually advanced to within six feet of him. With its potent scent glands as a defense mechanism, this gentle, easy-going little denizen of woods and many other environments is not as readily concerned as most critters must be of what danger might be lurking about.

Brilliantly thinking it was best to change the closing situation, Doug, still unnoticed, stealthily backed away. When threatened, Skunks can send multiple rounds of a pungent, golden-yellow spray from the scent glands located in their tail area. These glands are like little nozzles surrounded by gizzard-like-muscles, able to propel a sulfur-alcohol compound eight feet or more. Striking a victim in the facial area, the nasty fluid can cause temporary blindness, coughing and choking, nausea, and even fainting.

From a hopefully safe distance, Doug then made himself known with deliberate, but non-threatening, noise. The Skunk took a startled stance, backed up slightly, and raised bushy black tail straight skyward. Clearly this small creature would hold its ground. It did not act aggressively by facing its artillery toward the tall invader, but obviously it planned no retreat. Doug spoke softly, inching constantly further back. With its furry fan still at attention, the skunk moved off to one side and resumed scratching for food as Doug proceeded in a wide arc around the occupied part of the path. Once the distance of separation between them enlarged, the tail of the striped little scavenger descended, and it faded into the forest background with the other seldom-seen creatures of mostly the night.

Evidence of chunky Porcupines—stripped bark or droppings at the base of mainly conifer trees—we occasionally found, but we never saw these gnawing, forest-dwelling rodents of less than two feet in length, as they, too, are usually nocturnal. Porcupines will sometimes, however, shuffle over the forest floor during daylight hours, and a neighbor's dog had a very close daytime connection with one, bringing home several barbed quills sticking painfully from his nose. The spiny Porkies are fearless but never attack, nor do they "shoot" their very sharply pointed quills, as is often supposed. So the dog in its blissful, sniffing ignorance had to have come up close enough for the defensive animal to have rotated and swung its spine-armed tail into the canine's face. As with the claws of both animals, the Porcupine's quill's are composed of that familiar fibrous structural protein, keratin.

While most animals of the forested duneworks are primarily nocturnal, White-tailed Deer are both nocturnal and out and about during daytime, and are occasionally seen just about anywhere. They roam from along the lake's edge to the forest and out into the countryside, though their movement into the exposed beach area has only been noticed in the early mornings and in the evenings. Young and old, they come within yards of the cottage, dining on the edges of our miniature lawns. One afternoon, Doug, resting from a half-day of chores, lay in the hammock he had installed between two trees in the Balsam Poplar grouping on our front dune bluff. Opening one eye in response to a slight sound, he watched without moving as three does, coming from the park, walked leisurely along one of their normal pathways barely ten feet away, unaware of his presence despite their very excellent sense of smell, their most important sense. After their passing, he raised up to watch their progress and found himself staring at—and being stared at by—a straggling fourth Cervid. Following a moment of indecision by both parties, the White-tailed wheeled about and quickly retreated with graceful arching bounds in the direction from which the quartet had come.

To view the White-tails of tawny tops and white chins and underbellies is universally delightful. White around their eyes and nose softens their fine faces. Few people, if any, would say they are not handsome creatures. The fawns are simply adorable. This ungulate of the Great Lakes region is a northern sub-species that is larger than other groupings of White-tailed Deer to the south. And the species is fascinating in so many ways.

Doug or I have come down our driveway from the cottage at times and been startled by several quick, harsh, wheezing snorts coming from the steep wooded slope across the access lane. There, partially hidden by trees and shade, will be a stationary, highly-alert Deer, probably a doe, giving us a warning of sorts—or so it seems. If we do not advance, it will remain for a while, watching to see what we will do, snorting some more, and then begin moving up to the dune ridge and away, usually stopping at least once to check our location.

Why don't these very wary creatures bolt when we appear? We are always less than one hundred feet away when we halt to observe. However, with their vision highly geared to detect motion, there's no question they have seen our movement before we reach the driveway, early on hearing us coming, and probably have detected our scent as well, so it must be that the speed of our walking does not seem threatening, nor does it appear that we're on a chase after them.

Unless surprised or quickly come upon, Deer seldom panic, I have read. They evidently prefer to identify any suspicious newcomer or sound and assess the situation before deciding what to do. Also, in our coming down the driveway, they surely are well aware that being on opposite slopes is a divide between us and them that is greater than the straight-line distance, and their remaining in place provides an opportunity to

further gauge the extent of danger we may pose. These large mammals also know that, when necessary, they can instantly bolt and fly through the terrain with breathtaking speed, readily distancing themselves from most pursuers. Furthermore, it is known that Deer do have a sense of curiosity—and possibly stay to wonder a little about us, as we wonder a great deal about them.

While the wheezing deer snorts seem like a warning to us, the air being forcibly passed through their nasal passages is really a warning alert to other White-tails in the immediate vicinity that there is perceived danger in the area. An alarm call is just one aspect of this species' elaborate social communications system. Then, again, a snort or two might have been primarily for Doug or me. Perhaps, one or more of the Deer had been announcing to us perceived predators that we'd been spotted and was broadcasting, "Hey you, you're not going to be surprising me. Come any closer, and I can be outta here in a flash. Can't sneak up and catch me now—so don't even try." The Deer tentatively concludes that we're smart predators—no longer advancing and not willing to waste valuable energy going on a fruitless pursuit—and then the wily White-tail watchfully ambles off, having avoided depleting any of its energy reserve on a bounding escape action. Who can tell?

While does are commonly observed, the more reclusive older bucks are almost never seen. Only once have we spied the antlered variety. On an early evening beach walk accompanied by friends, with the late summer's descending sun coming to cast an orange tint to the coastal landscape, we noticed a large stag perched atop the high shoreline dune at the forest's edge. He stood regal and motionless there in the elevated distance as we ambled north toward Big Flower Creek, we watching him, he watching us. On returning, His Majesty was still there, evidently curious about the lowly two-footed variety of creatures plodding along the water's edge well below him—odd creatures he's surely seen at other times.

Evidence of male White-tails is infrequently found in the duneworks. Once we came across a skull with a single short antler still attached, but never have we found just the antlers, which are lost by the bucks each winter after the mating season. These male adornments are not horns, which are permanent head structures (made, of course, of the protein, keratin!), but bony structures, the fastest form of bone growth known. This speedy development is necessary, for antlers (some becoming quite large) are deciduous, like the leaves of broadleaf trees that grow, are cast off, and then re-grow to go through an annual cycle, again and again. It's been determined that antler growth is triggered by the increasing daylight hours in early spring—another solar-activated biological process.

In answer as to why we have never found any of the yearly-produced and winter-shed antlers is that these bony structures are a source of minerals for the many gnawing mammals of the Rodent Order and generally disappear rather quickly, once they end up on the ground. Porcupines particularly have a craving for bones on account of the mineral content. And, of course, many antlers don't end up on the ground, as bucks are more prized by hunters than does, and the racks tend to become wall decorations, many never ever leaving the head of the male deer. But some late winter, perhaps we'll find a nice set of many-pointed antlers on a cold woods walk.

Our bow hunter friend clued us in on another sign that bucks traverse the woods by pointing out the occasional bark scrapings that can be found on smaller trees where the "velvet" covering is rubbed off the matured and hardened antlers in the fall. While growing, the antlers are covered with a fine-haired "velvet" skin, which is rich with veins and arteries that supply blood to the bone—and is the only regenerating skin found among mammals. Tree rubbings by male White-tails also occur during the subsequent mating season of late fall.

On a cold and gray November late afternoon, with a blustery wind that created waves on the lake of three to four feet, Doug walked south along a now-wide beach. As he looked down the shoreline toward the far end of the park and the cottages beyond, three Deer (seemingly does) suddenly emerged from the park's high dunes and raced across the wide beach several hundred yards in front of him, heading straight toward the water. They bounded into the cold lake full speed, and continued away from shore until they had to begin swimming. We had seen White-tails drink from the lake and even frolic along the shallow shoreline on nicer evenings, but Doug was not prepared for what happened next. Instead of turning around when meeting the advancing waves in deeper water, the trio continued swimming outward into the lake until beyond his sight, hidden by the height of the waves.

Racing back to the house to get binoculars, Doug was still unable to pick out the Deer in the water even from the higher vantage point of our bluff. Then a large motor boat appeared far to the south, coming out of the horizonless gray of sky and water, about a fourth of a mile off-shore. As the roaring craft came nearer and approached the area where the Deer were heading, the binoculars picked up a glimpse of bobbing spots far out in the lake. The spots were the Deer, now headed back toward shore, being helped by the wind-driven waves. Emerging eventually from the lake, they briefly shook themselves before dashing back toward the dunes from whence they had come.

Having gone back to the windswept beach, Doug stood alone as he watched the four-legged forms materialize out of the lake and retreat inland, totally puzzled, trying to figure out what had actually taken place in the last half hour. Were the Deer fleeing hunters? But there had been no gunshots or hunters appearing to take shots at the animals while on the open beach. Fleeing from dogs? But no canines had come bounding out of the dunes in pursuit of the Deer and none were heard barking. And if fleeing some danger in the forested dunes, why did they head back in the very same direction of that danger on their return from the lake? If the boat with its roaring engine had not come along at that particular time, would the Deer have continued onward into ever deeper water until they died from exhaustion? If they were indeed trying to escape some predator, two-footed or four, were they taking to the water as if it were a river that would separate them from their pursuer once crossed? Do Deer have any understanding of the size of a body of water in which the other side can't be seen—or even an expectation of "the other side?" And how can these land-based animals with their very slender long legs made for explosive running be able to swim so well against on-coming waves?

As with so many aspects of the natural world, we were coming up short for explanations on our own. But as with the bird guides that I've found so helpful, there fortunately are excellent books on animal behavior by a range of wildlife specialists to help out. And in the case of White-tails, they are perhaps the most studied and researched of all wildlife species. First of all, it turns out that Deer are capable swimmers, able to swim relatively fast and for long distances. Doug saw a measure of this—but we still don't understand *how* they can do it. Deer will take to water to elude enemies, and that must be the explanation for the three having entered the lake, though there was no clue as to what the trio had perceived as a threat.

One source reported that White-tails have been seen swimming out into the Atlantic Ocean up to five miles (but whether the animals made it back to shore was not stated). And Deer cross large rivers and even swim long distances between islands. So these three deer could have gone into the lake, with or without a conception of "the other side," and at some point, after swimming miles out, have decided—absent the boat appearance—to turn back, either giving up on reaching land or thinking the original danger was gone by then. This may be attributing too much mental work to the Deer, as their brains are small, and one authority states that reasoning is impossible for them—although we lean with others who have seen enough Deer ingenuity to decidedly dispute the latter point. Also, Deer seem to forget about specific dangers once they have distanced themselves from the threat—which would explain the trio running right back in the same direction from which they had fled upon returning from the lake.

In any case, the three does certainly would have been exhausted from such an extended, vigorous ordeal in the cold water and, very importantly, have used up a portion of vital fat reserves that had been recently stored up for the lean winter months that were beginning. Then again, the Deer might have continued on too far to have made it back safely. Some of the mystery of the occurrence cleared up, but plenty remaining to keep us wondering.

One unusual and extended encounter with a White-tail brought deeply engaged interest, but it was laden with sadness rather than pleasure. A doe was seen on a summer morning moving slowly through the partially wooded swale down in front of the cottage. It was difficult to tell at first, but we came to detect in her labored movement that both front legs were broken, or severely dislocated, at the "knee" joint. Like the does that had passed Doug lying in the hammock, this critically damaged creature had come from the park, and was now slowly browsing her way along that same path between the edge of the bluff overlooking the beach and the rising wooded slope leading up to the cottage. The lower leg sections still clung to the upper front limbs, and as she made her way through the vegetation, tilted forward, the useless foreleg bottoms flopped with each step. Viewing with binoculars, we could see that these were old breaks, with the upper stubs having healed and enlarged from use as feet. Knowing that Deer often went down the bluff slope to get to the beach and the lake water, we theorized that this doe may have started down the bluff quickly, had her thin front legs suddenly sink deep into the sand, and her body went tumbling over them, dislocating the legs at the joint.

We subsequently saw the injured female a number of times in the varied vicinity of the cottage during that summer, and as lame as this animal was, it proceeded about its survival business in what we could only regard as courageous determination. Thinking she might not be able to get to water, Doug filled a bucket and put it beside her often used swale path in front of the cottage, but she never seemed to have drunk from it. We were surprised to see her able to negotiate up and over the high wooded dune between us and the park one afternoon.

The two of us were granted a close-up view of the doe on another afternoon when Doug, standing on the cottage deck, happened to notice the animal's passage through the vegetation along the swale deer trail down in front. She then seemed to settle in amidst the shade and thick growth at the front of the cottage deck next door. No one was home there, and Doug quietly slipped around behind the building and slowly out onto the front deck of the A-frame. Peering over the deck railing he could see the lame one laying some ten feet below in good view, facing away from him and the building toward the lake. A stiff sea breeze kept the resting doe from detecting his presence by sound or smell as he observed her quiet, solitary activity.

Returning for me, Doug and I crept back to the deck to view the injured ruminant eating twigs and leaves and then alternately chewing her cud. She browsed in a semi-circle around her resting position, the lower portions of her front legs splayed out at odd angles. Then, the injured lady got up and hobbled off on her shortened limbs a few yards into a fresh resting spot for more browsing and digesting. Deer have an unusual mouth arrangement for amputating the ends of twigs, small branches, and

other tough vegetation. Over the years, we have found several elongated deer skulls in the woods, and have noticed the absence of teeth along the front half of the upper jaws. It's not that the teeth were missing, they were never there. For Deer, we have learned, have a tough pad across the upper mouth area instead of upper front teeth, with the lower jaw teeth chopping off the vegetation against this hard pad. This leaves a slight tell-tale torn edge on one side of the branch that's been nibbled. (Rabbits, for example, with sharp upper and lower incisors, chop off similar vegetation with a clean, slanted cut.)

As we quietly watched leaning on the deck railing, occasionally the slight, tawny-colored creature below would look out towards the lake for a while, chewing away, but evidently feeling safe in the surrounding vegetation, never glanced up and backwards in our direction. In her moment of restful peace, the doe's lakeward gazing even appeared to be a contented absorbing of the pleasant afternoon scene of gently rolling blue water.

Here we were, in a most unusual circumstance, closely observing a wild deer as she was coping with a diet of vegetation difficult to digest, and avoiding potential predators—such as humans, large dogs, or coyotes. Deer need to take in large amounts of plant material because it is generally of rather low nutritional value. While the animal is roaming about, browsing, the tough vegetation is not thoroughly chewed, but stored in the first chamber, the rumen, of a complex stomach of four chambers. This "strategy" limits the time Deer need to spend out and about feeding and being exposed to predators, a "feed and gulp" practice. This procedure is similar to that of birds storing food in their crop while foraging, but there is a difference in what happens next.

Later, with the ruminate often bedded down in a safe place, the partially chewed twigs and leaves are returned to the deer's mouth from the microbe-laden rumen for proper masticating, which is repeated multiple times, before the pulverized material is passed on to further stomach chambers. Our doe was going through this process of regurgitation and re-chewing of her "cud," breaking down the cellulose-laden material further and further with the many pointed edges of her multi-surfaced back teeth to increase the effectiveness of stomach micro-organisms and acids in the digestion process.

We left, pleased that she felt, for the time being at least, somewhat at ease—and very privileged to have been so close in her presence.

This was nearly the last we saw of the lame one, for summer was closing out and the ensuing school year provided far less opportunity for us to be at the lakeshore. We knew her days were numbered with winter coming. Her caloric intake would soon need to substantially increase with the advancing cooler days followed by the extended frigid weather, and foraging would become harder and harder for her. White-tails are highly social animals, functioning cooperatively through living in family and larger groups—usually headed by older does—but this doe was on her own to make her way through coming snow and in finding suitable shelter and bedding spots.

Winter is a season of particular hardships for Deer.

Unlike some other of our area's creatures, they neither migrate south nor hibernate, nor are they nomadic. No cozy den or hollow log can offer them shelter either, and thus Deer are the only wild animals that I can think of in this region that go through winter continually exposed to the elements. The best they can do is retreat into a low area or a somewhat protected cove where the wind is blunted or huddle together amidst some thick stands of vegetation. Fur thickens and fat reserves are built up in the fall to provide insulation and future heat energy, and that's it. Even the physically well-prepared can have difficulty surviving the lean, harsh months of winter—and "our" lady was seriously handicapped and alone. For a brief interlude we felt emotionally connected to this struggling and doomed individual of a different species.

The following spring, two deer remains—bones with some hide still stretched across—were found among the sparse vegetation in the front dunal area of the park just to the south of the cottage. One seemed that of a yearling; the other may have been her. Not enough was left to be sure. Nearly a whole carcass can disappear within months, scavenged and recycled back through other life forms and the action of weather into the landscape and the nutrient chain.

Of all the varied creatures of the forested duneland, White-tails are the most connected to the vegetated landscape in terms of their impact upon it. They are the largest wild herbivores in the eastern United States, with the exception of a relatively few American Elk (which are really a larger deer). White-tails are also by far the most abundant large wild mammal on the continent, if not the whole world, as of the past half century or so. And they roam the state of Michigan in greater numbers than in any other state except sprawling Texas.

As generalist vegetarians, White-tailed Deer are one of the most adaptable animals in the world and exist over a wide range in this hemisphere. They can browse on hundreds of different types of plants, graze on grasses, and chomp on acorns, corn on the cob, and fruits. Many suburban and city dwellers know that the deer menu includes flora found in their gardens and urban parks, as well as in wooded and agricultural landscapes. It's perhaps easier to list species they won't eat at some point than those they will.

While White-tails have had only a slight impact on our Indiana semi-urban home landscape (bordering a woodland area), the cottage dunal area is another matter entirely. The second winter of our lakeshore residency, a number of Deer visited the low, gentle slopes immediately on either side of the Canada Yew that we had recently identified there. A low, sprawling, evergreen shrub, it is a species we were pleased to discover here, as it is the only yew native to most of the eastern North American continent and is relatively uncommon in our region. It is now even more uncommon locally, as Deer have recently, in effect, extirpated this plant in these forested dunes, for we no longer find it anywhere.

But it is fortunate we knew about it in time, for as the Canada Yew is a more northern understory shrub of late successional forests, it would certainly be another remnant species here of the pre-logging period—and one more of our dune species whose habitat reaches into the Boreal Forest.

Elsewhere in the duneland forest, the abundance of large herbivores has meant heavy browsing on ground level herbs and on younger trees, leaving a sparser understory of saplings and shrubs, a more open woodland landscape. It seems to us that species of woodland flowers are no longer as great as should be expected. The lovely spring

and human settlements into the early 1900s, significant and substantial habitat changes favorable to these opportunistic herbivores gradually increased as the twentieth century wore on.

Although the vast pre-settlement forest of the region had vanished, the great ecological transformation had not happened all at once, nor had every wooded area been clearcut. Thousands of tree lots remained across the chopped up landscape, and banks of stream courses and wetlands (not drained) usually retained smaller trees. And not every acre denuded of trees had lent itself to being converted into food production. While trees went down by the tens of millions over the decades, young ones were coming forth in thousands of locations as the small wooded "refuges" filled out. By the 1930s, many deforested areas and abandoned fields were coming into brush, and second-growth woodlands were emerging in the Great Lakes region, prime food and shelter for White-tails.

When Charles and Mary Huston gave up farming and livestock raising to move into the city of Muskegon Heights in 1912, it didn't take long for the sandy acres that had been cleared after their move to the Little Flower Creek area in the early 1890s to begin reverting to a more naturally vegetated landscape. The Huston story of leaving marginal land really not suitable for agriculture was but one of many hundreds of thousands of those taking place nationwide in the early decades of the twentieth century. And then there was the dunal woods the Hustons left behind; opened up from several decades of logging and exhibiting new woody and herbaceous growth, the local landscape was being transformed into near-perfect White-tail habitat, as was happening in numerous abandoned places elsewhere. Exit humans and their manipulative ways, enter Deer and theirs.

Trilliums are clearly much fewer than when we first came to this setting. Some tree species are more resistant to deer browsing and will likely be promoted, versus certain others, as the forest goes through its long-term regeneration. Interestingly, Eastern Hemlock twigs are supposed to be a desirable browse for White-tails, and young Hemlock shoots poking up through the snow in winter have been called "ice cream plants" for Deer. But we find that Hemlocks of all sizes are doing quite well in their numbers and growth in the duneland forest. As elsewhere in much of the eastern United States, an uncontrolled deer herbivory threatens forest regeneration, many plant species, and habitat for other wildlife forms in this dunal forest.

It is common to speak of an "overpopulation" of Deer almost as if it's their fault. There very likely are more of the highly adaptable White-tails in America today than when Europeans descended upon the continent. In Michigan alone, the deer population has been estimated to be hovering around 1.7 million animals during the first decade of the twenty-first century—and that's with hunting taking anywhere from a quarter to a half million Deer annually, according to Michigan Department of Natural Resources information.

The vast and often dense forests that originally covered most of the Great Lakes region (and much of the rest of eastern North America) provided generally poor habitat for White-tailed Deer, which thrive along fragmented forest edges and scattered openings, and thus it is thought by some that their numbers were not great to begin with here. Woodland Indians depended heavily upon Deer, and predation by both Gray Wolves and Cougars were also factors in limiting the size of Cervid populations in the millennia before the coming of Europeans with their guns and axes. And while Deer numbers drastically fell with the extensive clearing of forests, heavy and unregulated hunting, and the establishment of farming

The extent of overgrown fields and young woodlands expanded during the Great Depression of the 1930s, with an increased exodus of rural human occupants migrating to towns and cities and to wherever they could make it. In the droughty conditions and the great economic difficulties of the 1930s, tens of thousands, particularly in the Plains states, became refugees in their own land. Abandonment of land in poorer areas led to substantial acreage reverting to public ownership in the 1920s and 1930s, with much of that landscape in the East being set aside to help establish or enlarge numerous state and national forest areas—

although it was decades before any of the government-owned landscapes resembled forests again .

Along with natural habitat improvement coming from a "benign neglect," there were growing conservation and state game management measures to protect and increase deer populations. And with the virtual elimination of any wild "top" predators completed in the previous century, the numbers of White-tails in Michigan and elsewhere came to surpass those of pre-settlement times.

This prominent deer trail in the heart of the woods has become one that Doug and I often follow, too, in our trips through the multifaceted duneland. The dark green foliage is that of young Hemlocks, which are doing just fine in spite of the resident browsing herbivores.

By 1950, ever-enlarging deer populations in an expanding number of areas were killing forage plants by over-browsing. Stress in the Michigan deer population was evident as their numbers dropped to roughly half a million a dozen years later. Game management efforts then helped bring the herd size up to an all-time peak of two million animals in 1989. That was deemed too high, and measures were implemented by the Michigan DNR to reduce the herd by several hundred thousand and to generally maintain it at the size now existing during the first decade of the twenty-first century.

I have learned that the rise and fall of deer populations is a complex situation, and the reasons for past and more recent fluctuations are far more complicated than given here. For there are other factors, such as, disease outbreaks, legislative directives, winter feeding by humans, changing agricultural practices, and mildness or severity of winters. And in the end, not all can be known by us humans, even though White-tails are the most studied and researched wildlife species.

In recent decades, another factor has emerged affecting Deer populations. White-tails have become quite acclimated to a growing human population that has spread out again, more and more, into rural areas. The interface between the two species has increased everywhere, as our living in the dunes illustrates, as well as Deer advancing into the same vicinity as our Indiana semi-urban landscape. Of course, our Indiana landscape was White-tail habitat to start with. Like humans, Deer can overpopulate an area to the point of degrading the landscape that sustains them. But in the case of the White-tailed Deer, their numbers are now primarily in response to human-induced landscape changes and practices.

As it turned out, the forested duneland of the cottage locale, in recovering from the logging period, served as prime deer habitat as the decades of the twentieth century progressed. Our early residency along its lakeshore edge, however, may have coincided with the peak of the deer population within the dunal forest, and is now likely seeing a decline in that population. With the ongoing maturation of the tree cover and the deer decimation of much of the understory, the habitat is changing once again, this time away from what is most advantageous for White-tails. The heart of the duneworks does provide good shelter, so they will continue to use it for that, but from our observations, the overall number of Deer inhabiting the dunal forest seems to have gone down.

Previously, I had not been aware of the extent of the substantial ecological interconnections between the fauna and flora of a forest. But I now know that, in the case of Deer, their numbers and choice of browse exert selective pressures on plant communities, greatly affecting forest species composition at several levels. Although there are always multiple factors at work, the White-tails of this period have been significantly determining the dune forest's composition for the decades ahead.

But, then, was it not the human fauna of the recent past that initiated the greatest flora change and opened the door to the Cervid impact?

The principal coastal landscape that Doug and I have lived amidst and explored within extends from the Little Flower Creek outlet and backwater north to near the upper end of the Big Flower Creek marsh—a distance of about one and one-half miles—and reaches inland from the beach to the back side of the forested dunes and the eastern edges of the two Flower wetlands—a width of less than a half-mile. Somewhat the shape of a long irregular rectangle, that area encompasses roughly 375 acres. However, as that landscape rectangle also includes a number of residences, campground and parking areas, and some public roadway, the actual natural area we've engaged is somewhat less than 350 acres—the size of a very modest Indiana corn farm. Yet the diversity of flora and fauna and the mingling of species within is rather astounding. As year after progressing year has gone by for us in our immediate world beside the inland sea, we have encountered much of the complexities, the dynamics, and the richness of activity of this biodiversity in this varied landscape, and have even come to slightly understand some of the myriad connections and relationships—feeling connected and related ourselves.

It is one of those nicely serendipitous occurrences that, as the foregoing words were being set down, I should come across the observation of that ancient Greek philosopher and sage, Aristotle, that "all things are ordered together somehow, but not all alike, both fishes and fowls and plants; and the world is not such that one thing has nothing to do with another, but they are all connected."

CHANGES

One Labor Day weekend in the early 1990s brought our two sons, now in college, to join Doug and me at the cottage for a family outing. The somewhat tepid water on one of the warm afternoons called for us all to enjoy a little seldom-done frolicking together in the tumbling surf. While the high lake levels had come down, there was still a series of offshore bars out there created from sand stolen from the shoreline formations in the 1980s. The weekend-long breezes across the lake had generated building waves that tumbled in forcefully, hitting sandbar after sandbar. That had potential for some fun. The four of us pumped up small, one-person inflatable rafts and struggled out against the rushing waves past the first bars to chest-deep water. Launching ourselves onto the rafts brought rolling rides toward shore that often flipped raft and rider into the surf on the way in.

Dozens of enjoyable rides later, the cloudy afternoon sky darkened and the wind picked up. Occupied by spillings, sputterings, and laughter, we hadn't been paying the far horizon any attention to see that something had been brewing. Three of us were on our way out for yet another jostling ride, a short distance up from our cottage beach, to take advantage of a greater series of waves, when all of a sudden that wind turned very strong, with storm clouds boiling in from the northwest. Quickly turning back, we ran in slow motion against the resistance of the less-than-waist deep water toward the cottage beach, trying to keep the wind-flipping rafts in our hands. En route to the shore, the blowing

turned so fierce that we could feel surface water being picked up and hitting us on our backs. Once beached, we fought the howling wind for continued possession of the inflatables as we struggled toward the deck stairs, whipped-up sand stinging arms and legs, and rain beginning to pelt us. Running for the cottage soaking wet, the four of us scurried indoors for shelter and to close doors and windows, but not before a lamp, a wall picture, and papers left on the table had been scattered to the floor.

While we had not ventured out into dangerous water, we had forgotten that day, in our group fun, to be adequately attuned to how quickly change can come to this shoreline setting. The turbulent storm front that had moved in so suddenly also passed on relatively fast. But when the rain soon ceased and the weather calmed down, it was no longer warm.

A season can be discarded in less than an hour, here. We learned to dress in layers and to subtract or add garments in tandem with the day's rhythms, exchanging an afternoon's swimsuit for warmth of sweater and socks by sunset. The change suddenly brought by this storm, however, seemed decisive on a bigger scale. It was almost a certainty that we had just experienced our last watery frolic of the year.

Although a Ruby-throated Hummingbird still frequented my plantings of deep pink Impatiens, the flowers came to look ragged from exposure to the newly chilling winds. Any hour, with its food supplies rapidly diminishing, this pugnacious little creature would be out of here. Flying at low altitude, the solitary bird will head southward, its unique skeleton allowing its wings to move rotationally and hover to feed from certain flowers along the way. Powered by wing muscles that make up 25 to 30 percent of its weight, Hummingbirds, with their hovering, forward and backward flight (even upside down), dazzling speed, and aerial displays are masters of the air, adding their unique twists to moving water. These plump, sparrow-looking shorebirds on stilted legs and with long bills are the premier feeders in the swash zone, quickly plucking up small organisms left momentarily stranded by the retreat of waves. While nimbly staying just behind the advancing and retreating wash of the waves, these tiny beachcombers were staying ahead of the colder weather in their marathon migration south from the treeless Arctic tundra—the Sanderlings heading for ocean and Gulf Coast shores, the Sandpipers on to South America.

All were announcements of further changes soon to come.

Late September rains rusted the leaves of the Beech trees, and the Red Osier Dogwood foliage was changing to match the deep crimson of the stems. Below the kaleidoscope of developing fall color, creekside plants to our south, too tired to withstand further insults of wind and weather, succumbed and lay limp upon the stream's surface. I looked out from our small bluff deck over the vast, cooling lake topped by intermittent blue sky. Billowy white clouds rolled overhead with darker, more menacing cloud banks following in the distance, their shadows creating silver islands of shimmering water pursued by darker charcoal bands that moved across the churning gray waves. The moments of sun were warm and intense, but I hunkered into my jacket as each blue opening filled with the endless, moving clouds that insisted upon interrupting the desired afternoon sunshine.

By this time, after a half dozen years of inland sea residency, we had been well immersed in some of the great variations that weather, sea, landscape, and wildlife offered here. Never fully prepared for the array of natural changes, we came to adjust as best we could to the alterations and transformations that flowed on. It had also come to be that it was necessary to adjust to the human winds of change that arrived as unexpectedly as many of the natural ones.

the astonishing phenomenon of avian flight. For me, I don't see these amazingly light birds flying, but shooting and flowing through the air, and dancing and floating.

Feeding primarily on sugary nectar (through its hollow "soda straw" tongue) on its way to a wintering habitat, "our" little Hummer will take on an efficient fuel by adding less than one-tenth of an ounce of fat to its tiny body—and nearly double its miniscule weight—before making a long, mostly nighttime crossing over the Gulf of Mexico. Hardly a speck in the sky over the vast water in its lonely non-stop flight of more than 500 miles, the most energy-intensive phase of its annual cycle. A journey that normally is completed in less than 24 hours can last many hours more if turbulent weather quickly develops and headwinds must be battled. There is simply no rest stop for the struggling creature in this case, and fat reserves will be used up and muscle mass next consumed to keep aloft over the open water. If successful this far on its arduous journey, the exhausted, diminished puffball of a bird will need to quickly find suitable landfall habitat for recovery before pushing on to wintering grounds in Central Mexico. How close to the amazing Monarchs, already on their own long distance nectar trail migration to Central Mexico, do the equally amazing, diminutive Ruby-throats end up, I wondered? And how many of the millions of the travel-driven Neotropical migrants drop helpless out of the sky, unable to carry on their Gulf crossing?

A few trees were now winking orange tips at us, and the Goldenrod near Little Flower Creek had become downy-topped. The shoreline, already responding in form to the force of the new season's angled waves from northerly directions, displayed deepening scallops, cutting well into the previously expanding beach.

Migrating Semipalmated Sandpipers and Sanderlings (a larger Sandpiper) ran in hurried stride along the beach's wet edge, in and out with the waves, agilely staying just out of reach of the rhythmically

Doug and I had been careful, in choosing our Michigan coastal home, to also consider who the neighbors were. We had done some homework in that summer of 1986 before making our final decision, meeting the nearest residents, both permanent homeowners and intermittent ones like ourselves, seeking a definition of the environmental consciousness of those in the small neighborhood. We happily found that the setting that had attracted us harbored a collection of outdoor-minded people, ones who generally enjoyed connections with the landscape in ways similar to us, by way of quiet, low-impact activities. In purchasing the cottage, the two of us assumed that everything would remain as it was upon our entry into the accommodating social environment, at least for quite some time. That assumption proved wrong rather early on.

The first change in ownership occurred next door within less than two years of our coming, when Bob and Toni left the A-frame with the friendly little guest house for the last time. They had built their cozy, modest second home on the lakeshore themselves more than a quarter century before, were now retiring, and wanted to live near their daughter, Amy, in northern Michigan—an only offspring who had grown up from birth with the nifty A-frame and the big lake. Their decision saddened us, for we had developed an immediate affection for the two of them and had shared meals and many walks and beachside conversations. In consideration of us, they sold their cabin to a Grand Rapids family they thought would make good part-time neighbors for us, foregoing a higher offer for their place. It was a gift of friendship that gave us some compensation for the absence of these two wonderful neighbors. Although we dearly missed Bob and Toni as next-door companions, connections were not severed, for we were drawn to visit them on Grand Traverse Bay for a few days as each subsequent summer rolled around.

The owners of the dwelling directly behind us to the east soon followed Bob and Toni's lead in moving to a new residence. With a

second child on the way, Greg and Dee's abode was now too small. When built by William in the early 1950s, the structure had been sized only as a vacation cabin. The position of park caretaker had become available, and Greg and Dee went for it, since part of the job's compensation included use of the county-owned house at the entrance to the park. As we and the other residents of our little neighborhood needed to pass through this entrance and into the park to get to our access two-track, we continued to see them often during their two-year tenure as caretakers before they moved away from the park. For a period, Greg and Dee rented out their cabin, but then it stood empty until it burned to the ground on Halloween, 1992. The cause of the fire was never determined, but because of the timing of the blaze, it raised concern among us all that someone had come through the park to commit arson.

Maxine, the widow who lived some 600 yards north of us and who, as resident matriarch of the little neighborhood, dispensed neighborhood "rules" and advice to us and others, then surprised us with her announcement of leaving very soon after Greg and Dee's departure. She and her husband had resided in the full-size lakeshore home they had built in the early 1960s, and then she alone, after his 1975 death. Now edging toward her mid-seventies, Maxine had decided that dealing with the demands of living year-round in an isolated shoreline location, and being there by herself, was really not a wise situation any longer. So, she had found a house close to the town of Montague on White Lake, six miles to the southeast, and put her Lake Michigan home and most of her 1773 feet of shoreline property up for sale in 1989, three years after our arrival. Again, a purchase by a Grand Rapids party—but one we were later to find quite different from the rest of us. The impact of that ownership change would reverberate down through the years.

The two small cabins a little further east into the duneworks that William had long ago built also came to have new ownership, and in little over a half-dozen years at the lakeshore, everyone we had known when first coming to the setting had left. Strangely, as the relatively new and the third generation owners of the cottage, Doug and I were now the neighborhood's "old timers." For several more years there were no full-time residents in the little neighborhood, and with us coming to the lakeshore and the woods throughout all seasons, we were also the most present on the scene.

To the east of us, widow Erna's large tract of mostly forested duneland—"the woods"—had remained for decade after decade the one constant in the neighborhood, as owners of the six residences on or close to the lakeshore had come and gone. Though long absent from the locale, the elderly Erna never entertained selling the parcel, even when approached by the County, which sought the land as an addition to the park in the late 1980s.

Since 1967, Erna's granddaughter Carole had lived with her husband Bob to the northeast of the woods, on a long, north-south tract beyond the duneworks that her grandparents had given the couple out of the original ninety-eight acres William and Erna were deeded in 1940. Carole and Bob's, home, fronting on Flower Creek Road, lay at the far end of the easement two-track that came from our area and was our route to the woods. From their house to our cottage was a nice walk of over a half-mile through sparse, returning shrubs and trees on the flatlands and on through Erna's more-heavily forested dunes. Since the two-track continued on to the edge of the park, it provided a way to the park beach for the several property owners, east beyond the duneworks. As Carole and Bob frequented this path to the park, we early on saw them passing just behind our cottage and soon came to be good friends with them. They were teachers, too, soon to be retired, and had also come from Indiana.

Stopping by to see our progress on various cottage and landscape projects was more than just friendly curiosity, for Carole had often witnessed her grandfather building the Chalet (later, our cottage) in the mid-1960s. Granddaughter and husband had interacted with the older couple for the few years of overlapping residency before William died and widowed Erna sold the Chalet and moved to Florida in 1968. Since then, Carole and Bob, in Grandma's absence, had been the overseers of the woods tract. For several reasons, they, therefore, had a strong connection to the area, and we were glad for their protective stance toward the enduring woods.

Then it came: the announcement that what had been for so long stable was soon to change.

On a November 1993 visit to our cottage, Carole passed on the news that her grandmother's land would have to be sold some time in the next year. Erna's strong heart was outlasting her mobility and reason, and, in her mid-nineties, she had been admitted to a nursing home. More recently, a court had placed her under the guardianship of a daughter-in-law, Carole's mother, in Indianapolis, Indiana, and had ordered Erna's various assets liquidated to help pay for her care. Everything had been sold now—except the woods.

Coming as something of a shock to Carole and Bob, this new development was also of great concern to us, for Doug and I, in deciding upon buying the cottage, had seen the adjoining undeveloped duneland forest as one of the great advantages of the lakeshore property location. And once the other neighbors learned of the situation, they, too, were concerned. For that remarkable and quiet natural landscape, connected to nearly all of our properties, was now to be cast out there as a piece of real estate, with its future unknown. Upon leaving after delivering the news, Carole promised to let us know when more was learned about the developing sale process.

The call came on an evening the following February, while we were at our Indiana home. Bob had seen a stranger walking the woods trail who turned out to be a local real estate agent. The court order to sell the woods property had been issued, and Carole's mother, as Erna's guardian, had called the agent's office in Montague to inquire about procedures for selling. The agent would evaluate the property and write up a listing contract for her to consider. It seemed like the woods tract could now be on the market in a matter of weeks.

Carole and Bob and we knew immediately what that would mean. A developer would drool over the chance to carve this forested duneland into high-end lots for large, upscale homes. Although there were recent statutory limits on how many lots might be created and what could be done to the coastal dunescape, there would still be substantial clearings for a multi-party access road, houses, garages, driveways, septic systems, utility lines—all creating openings in the tree canopy and fragmenting this special, maturing forest, now finally recovering after decades of exploitation of a century and less before.

The current easement way intersecting Flower Creek Road, and coming in across the back portions of four properties before entering the dunal woods, would become the access avenue for any new homes there. What was now merely a roughly seven-foot-wide, sand-based walking path, with trees and other vegetation growing beside and over it, would have to be substantially widened and hard-surfaced to meet new township zoning regulations for access to new residences—a roadway suitable for emergency vehicles, such as fire engines, to safely and easily negotiate. Add to that the coming and going of vehicles, including recreational machines, within the heart of the woods, and the environment and its wildlife would suffer a heavy impact, statutory restrictions or not. At this time, Doug and I were only beginning to learn about and understand the ecological importance of these forested dunes, but we knew enough already that looming "development" seemed like environmental disaster for this landscape.

I worried about the impact of subdividing and building, particularly, because songbird habitats suffer from both forest openings and various human activities. Keeping intact existing woodlands that form "green" corridors and adequate nesting habitat is one of the most valuable actions that can be taken to halt the decline of the migratory Neotropicals. Cats and dogs that might come with woods residences and be allowed to run loose would be bad news for ground nesters such as Veerys and Oven Birds, ones already hard-pressed in raising offspring by the likes of egg- and nestling-loving Raccoons, Weasels, Skunks, snakes, and other woodland predators.

And, from our selfish viewpoints, the lives of all of us surrounding neighbors, enjoying the solitude of the dunal forest, would also be negatively affected. Gone would be the opportunities for Doug and me to roam "the woods," to further our emerging connections to this special landscape, and to further flesh out the stories of its special natural and human history of which we were just becoming aware. Development would create a situation that both Carole and Bob and we, especially, dreaded.

"Surely, together we can find a way to save it," urged Doug after hearing the news.

"I don't know how," was Carole's discouraged response. "All of the neighbors would want it to stay as it is. Are you willing to try for a group effort?"

"Certainly," she replied. "But I don't see how we could possibly put anything together in time. You're in Indiana, and Bob and I are leaving for a trip to Hawaii in a few days. But I'll talk with my mother in Indianapolis before we go."

Carole's communication with her mother before she and Bob left on their flight to Hawaii brought an agreement by Erna's guardian than she would not rush the arrangements with a Realtor about selling the woods. But it was made clear that there was a limit in the length of time she could delay in putting the property up for sale through a realty agency. Erna's decision to hold on to the land to the end of her functioning life ultimately meant that she would not be the one to decide its destiny. We would later learn that that was not an uncommon situation, as many elderly property owners fail to make provisions for land disposal to their liking, while they still can. How important timing can be.

With the welcomed news that we had been granted a little time, and with Carole and Bob embarked on their winter vacation trip, conversations were begun with several neighboring property owners that we knew well enough to contact and could reach from Indiana. While each of them was interested in the goal of keeping the woods undeveloped, they appeared lukewarm to the concept of group ownership, which was the only way we thought enough money could be accumulated to purchase the property.

Sometime during the previous summer, Doug and I had had a visit from Maxine. She occasionally came out from her new home on

White Lake to keep tabs on the lake frontage of 442 feet, just a short distance to the north of us, that she had retained when selling her home four years earlier. She would walk the beach and gossip with us when we happened to be at the cottage at the same time. Her visit that summer day was somewhat special, however, for she wanted to show us "naturalists" a plant she had recently discovered in her foredune area. She seemed rather excited about the matter, and we dutifully followed her down our bluff deck stairs and north along the shore where this still sprightly woman, now into her late seventies, then cut up into the newly forming foredunes and through the Marram grass, stopping near the bottom of her dune bluff. There, in a slight depression of nearly bare sand, was a sparse string of plants less than two feet high with slender, deeply-lobed, pastel gray-green leaves. At the branch ends of each plant were several delicate, creamy-white flowers, tinged with pink. Both the leaves and the very pretty, many-petaled blossoms looked somewhat like various thistles with which we were familiar, and indeed it was such a species—Pitcher's Thistle.

Maxine proudly explained to us that here *on her beach* was a rather rare dune plant, federally and state listed as "threatened," which meant it was "likely to become an 'endangered species' within the foreseeable future," facing extinction. Telling us that she had given us a little talk about "her" Pitcher's Thistles to her garden club, we were now informed that this was a plant specialized for life on open sand dunes and beach ridges around the shores of the western Great Lakes—as far as is known, it occurs nowhere else on the planet. Somewhat fragile-looking, the plant sends down a lengthy taproot up to six feet long and hangs on for five to eight years of growing before flowering—blooming and setting seed only once during its long lifetime, and then dying. This species is classified as threatened because it faces substantial disturbance of its inland beach habitat from natural water erosion and increasing human coastal activities.

We were pleased to learn of this exceptional dune plant in our locale, and that Maxine had eagerly wanted to show us her find. In the months following her visit, the new knowledge regarding how much we had been experiencing and learning about this coastal landscape and how much more special it was than we had recognized when first coming here. It was now apparent to us that the two Flower Creeks and their wetlands, the relatively undeveloped shoreline between, and the forested dunescape behind were important enough an environmental setting to have a professional assessment regarding its ecological value and any measures that might be taken to preserve it from further development.

Some years back we had become members of a national land trust, The Nature Conservancy. The national non-profit organization had begun in the early 1950s as a local group effort in New York working to save sixty acres of a beautiful river gorge. Successful in that endeavor, the new organization continued on, expanding its mission to the preserving of natural habitats of ecological significance elsewhere, growing over the next half-century to become, astonishingly, the managers of the world's largest system of privately owned natural areas. More recently, we had joined the Michigan Nature Conservancy chapter and decided to write to them in Lansing, describing broad details of our local landscape and asking for an evaluation of the area. They responded by scheduling a visit to our setting in late November, 1993—not long before we were to learn about the woods having to be sold.

We told Maxine of the arrangement and the date, and, with me remaining at my teaching post in Indiana, she joined Doug and a Michigan Nature Conservancy staff biologist on a several-hour, chilly afternoon tour of the beach area, the south edge of Big Flower Creek marsh, and the woodland trail through the back dunes. The biologist was plied with information to go along with his observations, and after the exploratory hike he confided that he thought the area was certainly worthy of a conservation effort. However, the Michigan Nature Conservancy chapter had recently decided to concentrate on larger-scale habitat conservation initiatives that they believed would do the most good to protect the state's special biological diversity.

The Michigan chapter's effort would be part of The Nature Conservancy's Great Lakes Program for the conservation of biological diversity throughout the Great Lakes ecosystem. The Conservancy biologist explained that with limited resources, the state chapter couldn't work everywhere and needed to prioritize its land protection efforts. And since Michigan was blanketed with local and regional land conservancies or trusts, the Michigan Conservancy chapter would generally rely on those local conservancies to protect smaller natural areas. He supplied the name and phone number of the director of the regional conservancy closest to us and hoped that something could be accomplished with that organization. With the start of winter upon us and a busy schedule, we put the matter of contacting the regional land conservancy on the back burner.

With the return of Carole and Bob from Hawaii, we again checked with several of the neighbors about cooperatively purchasing the woods tract. But one told us they had a daughter's wedding expense coming up; another needed to borrow for a house addition; and another was simply noncommittal. While Carole and Bob were interested, it seemed no others were really accepting of the somewhat unusual concept of commonly owning land that would give no owner tangible benefit. Although a cooperative venture seemed a logical approach to us, in view of the benefit it would bring everyone, it never got off the ground. At this point, we wondered if the regional land conservancy could be of assistance in protecting the woods, and a call was made to the office in Grand Rapids sixty miles away. Executive Director April Schultz agreed to meet us at the cottage to tour the duneland tract and discuss what, if anything, could be accomplished through that organization.

On a day of light snow in mid-March of 1994, April rendezvoused with us, and after a half-hour hike together, we warmed ourselves and talked in the cottage. She was enthusiastic about the possibility of keeping the duneland tract undeveloped, for, increasingly, Michigan's coastal dune assemblages were being lost to many forms of fragmentation, development, and exploitation. That the woods property was adjacent to the relatively undeveloped Meinert County Park was another plus. She would take the matter to her board of directors of the Land Conservancy of West Michigan to see what the Conservancy could possibly do.

Several weeks later, April notified us of the board's response, and the news was not helpful. The Conservancy didn't have the money currently to purchase the property for a nature preserve. And the question we had posed to April about the organization lending us a portion of the purchase price was answered with a negative—the Conservancy, as a nonprofit entity, could not loan money to individuals for private purposes, even if the goal was land conservation and the funds would be paid back. We understood that position, but our options were now extremely limited.

Somehow Erna's forested tract had to be purchased with the goal of preserving it, or we all would witness the protection of this special place slip away forever. There would be no second chance—and time was running out. We conferred again with Carole and Bob. They previously had said they could not afford to buy Grandma's land and keep it in the family, but we asked if they would be willing to lend us a portion of the purchase price if we alone made an offer to buy the tract. A single buyer would be the least complex arrangement and could proceed the fastest,

and we would promise not to develop the parcel. Yes, they would make such a loan on trust.

The proposal of a personal purchase was somewhat crazy on our part. We didn't have a cent in savings and were already saddled with the cottage's land contract and two mortgages, having two years before purchased a small fixer-upper house in the away-from-home college town for our two sons' residency there. We now had only one family income (from my teaching job), as Doug had left the indoors employment of teaching and was doing volunteer environmental work and putting sweat equity into the cottage home, our Indiana residence, and the college town fixer-upper. We were doing a little summer renting out of the cottage and taking in several renters at our sons' place, but that covered little more than property taxes and homeowner's insurance on our holdings. Radical frugality was our other financial leg.

Although it was a long shot, we set about coming up with a way to create a viable purchase offer. Doug first checked into what Erna's property was assessed at for tax purposes, and found that it was not that high, which gave some hope. Then we applied for an increase of our second mortgage, or equity loan, on our Indiana house. With appreciation over the twenty-five years of our ownership and improvements Doug had made, we qualified for a new loan amount that went part way towards what we would need for the woods tract. Next, we looked at cashing out our one life insurance policy and foregoing such insurance coverage. With a loan from Carole and Bob, we could have enough to offer almost two thousand dollars over the assessed tax value for Erna's parcel.

With Carole and Bob's support, we wrote to Carole's mother telling her that we'd like to submit an offer-to-purchase direct—which would save on a Realtor's commission—and that our purpose was to keep the woods undeveloped. Her response was a reluctant "no." She really didn't want to accept such an arrangement as she didn't feel confident, under the circumstances, of handling a sale on her own—"As a guardian, I prefer working through an agency. That way I'll get whatever proper assistance I need."

We were disappointed, but there was nothing else to do but be persistent. Doug promptly called her and explained, "We've had some experience with property sales in recent years, and we can do the necessary beginning paperwork. Why don't we just send you an offer-to-purchase document. You can read it over and think about it and check with your attorney before deciding. It doesn't commit you to anything unless you sign it," Doug assured her.

Carole's mother remained hesitant, but didn't outright refuse our suggestion. First thing the next morning, Doug was on his way to the library, bringing back home sample copies of several purchase agreement forms to study to go along with such agreements in our files. We typed up what seemed to best fit the woods situation and quickly got a concise homemade document into the mail, along with an earnest money check. Our note explained, "If you accept our offer, just sign the line above your printed name and return one of the two copies to us. That will also be our receipt for the earnest money. If, after reading this over, you feel you cannot accept, then just return the check to us uncashed."

We waited for over a week—and then came a call. "I think you'll be pleased to know that I've signed the purchase agreement and mailed it to you." There seemed to be pleasure in her voice, too, as we listened over the phone. "Pleasure" wasn't really an adequate word for our reaction. "Ecstatic" and "grateful" came closer. Carole's mother had checked with the probate judge overseeing the guardianship process, and he was satisfied with our price which was higher than the assessed value. Sometime later, we learned that we had had the closest of calls in the acceptance of our offer.

As it was told to us, just hours after Carole's mother had signed our offer-to-purchase document, the real estate agent she had previously contacted called to tell her that he had put a contract in the mail for her to sign authorizing his agency to list the property for sale. It is very likely that he also told her that the woods tract could be put on the market at a higher price than we had offered. If she hadn't already just signed off to us, Carole's mother might have felt obligated to go with the realty agent's listing—and we would certainly have been priced out of the market. What fortunate timing for us—and the woods.

We also later found out that the agent had contacted Maxine seeking to list her lakeshore frontage, which had its inland boundary adjacent to the woods tract. Together, the two parcels would be a great deal more valuable for a developer. Maxine had turned him down.

Several months would be needed for an attorney to draw up the guardian's deed to us and have the sale approved by the probate court in Indianapolis. A property sale closing was targeted for early summer, when Carole's mother would be coming to Michigan for a family visit. A delayed closing date was helpful to us, as we set about assembling the purchase price from our varied sources to be ready for the big day. Everything proceeded well enough, but not without a sense of apprehension over our financial commitment—accompanied by a nagging worry, particularly as a court was overseeing the process, that some quirk would upset the apple cart before the closing could happen.

The momentous closing date of July first came, and we drove with Carole and her mother to a Montague bank for the necessary witnessing by a notary public of our signatures on the purchase documents—the bank setting also giving the proceedings an air of being "official." Although Doug and I were a little nervous, the event was a quiet, easy affair with no intervening third party as with most real estate exchanges.

In fact, neither the beginning of this remarkable arrangement, nor now the end, involved anyone but the buyers and seller.

When the cashier's check was exchanged for the deed to the woods, we sensed that this was too good to be true. Underneath much of our effort during the previous half-year had run the feeling that saving that special environment was likely an impossibility—and now, amazingly, we were the owners!

The day after we received and recorded the deed, Jovan and Derek pulled up the steep cottage driveway with their girlfriends from college, coming to spend the July Fourth holiday with us. It was, of course, an exceptional time to celebrate. In spite of a muggy stillness to the air that invites insects to tag along and harass, we hiked the woods, excitedly shepherding the troops to our new holding and some of its

more interesting locations. Exploring this wooded environment now took on deeper meaning, and Doug and I delighted in sharing the forested dunescape with our special visitors. Later, we swam and rafted, and all except Mom tried out the used sailboard recently acquired. This was indeed a time of celebration. The woods had been miraculously saved, and the world was cooperating with gifts of blue sky, warm waves on an ongoing receding lake level, good health, and all of us together.

Just after an easy darkness had descended over the cottage setting on their last evening, which on July third does not come until after ten o'clock, the "kids" called me to come outside. They had something to show me. "It's dark—and getting late," I complained from the comfort of the sofa and the spell of a good book. "Can't it wait till morning?"

"No way," they chimed. "This is something you've got to see now."

One son at each arm, they led me out across the cottage deck and down towards the dune bluff. Along the entire path—spaced along the descending sand risers, across the little sand bridge and the dune swale, and down the deck stairway to the beach—were homemade luminarias. The little votive candles shone through the white paper sacks with a soft, welcoming glow like that of fireflies beckoning me to follow. At the bottom of the lighted trail, on the beach, the others were sitting in a circle, and as I stepped from the last stair onto the sand, they all sang to wish me "Happy Birthday." The wishes were a matter of a few hours early because our sons and friends were leaving in the morning on the Fourth. But their timing gave the surprise event a memorable significance.

We sat in the sand beside the inland sea, with the dimmest of magenta glow on the horizon, tiny points of luminary light in the shadowy dunal forest at our backs, eating cake and savoring the sweetness of the day and night. We all felt part of something special indeed—participants in a story bigger than ourselves.

College visitors: Derek, on left, and Jovan.

EASEMENTS

With the remarkable acquisition of the woods came a heavy load of new responsibilities. There were now two more loans for us to pay off, and we had become the party responsible for paying the property taxes on the land. There was also the promise to Carole and her family members, and to a lesser extent the other neighbors, that we would not allow development of the dune tract. We had become the successors to Erna two months after her one-hundredth birthday and felt more like trustees of the land than conventional owners. We began thinking of ourselves as stewards, parties that were responsible for the woods' well-being, rather than property owners. To carry out that stewardship, it seemed important to know fairly well where the property lines were—even though that would be another expense.

As far as we could determine through multiple inquiries, there was no survey map available of the woodland tract. A legal description existed, of course, but we could find no identifying stakes telling where the property lines should be. In addition, we did not really know the acreage amount we had acquired. We had been told "about forty-five acres," but there was no documentation for that. Even the tax assessment statement was devoid of an acreage amount, listing only the known legal description, which included an irregular southern boundary. Of course, knowing all of that information precisely wouldn't have made any difference in whether we would have tried to save the woods or not—the

Later in the summer of our acquisition, Doug joined a survey crew of two young men on a quite warm, humid morning, as they began the woods surveying project we had contracted. He wanted to learn everything he could about the landscape boundaries the surveyors would be identifying. To our surprise, the two men started from a point a mile away from the property, to the east, setting up on a section corner stake recessed in the middle of the county road leading to the park and our access roadway.

After passage by Congress of the "Land Ordinance of 1785," much of the western two-thirds of the nation came to be divided, over the next one-hundred years, by federally-contracted surveyors, into a survey grid of one-mile squares called "sections." This measuring and marking was the first step in transforming wilderness into a commodity for sale, and it began in the Great Lakes territories. These section squares contained 640 acres, had their corners initially marked with wooden posts, were identified with a numbering code, and were subdivided further into quarter sections with the survey markers left for future use—lonely identifying points in the wilderness. After that original land survey, further subdividing and marking was done by private parties after acquiring the land from the federal government. Because of the inconvenient curvature of the earth's surface, a flat grid did not always allow for perfect 640-acre sections, but that was accounted for in certain ways. And then there were bodies of water, such as Lake Michigan, that provided incomplete sections of land along their shores. In any case, our crew was starting from a marker at the intersection of Sections 2, 3, 10, and 11, Town 12 North, Range 18 West, of White River Township, Muskegon County, Michigan—a survey point established in November of 1837.

general landscape outline that we did have had been enough. However, now it would be best to clarify the property boundaries.

Although that survey point is today in the middle of an asphalt-topped county road with agricultural fields and scattered rural home sites radiating out in all directions, in 1837 this was still wilderness territory. Late in that landmark year, a government-contracted surveyor, John Mullett, and his crew of perhaps eight men were making their lonely, difficult way northward from White Lake through heavily forested landscapes and chilling soggy wetlands, with early winter underway. Michigan had just become a state earlier in the year, and Mullett was measuring and marking out the mile-square sections and smaller quarter sections in this coastal area so the timbered landscape could undergo a new form of occupation. His survey field notes are still available, and the surveyor recorded that he set a corner post at the common meeting point of what was to be the fore-mentioned four grid sections, marking two nearby Beeches as "witness" trees.

After the momentary appearance of the ever-migrating surveying crew, that wooden survey post was to stand lonely in its tiny forest clearing for several decades before enough loggers and settlers came needing an established access route to their recently purchased land parcels. Trees were then cleared along the east-west section line leading to the lake, providing for a primitive roadway and heralding the arrival in this area of a transforming logging/farming frontier. At some point a metal stake was driven deep into the rough, sandy roadway later on, to replace that aging wooden landmark of enduring importance. Today, the top of a steel pipe can be seen level with the surface of the modern asphalt road, now named Meinert Park County Road. And throughout Michigan and many other states, the grid pattern of most rural roads sits upon the survey lines delineated by the early wilderness surveyors.

Using that survey point out of the distant past as their starting location, the two modern-day surveyors sighted directly westward toward the lake, one mile, to locate the next section corner inside the park. The

original survey post set in the dunes at that point in 1837 had long ago disappeared, along with the White-cedar and the Hemlock that surveyor Mullett had recorded as its witness trees. From that southwest corner of Section 3, which they re-established at a vehicle turn-around in the park, our surveyors sighted north, entered the forested duneworks proper, and proceeded to retrace the long-ago steps of Mullett and his men. While that larger crew of more than one and one-half centuries past laboriously moved along in the chill of early winter, our modest team and Doug endured increasing summer perspiration as they advanced 2,598.97 feet to a quarter section point that was the northwest corner of the woods tract.

In 1837, Mullett had recorded the existence of a 30-inch wide Hemlock along that north-south section line, a tree that possibly had started growing before Columbus had sailed—and that was almost certainly harvested in the period of the Huston timber deed some half century after Mullett's notation of the tree's exceptionally large girth. While the earlier survey crew had continued nearly another half mile north to the "top" of the section line being established, our men turned due east from Mullett's quarter-section point, the beginning of our survey delineation.

For nearly two and one-half unusually sultry days, our surveyors traipsed doggedly up and down the rolling and often steep wooded dune terrain traveling in a demanding straight-line fashion, such as we never hiked. Time after time, the surveyor set up tripod, the standard bearer with his tall measuring scale scurried ahead, up or down slope, and Doug, with his hand-held 30-inch bow saw, trimmed offending branches that blocked the path of sightings between the two men. Mullett would have had several axemen clearing a sighting line, but our tree cover was a much diminished one versus the unexploited and denser wilderness forest that the first surveying team had had to negotiate and delineate. Our hardy and congenial young men made multiple distance and compass readings to sight around the trees we would not permit to be cut and painstakingly added the numbers to their detailed logbook record. Meanwhile, I relayed over parking lot. Surveys are not about the land; they are about defining human ownership—about the boundary limits of control—at least on paper.

Primarily because of the unusual number of boundary lines resulting from the three odd lots that William, prior to building the Chalet, had carved out of the southwestern portion of the woods tract in the early 1950s, the final survey became nearly a half page of a new legal description: "Commencing at the West ¼ corner of Section 3; thence along the East and West ¼ line South 89 degrees 39 minutes 54 seconds East 1079.25 feet; thence South 00 degrees 41 minutes 25 seconds West 1806.47 feet . . . ." And so it continued with a litany of detail and precision in relating angles, compass directions, and distance measurements—all newly calculated with modern surveying equipment and procedures.

How strange the singular language of straight lines and precise numbers appears when it references a land of irregular ridges and rounded troughs—the undulating hills of dune country. Not a word about the terrain itself, which was anything but straight and precise. As if they were incidental, the aspects of the landscape within our boundaries were not divulged in the survey description. There was no mention of topography or soil type. No hint whether the parcel was forested, barren, or covered with wildflowers and ancient ferns, or home for a multitude of animal and other species that have been integral to the landscape for millennia, long before our appearance or the surveyors of yesteryear.

Although unique features occur here, none were listed. The survey grid system of measured squares was designed to maintain a definition independent of features of the land (although if there were a body of water in the woods, that would have been noted). In determining that the

tract was just slightly over forty-three acres, not forty-five, the survey did not say forty-three acres of what. The land between the new survey markers might as well have been perfectly flat and totally bare, a paved-cold drinks and snacks to ease the arduous task in the humid heat, a kind of luxury the nineteenth century surveyors could not even have dreamed about in their summer wilderness travails.

In spite of the physical challenges, our surveying team of Allen and Alan enjoyed their strenuous effort. It was a beautiful woods for hiking, and that can be one of the pleasures of surveying, we were told. And, for once, they were completing the requisite survey for a purpose other than subdividing the land to build upon. "It's a treat to work on a great piece of land that's just going to stay as is," they agreed.

"Stay as is" was our next area of responsibility and concern. Now accurately knowing the outline of the dunal woods tract, we needed a protection strategy to fulfill our promise of preventing development there. Just having the woods in our hands did not guarantee non-development. We could break our promise. Something could happen to us, leaving Doug or me unable to determine its future, as with Erna, and others might have the desire or the need to put it on the open market, making it available for development. In any case, we would be the owners for only a matter of decades at most. And we had learned that we could not, by ourselves, encumber future owners with a non-development deed restriction. It was April Scholtz who provided the answer as to how the woodland tract could be protected for the long-term.

Although the Land Conservancy of West Michigan had been unable to help in acquiring the property, April had informed us that land conservancies, or trusts, could provide private owners the means to ensure permanent protection of their special landscapes. With our land survey completed, we turned to her for an explanation of "conservation

Giving the matter the consideration necessary by both parties, and with a number of steps and variations in the concept. However, it boiled down to working out a legal agreement with the Land Conservancy in which we would retain private ownership of the woods tract, while granting, or "hold." By entering into such an arrangement, neither we nor any future owners could exploit the land—such as, to build on it, remove trees, drill for oil or gas, or mine minerals—because the rights or title to do so would have been given up by us and held permanently by the Conservancy as a public trust.

While the basic concept seemed relatively straightforward and simple enough, there were many elements to consider and work out. The Land Conservancy had, at this point in time, accepted only a few easements in its less-than-two-decades existence, and since each arrangement varies depending upon the landscape and the interests of the owner, every easement has to be negotiated with care, as they are legally binding contracts. There were a dozen categories of decisions to be made regarding retained uses of the land that would be compatible with permanently preserving the natural features of the forested dunescape. Specific permitted and excluded uses needed precise defining, and we dealt with issues such as trails, hunting, off-road vehicles, possible small temporary structures, firewood gathering, domestic animals, campfires, and subdividing.

April had field work to conduct to put together a "Baseline Data" document providing an inventory of the natural and human-made features of the conservation easement tract at the time of the easement donation. This would be the reference data for future monitoring of the tract by the Conservancy, and for ensuring that only permitted uses of the land were occurring, and that the conservation values were being preserved—a substantial legal responsibility the organization would be assuming.

easements," with which we had not been previously familiar. She detailed a number of steps and variations in the concept. However, it boiled down to working out a legal agreement with the Land Conservancy in which we would retain private ownership of the woods tract, while granting, or conveying, developmental and exploitation rights to the Conservancy to "hold." By entering into such an arrangement, neither we nor any future owners could exploit the land—such as, to build on it, remove trees, drill for oil or gas, or mine minerals—because the rights or title to do so would have been given up by us and held permanently by the Conservancy as a public trust.

The final, nine-page agreement document was eventually ready for signature at the end of 1995. It stated that "the Donor conveys and warrants to the Conservancy a perpetual Conservation Easement over the Property," and that "the Property possesses natural, scenic, open space, scientific, biological, and ecological values of prominent importance to the Donor, the Conservancy and the public." Further spelled out was that "this Conservation Easement assures that the Property will be perpetually preserved in its predominantly natural and scenic condition. Any use of the Property that may impair or interfere with the Conservation Values is expressly prohibited. Donor agrees to confine use of the Property to activities consistent with the purposes of this easement and preservation of the Conservation Values."

Among the conservation values, or natural assets, of the property delineated in the easement document were: "significant natural forested dune habitat in which native flora and fauna thrive in a natural state. The area itself represents a high quality example of a natural community that is becoming increasingly rare in the Great Lakes basin: a relatively undisturbed, mature, wooded dune and ravine system. . . . The Easement Property provides habitat for a variety of birds that follow the Lake Michigan shoreline during migration. The large block of mature woods is also important to nesting species that cannot live in more fragmented forests...." The property was thus being preserved "pursuant to a clearly delineated federal, state or local conservation policy and yields a significant public benefit."

Of particular importance, the Easement noted that these forested dunes fell within the State-designated area of "Critical Dunes" along the eastern shore of Lake Michigan—a landscape that had received special designation and protection just five years earlier by the State Legislature, declaring the dune assemblages "a unique, irreplaceable, and fragile resource that provides significant ...benefits to the people of this state... [and others]."

Not mentioned in the document is the value of the dunal woodland as natural history. For at this time, we had not yet fully learned that the woods, although greatly human-impacted, significantly resembles that early Michigan forest that those nineteenth century lumbermen first lusted after. That, unlike the larger Michigan landscape that was so thoroughly exploited and converted into extensive agricultural and numerous urban settings, here is a landscape not so drastically diminished in its original biological diversity—a tiny, salvaged portion of nearly natural habitat, almost a museum piece. Moreover, that remarkable repository of biodiversity includes tree species that are among the oldest life forms in the region. Adding further to the multiple conservation values, notation could have been made of the importance of the woods environment in sequestering carbon from the atmosphere. In all, a highly worthy list.

As if that litany of conservation values was not enough, "our" coastal dune area presents a very interesting—and, we think, significant—anomaly. Here, in a terrain that is one of the most recent geologic features on the continent, next to one of the newest of the world's great lakes, we find descendants of some of earth's oldest plants. This array of ancient flowerless and seedless species that we have found here begins at the frontal edge of the duneworks with the Scouring Rush. Moving just inland from that bluff location are the Bracken Ferns, and then immediately into the woods are the woodland ferns and, a little further, the Clubmosses. Just yards beyond the inland edge of the

dunes I found the Meadow Horsetails along the Cedar Swamp. In this slightly newer terrain than the dunes are also the gorgeous Cinnamon and Sensitive Ferns. Along Little Flower Creek, as it winds it way through the dune forms to the beach and lake, are several other fern species. Even more primitive species on this juvenile land are the fungi, lichens, and mosses in the woods and the swamp, with these hardy, rootless plants attached along tree trunks or growing in organic matter, not even needing soil for their existence.

I don't understand the apparent disconnect between this very young terrain and the most ancient of plants. One might expect that a primordial ground needed initially to call forth a primordial life. But I don't think that adequately explains the conundrum, for it took the emergence of a dunal forest that included more advanced biota to first provide the habitat for the simpler woodland ferns and the relic Clubmosses. Succession doesn't seem to sufficiently explain it. In short, I find this association of the "less-advanced" and the "more-advanced" plants, along with a young terrain, surprising, and don't believe it is very common. Remarkable it is, another of those nature mysteries, and another plus for "the woods."

In a section entitled "Prohibited Actions," it was clearly spelled out that we or any future owner could not, upon the property, conduct commercial or industrial activities, build, alter the land surface, dump waste, keep livestock, operate off-road vehicles, and place signs (except for no trespassing, for sale of the property, and for identification of it being a conservation easement property). Cutting of trees and vegetation was prohibited, except for reserving to the owners the right to "limited gathering of downed wood for use as firewood" and "to trim vegetation as needed to create and maintain footpaths through the Property." And last, "hunting and trapping are prohibited except to the extent specifically pre-approved by the Donor and the Conservancy as necessary to protect the ecological balance of the Property." Of course, the impact of White-tailed Deer was the prime reason for the exception here.

are protected. We short-lived humans have not time left to see but an inkling of that glory, but it would come for others to marvel at.

Among the many other sections in the document there were those allowing for the Conservancy to carry out its responsibilities in the future for monitoring the condition of the conservation values, to establish remedies for any violations, to provide for a number of contingencies that might arise, and for defining liabilities. We had no idea how extensive our agreement with the Conservancy would be, but were pleased to find the process so congenially and professionally carried through by April and the organization. They had become essential in enabling us to fulfill the most important responsibility we had assumed, for the protective conservation easement Doug and I signed was irrevocable—"running" forever with the land.

It was now possible to dream of a future return to glory for this narrow strip of coastal forest community. There are already many monarchs on the rise, thick, tall trees of several species that should some day match those outstanding ones of the past. Among them stand aged ones to lead the way. And there are the younger, smaller trees that have centuries ahead of them, now that their numbers

Ironically, as we were going through the lengthy process of working out extensive protection provisions for the woods, there emerged a threat to that environment that a conservation easement could not prevent. The matter was another easement issue that was to be even more drawn out and not at all congenial. It began with us receiving word that

212

the person from Grand Rapids who had bought Maxine's lakeshore home some years before was planning to upgrade the half-mile stretch of sandy two-track across the woods parcel and the four properties to the east and make that roadway his access route to a substantially enlarged and remodeled version of Maxine's former home.

The old two-track beginning at Flower Creek Road just east of Bob and Carole's home, angling south and west to the lakeshore properties, and then dropping south to the north end of Meinert Park was the product of a 1949 access easement agreement. An easement is a right one party has for a specific use or enjoyment of the land of another, and this roadway arrangement was a "reciprocal easement" created by William and Erna and the party to the west that owned the lakeshore area in 1949 (north of the park) before it was partially subdivided. Each of the two land-owning parties granted passageway (an easement) over the other's land—a reciprocity.

The roadway easement was to provide for vehicular access from the northeast, off of Flower Creek county road, to both the other party's shoreline tract and to William and Erna's land immediately to the north of the park prior to the establishment of a more direct and suitable driving access through the park. As their benefit for granting the long access route across their property, and for preparing a primitive roadbed, William and Erna were given a 200-foot lakeshore lot by the other party—the parcel they later built the Chalet upon (now our cottage), after selling the north one hundred feet of frontage to Bob and Toni. William and Erna quickly took advantage of the new easement arrangement by selling three small lots in the southwest corner of their woods tract, land adjacent to the park and close to its beach. The owners of the little summer vacation cabins that William built for them could go onto the easement two-track north over the lakeshore properties and then back eastward onto William and Erna's property out to Flower Creek Road. That is, if heavy rains didn't

make the sand roadbed impassable.

A decade later, a much shorter driving route from the south over the park's newly hard-surfaced parking lot was made available for the several lakeshore parcels and the three cabins just north of the park. Thereafter, the northern portion of the reciprocal easement right-of-way eastward over William and Erna's woods tract and beyond was no longer needed for vehicular access, but the agreement was not revoked or amended. Over the decades, that half-mile section of unimproved two-track easement roadway gradually deteriorated into little more than a 7-foot-wide walking, jogging, and bicycling trail, through pleasant terrain, occasionally used by the owners of the various parcels that were created over the years out of the two original, larger parcels. It also provided an exceptionally nice walking pathway to the park and its beach for the owners of the four lots that had been created years ago by William and Erna east of the woods. And with people traveling back and forth on foot, it became something of a social conduit, with occasional meetings along the way and stops at one another's abodes. We had first met Carole and Bob in this manner, they from the far northeast end of the easement-way, we at the southern-most terminus.

In the 1950s, Maxine and her husband acquired in a tax sale all of the lakeshore parcel north of William and Erna's lot for a distance of 1740 feet. Soon after, the access through the park became possible. And to prevent unauthorized vehicular traffic coming onto their property over the two-track route from Flower Creek Road, Maxine's husband took it upon himself to install a locked gate across the roadway in the mid-1960s at the common north-south border between their property and William and Erna's woods. A little later, Bob and Carole chained the entry point at Flower Creek Road. Thereafter, the roadway section across the woods tract and eastward was blocked to motorized vehicles during the succeeding decades. While our conservation easement took note of the only ones to use it. If one party opened up and improved the old roadway section, it would be available for all reciprocal easement holders to use. There were now ten property owners/easement holders. And, in time, at least some current or new property owners would possibly end up using the route, and that would likely include recreational use with motorcycles, snowmobiles, and other machines. In the past, one of the cabin owners just east of our cottage had brought small, all-terrain-vehicles (ATVs) to his place, and that could be repeated by other easement holders. Also known as off-road-vehicles (ORVs), there is the distinct tendency for owners of such big toys to use them as their designation suggests.

Service and delivery trucks and snow plows would also ply this intended new road. And, with its connection to Flower Creek Road, a new, very visible, and substantial easement roadway would certainly attract trespassers—particularly as an upgraded right-of-way would now make for a fully drivable connection southwest to the county park, a "back door" (and free) entry to that popular county facility. While gating can dissuade trespassing, unlocking and locking, swinging a gate open and then closing it, becomes a nuisance and gates are often just left open. Ways around closed gates can be found by the determined trespasser.

Like us, Carole and Bob and several other neighbors saw that such a roadway, both the roadbed establishment and its subsequent use, would bring too much disturbance to the landscape and the wildlife—and to the long-time peaceful setting of the woods and the adjacent properties to the east over which the easement ran, a very pleasant situation we all enjoyed. This was precisely an aspect of development that we were seeking to prevent by acquiring the woods—and establishing a protective conservation arrangement with the Land Conservancy. So, as Doug and I were finishing up in late-1995 on our conservation easement agreement, the two of us were forced to begin wrestling with the reciprocal roadway easement situation. While the worrisome concern about the

existence of the reciprocal easement, it could not, however, extinguish or limit the use of the pre-existing, legal right-of-way agreement across the woods tract—an agreement that provided for a roadway width of up to an expansive thirty-three feet. Now, after three decades, a new easement issue was rearing up, entailing the two-track.

As the first half of the 1990s went by, the well-to-do owner of Maxine's former home had so up-scaled the building that it was no longer recognizable as having once been hers—and it was still growing, with decks, bricked patio, and outdoor hot tub. After a half dozen years of being a second home undergoing continual metamorphosis, the expensively transformed structure and the site were on their way to becoming the man's primary residence—although he was retaining his other home in Grand Rapids, a 60-mile one-way commute. The new lakeshore owner had made no self-introduction to any neighbors in his more than half-decade of coming and going. Occasionally sleek cars, usually black, were seen quickly driving past us older lakeshore residents without pause, no head turned with interest toward what neighbors might be doing. Our rare glimpses of him were to come in conjunction with his use of a growing fleet of motorcycles, jet skis, and snowmobiles. Ownership here along the lakeshore was becoming a statement—and playtime.

It was now quite disturbing to learn about Maxine's successor's intent to turn the half-mile eastern stretch of easement two-track into his personal driving access instead of continuing with the shorter route through the park as the rest of us lakeshore area dwellers were doing. Making a suitable year-around private roadway of the existing woodland path would require clearing to widen the right-of-way opening and some sort of raised, hardened roadbed. We knew that if such a road came into existence, the new lakeshore owner and his visitors would not be the return of shoreline erosion had faded over the past few years, we now found ourselves with a new concern—the environmental welfare of the woods. Hopefully, somehow, the man's private drive ambitions could be forestalled.

Through occasional contact with the stream of contractors and workmen who came to do the drawn-out, grandiose makeover of Maxine's house and adjacent landscape, we learned that the owner had the reputation of being a difficult person to work for. Hard to satisfy, he wanted things exactly his way and wasn't averse to changing his mind and having construction work torn out after completion and redone in another manner. As one builder told Doug during a gossip stop at the bottom of our driveway, "I spend half my time building and the other half tearing it down. I've never had such a job." Another general contractor either quit the job or was fired, and a frustrated craftsman told Doug that his employer sometimes wanted the near-impossible—and pushed till he got it. It was only through a contractor that we learned of the man's private drive plans out to Flower Creek Road. No discussion of his intentions with any of the property owners over which the easement ran was ever initiated by him. All in all, it didn't seem that simply appealing directly to such a person to abandon his plans would meet with success, particularly one who showed no apparent interest in the rest of us. We had to think of an alternative strategy.

Speaking with various neighbors, it appeared to us that everyone was very interested in keeping the use of the eastern portion of the right-of-way just as it had been for the past several decades. Even if the lakeshore owner would agree at this point to no private drive, he could press ahead at a later time, or some future party might come up with the same roadway desire. The only way to make permanent the current trail-type usage would be to obtain an attorney's opinion (followed by a court

action, if necessary) that supported those parties burdened by the roadway going over their properties in preventing a development action of a single benefiting party. Or, better yet, although far more difficult, amend the 1949 easement provisions. Even though Maxine's successor would likely not agree to an easement amendment, if every other easement holder did, that might be enough pressure to encourage him to at least suspend his road plans.

Since amending the easement arrangement would take unanimity among all easement holders and be involved and time-consuming, we needed first to find out if there was legal standing for us and the other burdened parties being able to simply impose a no-drive condition over the woods and properties to the east. It would be worth a try. A search for an attorney familiar with property law was begun.

Unfortunately, we got sidetracked when we followed up on a friend's recommendation of a young lawyer who, we were told, was environmentally minded and energetic. Visiting us at the cottage and briefly touring the easement passageway, he seemed eager to take on the legal work and was positive about the outcome. Encouraged, we passed on a number of easement and map documents to him. The problem came when he failed to make future appointments, and then we couldn't even reach him by phone. After several frustrating months had been used up with no results, we wrote to him stating, "We can't go on not meeting like this," and would he please return the information we had supplied so we could proceed with another attorney. We never heard from him and never learned what his problem was.

Our decision was now made to go with a sizeable legal firm with offices in the city of Muskegon. Assigned to a very business-like attorney, Michael, our situation was again explained. He would assess the easement matter and get back with us. Again, weeks went by, but we then did get an opinion this time. After consultation with others in the firm, Michael told us that even though the easement right-of-way over the woods tract and the four properties to the east hadn't been used for ingress and egress for three decades, we likely couldn't successfully assert that it had been legally abandoned—or prevent some easement holder from now reactivating it for his vehicular use. Even though there might be a case to prevent such usage on certain technicalities, his opinion was that we had no better than a 50-50 chance of getting a positive ruling in court if either we or the other party took the matter to that stage. We were now left to try amending the easement agreement to eliminate, or at least forestall, roadway development and vehicular usage over it.

As the months went by through 1997 and on into 1998, rough drafts of an amendment document were worked out between us and Michael, and then reworked. Complexities conspired to draw this procedure into a far more difficult and lengthy process than we had imagined. For the reciprocal easement was not a conventional agreement, the interests and desires of the various neighbors were nuanced, some even a little divergent, and conditions had changed over the decades. For the parties who come to succeed the original agreement makers, as in this case, a reciprocal easement is at best an arranged marriage of previously unacquainted persons using one another's territory, hopefully in a considerate manner. When the number of successor parties greatly increases and new styles of behavior are introduced, it becomes for those successor parties a difficult situation, if not a battleground, as we were to soon discover.

By mid-year, Doug and I had a final draft of a letter to be sent out to all easement holders, including the one who wanted to build the roadway, announcing that an amendment document would be forthcoming and expressing the hope that all would find it suitable for

adopting. The letter sent was signed by us and three other property owners. It stated that the amending purpose was merely to legally ratify the current status of the right-of-way usage, assuring that the quiet, undisturbed natural setting over which the eastern portion of the easement existed would remain as it had been for the past thirty years, a distinct benefit to all surrounding property owners—even the lakeshore owner, who had now been seen walking it with his dog. Motorized vehicular traffic therefore would be prohibited. And as part of our communication, we included a letter from April of the Land Conservancy to explain why a bisecting, operational road would be detrimental to ours and the Conservancy's efforts in protecting the woods tract.

She wrote in part:

In general, a natural area has greater ecological integrity and habitat value when it does not include roads, especially those with higher levels of use, maintenance, and hardened surfaces. Roads used by motor vehicles fragment a natural area into smaller functional blocks of woodland. They create [a wider canopy opening and] an additional "edge effect" that promotes the invasion of aggressive and exotic species that can have a negative impact on native populations. An example of this is nest parasitism by cowbirds on warblers that nest in the woods of Michigan, or the spread of spotted knapweed along Michigan's roadways, replacing native meadow plants.

While some animals will cross roads freely (such as deer), others are reluctant to do so [which means that their habitat becomes partitioned into smaller, less sustainable parcels]. Smaller, slower moving creatures that do venture across roads can be run over by vehicles. In addition, the noise, activity, and exhaust fumes of motorized vehicles of any kind can be very disruptive to a variety of species, particularly in nesting and denning situations.

[With this wooded duneland area,] road development

and vehicular use can be expected to have a negative impact on its natural and habitat values. It is the Conservancy's position, therefore, that the conservation values of the woods (and the adjacent natural area on the properties to the east) would be enhanced if the unused road easement remains undeveloped and is allowed to further revert to a footpath.

I could have (selfishly) added that for those taking a quiet stroll along the easement passageway—listening to the raucous call of a Pileated Woodpecker or the evening serenade of the Veery, or hoping to have a close-up wildlife encounter, or needing simply a measure of solitude, an interlude of escape (or perhaps all those together)—then, having the engine noise of approaching and receding vehicles and needing to step aside to let the machines pass robs one of those special offerings of the woods and significantly degrades the natural experience from the unique to the commonplace.

While the disturbance of which April wrote would not be as great from a private drive as from a public road, nevertheless, our appeal for voiding the right of vehicular use on the lengthy easement road was based on what would be clear negative environmental impacts upon the physical and living landscape.

The mid-1998 letter to each easement holder was followed by a copy of the amendment document, with signature sheets that were to be returned and which we could record in the county's Register of Deeds Office. Slowly, over the next several months, the signature

remained closed and winter passed uneventfully, as did the following spring—no additional signature sheets unfortunately, but no trail disruptions either. Perhaps the lakeshore owner was too busy with putting finishing touches on his compound, traveling back and forth to Grand Rapids, and entering into a new marriage.

But into the spring of 1999, a new lock on our gate again appeared, and this time the lock on the chain at Carole and Bob's end of the easement right-of-way was surreptitiously replaced as well. We shortly thereafter found that a number of small trees close in along the woods trail had been cut down, and one large Black Cherry tree leaning over the pathway had been removed. Tire tracks in the sandy passageway were clearly visible all the way out to Flower Creek Road. Some old landscaping materials we had stored just inside our property along the trail had been removed as well. The man was on the move.

We and several other easement holders had openly and courteously communicated our reasonable views for retaining the right-of-away condition and usage as it had been for decades, and we were due some measure of communication back. The ball was in our easement opponent's court. Nevertheless, Doug and I now walked up his lane one weekend to initiate a discussion of the situation with the man, knowing this was not likely to turn out pleasant. But he was not at the residence. We may not have had adequate unanimity on the easement amending, but one party removing locks and materials and cutting trees on other's property without even consulting with them first was to be resisted. Again, Doug superglued the locks shut. Shortly afterwards, we re-engaged our attorney, now in partnership with another lawyer, explaining to Michael the new situation.

A month later, Doug was going down our driveway as the lakeshore owner came speeding in on the access roadway from the park.

218

sheets began arriving until we had received six in addition to our own. We didn't expect one from the roadway advocate, of course, but were surprised there was no response from several others who had expressed early support for assuring that the easement way remained simply a nature trail.

As we waited for those other hoped-for signers, a disturbing event occurred. The locked chain on our gate at the west entrance to the woods' easement passageway was cut and replaced with a new lock. This was the gate Maxine's husband had installed and secured more than thirty years before. However, it had been placed, either by mistake or intentionally, some ten feet inside the woods tract, and we took the gate to be ours now that we owned the woods. In any case, Maxine's locked chain came with it and, as we had not been presented with a key after several years of woods ownership, had not that long ago replaced her lock with our own. We didn't think Maxine would have turned around and replaced our lock now that this section of common boundary was ours and her successor's. Was this the beginning stage of the man's road development intentions, gaining driving access to the long eastern segment of the easement right-of-way? We decided not to make an issue over the matter as we had the easement amending process underway, although it clearly had stalled.

On through the latter months of 1998 nothing occurred regarding the woods trail, although once we found what seemed to be motorcycle tracks on it. However, with the setting in of winter, Doug noticed that snowmobiles were now parked at the lakeshore owner's place. We certainly didn't want him roaring through the woods with those machines, particularly since our infrequent wintertime trips to the cottage would not allow us to adequately monitor the possibility of there being off-road snowmobile forays into the woods tract. To dissuade use of the woods trail, Doug decided to make the mystery lock non-operable by supergluing it shut. Whether the man tried to open it or not, the gate

Going on past, he suddenly stopped, and Doug noticing, stopped our vehicle. Swinging open his door, the fellow jumped out and stalked towards Doug, his manner conveying agitation even before he spoke.

"Do you know anything about my locks?" he barked.

"Yes," Doug responded quietly.

"What are you trying to do?"

"Did you read the letters we and others sent you?" Doug kept his voice steady in spite of the growing anger in the other man.

"Oh, that's just a lot of gobble-de-gook! You're just trying to take away my rights."

"Well, you'll be getting a letter from our attorney," Doug responded.

With that, the man turned red-faced toward his SUV,

"You'll be hearing from MY attorney. I'll have what I want!"

An appropriate setting for pavement, lights, cars, trucks, motorcycles, snowmobiles, and ATVs??

ACCEPTANCE

"You would not have to seek the permission of the current owners of the [woods] property to clear the easement to its full width of 33 feet, to install lighting, or to asphalt the roadway portion of the easement…." So advised our adversary's attorney in a copy of a letter sent by the lakeshore owner, along with his own, to us and other easement holders in September of 1999. While the man's letter suggested a meeting of "open and direct dialogue" with us and others, he made it clear he had always intended to have the easement way "as my primary thoroughfare for ingress and egress" and that he did "not think there will ever be a 'win, win' solution to our disagreements…."

The attorney had asserted an extreme position, but statements were not then followed up with any roadway actions to match them. On our behalf, Michael replied to the other attorney, contesting the points that attorney had made regarding his client's legal position. Michael especially countered that such modifications of the easement roadway, as put forth by the other attorney, "clearly…were not within the contemplation of the parties at the time the [1949] Reciprocal Easement was entered into." And that "a servient estate [Doug and I, in this case] may not be burdened to a greater extent than was originally contemplated." In its short service of the past, the easement roadway had been never more than a sandy two-track.

There was reference, as well, to the lakeshore owner's recent removing of some landscaping items that we had stored inside the woods parcel beside the easement passageway.

Michael also sent along a letter from us to the lakeshore owner clarifying that we were not so much opposing his intentions as we were seeking what was best for the environment and the neighborhood as a whole—in other words, that we were operating on a higher ground than just one set of landowners opposing another landowner on merely a self-interest, territorial basis. We concluded our letter by stating to the man, "if you see an option other than litigating this matter, please let us know." We didn't think the reiteration of our position of protecting the woods environment would dissuade him, and we did not get a response to our letter. So, Doug and I still had to continue wrestling with what to do regarding the unpleasant roadway situation.

Earlier in the year, we had received word that Erna had passed away in her 105th year. The last of those whose livelihood had been directly connected with these forested dunes was now gone. Gone, too, was the last of those parties that had created the reciprocal easement agreement. In a somewhat twisted case of fate, here we were, an Indiana couple, now struggling with the legacy of a pioneer family and a German immigrant couple regarding a Michigan landscape that had recently come into our hands by unusual circumstances and with which we had only an aesthetic and emotional connection. Once again, we had taken on more than we had bargained for in coming to this inland sea setting.

Along with Erna, the easement amending process was now obviously dead. But was there any other possible legal route to keeping the passageway closed to vehicles, one overlooked previously? We raised the point with Michael that since Maxine and her husband had maintained a locked gate for three decades—and early in our residency Maxine had told us that property owners were free to go around the gate and walk the right-of-way out to Flower Creek Road, but could not drive it—and had prevented motorized passage by easement holders, could we now assert that the successor to Maxine and her husband had no right to do what his predecessors had prevented others from doing? Was there not some legal angle for keeping in place the long-standing status quo?

An extended exchange of communications then ensued between the two opposing attorneys—new issues raised, information conveyed, legal points made, then countered. In between, conferences with clients.

The months went by, and as winter was winding down in March of 2000, Michael convened an office conference with his partner and another attorney, Mary, and Doug and me. Background information was hashed over, questions raised, legal avenues probed, but the consensus of the attorneys ended up as before: that which Doug and I saw as just and warranted would possibly not hold up in court. And it would be an expensive proposition for us, win or lose, if either we or the other easement holder forced the issue to go down that road.

Then attorney Mary asked us, "What would you see as the long-term outcome for the woods tract with your conservation easement on it?" Knowing that the county had, more than a dozen years before, approached widow Erna about selling her property so it could be added to Meinert Park, we replied that the woods might at some future time end up being sold for a park addition. Mary gently responded, "Why don't you consider doing it yourselves?"

That was a shock! We had invested so much of ourselves into the woods, not just the hard-to-come-by money but getting to know and acquire and protect it, that to turn around after only six years and divest ourselves of that which had become a part of us was difficult to consider at the moment. Mary then pointed out that the County as a public owner could perhaps block vehicular traffic through the woods where we couldn't. We had to have time to think about all of this.

Into spring, as outdoor temperatures finally warmed and, as had become my custom, I filled the planters outside the kitchen with Impatiens—a gorgeous combination of lilac and deep magenta. This year I placed the long planters between the uprights supporting the sheltering roof overhang that Doug had extended across the walkway and steps to the cottage's side entry. Two hours later, I walked out the kitchen door to find three plants from the center of one of the containers dug up, lying beside the box. Perplexed, I poked them back into the soil. The next morning, the same plants were on the ground.

"What is going on?" I complained.

With some aggravation, I this time moved the long box onto the walkway to better replant the discarded flowers. It was then I noticed the Chipmunk hole directly below where the planter had been placed the day before. The confused creature had been tossing aside the flowers as it dug through this new mound of dirt covering its original entryway, only to be prohibited access by the bottom of the container. The Chippie certainly had a right to be more agitated than I was. Doug and I supported the planter slightly above ground level to allow the little ground squirrel its previous subterranean burrow access. Once again, we had become entangled in an ingress-egress issue. Involvement in such matters seemed to have become a way of life for us.

In the few weeks after the conference with the three attorneys, we poured a lot of agonizing thought into their conclusions and advice to us. We couldn't chance an expensive court battle that might not go our way, particularly as no one else wanted to financially join in. The route of selling to the county therefore came to make sense, on several levels seemingly, in spite of us seeing it as a drastic step. We finally gave in to that option—although not one hundred percent—and asked Michael to quietly inquire of Muskegon County officials regarding any interest they might have in buying the woods from us. There was interest.

As spring 2000 was ending, Michael presented our tentative terms and conditions to the County Attorney and negotiations eventually began. We had an appraisal of the woods tract done to give us an idea of a price we might present. But our overriding concern was the protection of the woods. We would consider selling to the County contingent upon that governmental body agreeing to utilize their public welfare authority, such as proceeding with eminent domain, to extinguish the reciprocal easement over the woods tract once they owned it. And, also, if County officials would assure us that the conservation values delineated in our granted conservation easement would not be impaired by public use of the woods tract. We did not want to trade one form of the expansion of human activities in the woods, via an opened roadway, for another, in the form of unregulated public use throughout the tract. To work on that issue, a letter was dashed off to April and the Conservancy explaining the situation and our intentions. Would they suggest any amendments to our conservation easement that they felt necessary, in this possibly new ownership arrangement, to adequately protect the woods landscape?

As negotiations via attorneys and their respective clients slowly advanced, we remained anxious and uncertain about crossing such a bridge. It had been very difficult to arrive at this point, particularly for me. Exploring, journaling, and studying had written this place of wonderful forested duneland indelibly across my mind's heart. It was now a part of me. And we had now come to learn of the woods' special history and importance—and to know, almost as friends, the special owners who had preceded us. But the efforts, now extending beyond half a decade, to preserve and protect the woods had become a financial

and an emotional burden—especially for Doug. He wrestled most with its issues and costs, such as mounting attorney's fees, and handled the majority of the communications and interactions, sometimes having to make solo trips to Michigan as I was teaching in Indiana.

Into the summer, we learned that, in addition to evaluating the woods parcel for its suitability as a park addition, county officials were assessing the implications and costs of forcing the extinguishment of the road easement. As word got out about our proposal, the County Attorney undoubtedly learned from our adversary's attorney that there would be an objecting court case if extinguishment were attempted, for Michael began getting the message that the county had qualms about taking that action. Then we learned that the conservation easement on the woods tract and the further use restrictions advocated by the Land Conservancy and ourselves were being viewed by park administrators as too limiting in the recreational use of the property as public space. We were proposing that, as an addition to the park's other recreational offerings, the woods be set aside or given status as a nature preserve with minimal human activity and impact within, leaving a special place for quiet walks of observation and solitude. By late fall, 2000, the tight county budget was presented to Michael and us as the main reason for the county passing on our land proposal at that time.

Doug and I felt both disappointment and relief. Actually, great relief, for this had not been a route the two of us had wanted to accept, but had felt forced into it by the circumstances. We had given it a shot, and the other party had made the declining decision. There was also a measure of tentative relief regarding the right-of-way through the woods itself. While the superglued lock of last year had been cut and removed at some point by the lakeshore owner, no new lock of his appeared on our gate. It was left unchained, both by him and by us, and only once or twice had we seen what appeared to be motorcycle tracks along the pathway, her 1989 sale's survey, the gate is more than ten feet into our property. We saw now that Maxine's successor had assumed it was on his property because Maxine would have told him it was *her* gate, as her husband had installed it many years ago. Perhaps only half accepting this new fact, there was no apology from the man for his mistake.

He then stated that everyone would probably agree that our retaining of the woods in its natural state was an advantage to the neighborhood, and maybe we all could work out something of a compromise about the roadway. Doug and I briefly reiterated our view that the woods was a special area and that a developed, active road would be too disruptive, especially to wildlife. We would prefer no roadway suitable for vehicles, only the current path.

But the foot-dragging regarding our position came not from the host, but instead from the other two parties. Maxine and our next door neighbors had early on told us that they favored no functioning roadway, but later had been hold-outs in signing on to the recent amending attempt, for which no reason had been given. To add to that disappointment to us, there now came overt resistance from their direction.

They spoke instead in favor of having a useable roadway in case of an emergency when access in from the park might be blocked. That an emergency situation and access blockage would both occur at the same time was a highly problematical situation, but we could see merit in a modicum of passable roadway for such a hypothetical situation. "Would everyone be willing to accept a written agreement or amendment limiting use to emergencies only and prohibiting use for other purposes, especially with recreational vehicles such as ATVs?" we responded.

"I don't believe in agreements that tell you how things have to be forever. If, a hundred years ago, they had said the road to my home could only be used by horses, I'd be up to my knees in horse poop by now. We just don't know what's going to happen in the future," came a response

but no further attempt to alter the roadway. This pleasantly surprised us as we went into 2001, for the man's compound finally appeared to be finished, and he seemed to have somewhat settled in with his new wife.

By spring, we felt that the positive situation "on the ground" warranted a last-ditch effort to work out a compromise easement arrangement by way of a face-to-face meeting with the principal lakeshore easement holders. Our letter received an agreeable response from each, including Maxine's successor. Although we suggested meeting in one of the attorney's offices, with both attorneys present so we could have their counsel, the lakeshore owner surprised us with an invitation to his home. He and his wife would host the gathering.

On a muggy August evening, man and wife escorted their guests to a large round table on their elaborately bricked patio facing the calm lake that stretched out some distance below and beyond. Maxine's daughter was now handling her elderly mother's affairs. Strangely, the woman was sitting in a house setting where she had spent much of her youth, but was now not recognizable as such. The couple now owning Bob and Toni's A-frame completed the group of lakeshore owners tied together by both their coastal adjacency and the southern stretch of the easement-way that connected with the access through the park.

The conversing began well enough as we settled in, with some brief exchanges on backgrounds and families—a little awkward, but gracious, beginnings. The host took the lead in shifting to the subject at hand by admitting that he had perhaps been a little too brash in dealing with the roadway situation—and, in turn, felt that Doug and I had been somewhat extreme in responding to his actions, such as disabling the locks on his gate. On "his" gate? "That gate is on our property," Doug quickly corrected. The man questioned this new revelation, and we responded that if one sites along property stakes placed by Maxine during back from our next-door neighbor to our compromise position. Wasn't that basically *our* point—seeking to amend an arrangement of over a half-century ago to reflect changed conditions and to protect a certain, current desirable situation, rather than being under the same agreement "forever?" In the future, the document could be updated again, if the need arose, we contended.

"Why can't we just continue with the gentlemen's agreement we've had in the past?" asked Maxine's daughter, seemingly somewhat annoyed—and sitting across from the party that had sought to upset that so-called "agreement." Whether she remembered it or not, her father had unilaterally imposed a no-drive situation with a secured gate to prevent anyone from coming onto their property via the eastern easement segment, or going out that way. That simply had become a long-standing situation—with no "agreement" ever sought or involved, "gentlemen's" or otherwise. And people, such as ourselves, had been told by Maxine that the roadway was not open for driving. "Even if everyone now agreed," we countered, "to simply go along with the previous status quo, that situation could be upset at any time, by any easement holder, in any way, if there were no legal document change to prevent it."

Since Maxine's lakeshore parcel would likely be put up for sale in the near future, we saw that her daughter was leaving the door open for future roadway development as a possible selling point to a potential, well-to-do buyer of her mother's parcel—as it very evidently had been mentioned as a possibility to our host a decade earlier. We also knew that Maxine's successor had employed her attorney, and as attorney for both clients, the man wasn't likely to be advising them to be at cross purposes with each other.

And so it went around, with the occasional minor or irrelevant point, but with our host saying very little. It ended with an attempted show of cooperation by addressing the matter of preventing trespassing

on the easement way and with everyone agreeing that a gate should replace the less-than-substantial chain across the entry at Flower Creek Road. We said we'd look into doing that, and the gathering adjourned with us being no closer to having lakeshore property owners agreeing to accept any written restriction on personal use of the eastern easement segment. Although we could accept the existence of a passable roadway for emergency conveyance, no actual compromise was worked out—at least not verbally or openly.

We left the meeting feeling more distanced from our closest lakeshore neighbor, but sensing something had been bridged with the farthest one, for our easement opponent seemingly had now come around to some measure of respect for what we had been willing to do to protect the woods. His wife had been very friendly to us, gracious even. One could easily deduce, we thought, that an attractive, younger, and personable companion had mellowed the belligerency of the man.

That meeting of August, 2001, came to be a turning point for us. In a last-ditch attempt at an agreement, we communicated by letter to all easement holders our willingness to work toward a formal arrangement for a roadway able to accommodate emergency access to and from Flower Creek Road, but restricted in other vehicular use. Several favorable responses came back, matched by two very negative ones from the lakeshore hold-outs. Our recent host was quiet, both in responding to our letter and in continued non-action on the woods two-track. The rest of the easement holders were evidently tired of the issue or just willing to let matters take their course. We hadn't expected success in getting an agreement, but needed to take this last step before accepting as final that this issue would remain, sadly, unresolved. As with so many other cases of land conservation and environmental protection efforts, obstacles always exist, and success, if it happens at all, is often only partially achieved.

The cottage, the driveway, the landscape, the access way in from the park, all had been worked on by us every year since our purchase, essentially during every lakeshore stay. Much had been improved, but there were major cottage renovations still needed. However, the costs for those were too great for us to take on, having put so many dollars into maintenance, lesser building upgrades and repairs, and especially into the woods tract, along with its substantial protection requirements and legal fees. Various expenses such as property taxes and homeowner's insurance kept creeping up.

We had come to the lakeshore while Doug and I were still in our forties; now Doug had entered his sixties and I was on the edge of that many decades. We didn't want to go into retirement still in substantial debt, with income reduced while expenses continued to climb. Selling either the woods or the cottage would take us out, but letting go of the woods, as we had been reluctantly willing to do, would not solve as much as selling the lakeshore place, nor would it be as marketable. Finally, the half-decade-long reciprocal easement struggle had exacted an emotional toll. A measure of the joy in coming to this place had been forfeited, particularly for Doug, the one who had initiated the search for such an environment. So, what once would have been unthinkable was broached. The sale of our cottage home made the most sense.

I argued against it, dragged my feet on decisions, cried in secret, and denied the obvious. The view, the lake breeze, the solitude, the tending, the readily available beach and nature walks, the songbirds (especially "my" Veery!), the revelations and the feeling of connection, the dreams, and more—these were mine. How could they be offered up for sale to strangers? But if the timing were such that our leaving now could help protect the woods.....

We were encouraged, however, by the lakeshore owner's continuing restraint in not traveling or modifying the woods easement-way, and were glad each of us two principal parties had gotten a new (and favorable) slant on the other. Could it be that the other party was accepting a sort of unannounced easement compromise? And, it now occurred to us, would it perhaps be helpful, under these somewhat favorable circumstances, if we were to back away from the lakeshore scene, the arena of disagreement?

There had come to be other reasons for considering this new course. The ongoing changes of the natural setting had been matched by many others of a different kind since we had come so excitedly to this marvelous lakeshore. The complete turnover of the immediate residents here had brought a significant alteration in the social dynamics, with a diminishment in the friendly and enjoyable interactions and support of the "early days" which had been so important to us. We had long missed the nearby association with compatible Bob and Toni, spunky Maxine, and Greg and Dee, for like the White-tails, we also are social animals. For a while, we had had a sense of home here, and had even become involved in the broader social-civic scene, contemplating that the cottage would become our primary residence upon retirement.

Although we had friends and a few relatives from afar visit us each summer at the lake, no longer were our sons close enough to make trips. Having finished college, they and their fiancées had ventured west in the late 1990s—first Derek and Emily to the far side of the continent and San Francisco, and then Jovan and Stephanie crossed the Rocky Mountains and the Continental Divide to western Colorado. Evidently, we had taken the two boys on too many camping trips and to too many interesting far places for them not to roam further afield for their own adventures as adults. If we were to see them much, we had to take the time to go to them.

Several years back, on a sun-filled afternoon in late summer, two visitors appeared at our kitchen door. Brian and Belinda had stopped by on their walk to the beach from Carole's home. They were visiting Carole, Brian's mother and the grandmother of his and Belinda's three young children. Grandfather Bob, sadly, had died suddenly and unexpectedly in 1998. (His passing had meant the loss of a strong partner-advocate for protecting the woods.) Having only briefly talked with the young couple in the past, we barely knew these visitors, but that was to change significantly with the invitation for them to come in.

Brian told us about having grown up in the area, living at the other end of the woods trail as a child and a youth, and he explained that the cottage and lake setting was a significant part of his memories of that time. We were complimented on the improvements to the cottage, and Brian pointed out that his great-grandfather had built this house, which we, of course, knew. The great-grandson, as a toddler, had hardly gotten to know William before he passed away; but the professor was another matter, as Brian told how, as a teenager, he had done yard work for the old man, as well as helping in other ways. Belinda commented that her family in Kalamazoo had vacationed along Lake Michigan shores and that she as a youth had developed a great fondness for such a setting.

Sitting in the wood-paneled living room of the cottage, watching the somewhat-distant waves out beyond the greatly expanded foredunes and beach burst into little sparks of sunlight as we talked, there was a pause in the friendly exchange of information and reminiscences—and then Brian revealed the underlying reason for stopping to see us.

"If you ever want to sell this place, we'd like to have first chance to buy it."

Surprised, we smiled and said we'd keep that in mind, but that we didn't anticipate parting with the cottage. The very pleasant couple soon went on to the beach, and after their leaving we thought it was nice to

have someone interested in the place, but we hoped that they wouldn't get *their* hopes up.

"We are considering selling the cottage and are checking whether you were still interested in buying it," announced the letter we had now sent to Brian and Belinda at their home on the other side of the Michigan Lower Peninsula in March, 2002. They were, and a meeting at the cottage was arranged for a tour of the house and further discussion in early spring. If we were to leave, what better ending could there be than for a descendant of the original builder to reclaim the home, perhaps even having an attachment to the building's idiosyncrasies because great-Grandpa had fashioned them. They would harbor a built-in affection for the area's natural and human histories. And mother and grandmother would be just a nice walk up the two-track from this second home, with widow Carole in closer connection with a significant part of her family. It was almost like we owed it to Brian and Belinda to sell, even if we didn't want or need to leave, ourselves.

With this new development, my wall of defense against parting with the cottage scene had severely crumbled, and my struggling to hold on to our home finally ended. For the near future at least, we would keep the woods, but I finally joined Doug in accepting that the home on the lakeshore should be sold. The arrangements between the parties went smoothly, and, by agreement, closing was set for several months distant. It arrived, just the same, all too soon.

The August afternoon was warm, the sky clear, and the waves reflected that beautiful shade of Caribbean blue I had come to love. In short, it couldn't have been a harder day to walk away. Indeed, it was very much a replica of our grand first day of possession here. Quite different in another way, however. For we might have noted to Brian and

Belinda that when Doug and I came to this lakeshore spot, we purchased less than an acre of dunescape, with essentially no beach. Now, with the beach and foredunes stretching almost 400 feet out from the bluff, we were conveying nearly *two* acres of sandy landscape to the new caretakers. Change after change here.

We offered a final inspection, exchanged the necessary papers in the comfort of the living room—deed prepared by Michael—posed smilingly with the buyers for a picture on the cottage deck, and wished the happy couple well. Along with the keys, we handed over the joys and headaches of ownership, reserving for ourselves sixteen years worth of exceptional memories and dreams.

As we eased into our fully packed vehicle, my eyes were not the ones wet with tears. My tears had been used up along the way in coming to accept this day.

Doug started the engine and turned the vehicle to face a new direction for our lives.

Just months after the cottage sale, we returned to my heart's place to meet with a Land Conservancy staff member for the annual monitoring of the conservation easement tract. We parked at the bottom of the cottage drive and first walked up to the closed-up-for-the-winter building, observing the new metal roof shingles that Brian and Belinda had had installed, ending the long, on-again, off-again roof leaking. Strong feelings of loss wavered back and forth with those of relief from having to deal with the seemingly endless needs of the structure. A quick walk to "our" delightful bluff deck and a view of the gray lake, and it was time to join Melanie for the woods inspection.

It was an early November weekend that promised freshening accumulations of snow. The three of us roamed the woods' rugged periphery, checking for anything amiss in the landscape, until the weather began to fulfill the forecast in earnest. Upon our return, I hurried up the lane to catch one last glimpse of the center of the woods before heading for the car, as the front of heavily-laden clouds was even now paving the roads in slippery white. Standing a moment at the hillock that obscured the gateway to my favored view, I breathed deeply to relax tired muscles and clear hurried thoughts from my mind. Then I rounded the turn and slipped soundlessly through our gate stile.

Looking full into the heart of the woods, the beauty of the spot struck me, as it always did. But this day, it momentarily made me catch my breath. Basketfuls of frozen petals drifted earthward, landing in soft wetness upon my cheeks and collecting in gentle nests upon the welcoming arms of the evergreen and ever-graceful Hemlocks. It was a luscious, thick, and comforting snow. I stood motionless until it ran in rivulets from my hair and washed my face like tears.

As we headed toward the car, I felt thankful for this special moment and for a realization that came with it. I no longer needed to see this special woodland as belonging to Doug and me—it was wonderful that it still did—but it was enough just to know that it was there and would continue to be there, as it is. We had our deep connections here, knew of those sturdy people who had preceded us, but such unique environs exist beyond the realm of human ownership. This rugged terrain had never truly belonged to any of its "owners"—although all of us who had intimately engaged this landscape had benefited from association with it. As with the cottage beside the inland sea, it is we who belong for a time to this land. And that is as it should be.

AFTERWORD

Doug Paprocki

There is no more poignant illustration of that constancy of change which Gretchen observed and wrote about than to relate that, as she was working on the final draft recounting our lakeside saga, author and wife died rather suddenly of brain cancer in mid-2009. As her co-traveler through this world—and so fortunate to be—I have labored to suitably convey in finished form Gretchen's impassioned endeavor and to provide an epilogue to our having sold the cottage. For the story of our Lake Michigan coastal connection did not end then—nor has it yet finished.

The ownership divestment of our cottage in 2002 was a major turning point in our lives, as had been its acquisition. Letting go was a wrenching step for us, but also a very freeing one. Relieved of varied financial and time-consuming ownership demands, we were able to see our distant sons and families more often, chart some new courses, and very importantly, Gretchen had more time to set down her story. The year of the cottage sale coincided with her taking early retirement from teaching, as well.

The happiest development of our leaving the cottage scene turned out to be that we didn't really have to leave after all—not entirely, that is. In a most friendly move, Brian and Belinda offered us the opportunity to stay at the cottage—without charge—when they were not using their newly acquired second home. We, of course, took grateful advantage

231

of their very gracious offer, and with lodging elsewhere in the area at other times, our visits to the cottage and explorations of the environs continued annually throughout the rotation of the seasons until the year of Gretchen's passing.

I must make a few comments about our ongoing relationship with that dwelling, for how often does one encounter such a delightful situation? While making several major upgrades to the building which we ourselves could not afford, Brian and Belinda left the cottage very much as it was following our myriad accreted improvements. We felt quite comfortably at home while visiting, still in "our" place—even with much the same old make-do furniture. Despite their and our changes, this home, though, still remained William and Erna's—and a little bit of the professor's—for there had been no major makeover in some forty years. To make the connection back to Brian's building-conceiving great-grandparents even stronger, he and Belinda rechristened the cottage, "the Chalet."

Particularly with periodic availability of the cottage/Chalet, Gretchen and I hardly skipped a beat in continuing our engagement with the coastal environment, one that sharpened and enhanced the descriptions and extensive information that she was incorporating into her writing. More time was available for the "search and research" that brought greater breadth and depth to her compositional offering. And we enjoyed the increased number of trips now possible to the offices of Registers of Deeds and Clerks in nearby coastal counties, visits to several area museums and libraries, and jaunts to the impressive Michigan State Library and Archives in Lansing. There were the annual late summer reunions with Bob and Toni northeast of Traverse City, and their taking us to the delightful musicals at the Interlochen Arts Camp. Each lakeshore and woods visit also included time with friends we had made over the years in the nearby vicinity and in the White Lake area. Our new chapter beside the inland sea was good—and a great deal easier.

In the period following Gretchen's death, when the jolt of her passing had somewhat subsided, I made a number of pilgrimages to the lakeshore scene. A stickler for detail, she had wanted me to check on various aspects of what she had written before her manuscript was finalized. Also, enough changes had taken place in the locale since the cottage sale that a brief update to her story was needed. Moreover, it seemed of value to consider and note some of the significant broader and longer-range changes that had transpired since our coming to this special environment a quarter of a century ago. To accomplish all of this, I needed to re-immerse myself in the landscape the two of us had so wholeheartedly engaged together.

As the generous owners extended visiting privileges to me, my stays were mostly at the Chalet. In taking advantage of that generosity, I could even write the heart of this epilogue in the setting that Gretchen loved—a task of strongly mixed emotions. I knew not how to do this, however, except to follow in her presentational footsteps, to attempt it as best I could in the form that she had brought forth:

.

In the lingering dawn of a morning in late May, 2010, I walked down the tree-lined path from the Chalet to the bluff deck. Pausing there, cool air draining down from the forested dune ridge behind me, I searched the shoreline briefly for any early activity and, with cloudless sky and quiet, smooth lake before me, descended the long stairs. Progress was momentarily interrupted as I had to make my way over a prone Balsam Poplar that had recently toppled, hit the deck, broke its surrounding railing, and then cascaded down, breaking the stairway railing at

the bottom. There were now only seven trees left from the more than a dozen of the cloned circle that had greeted Gretchen and me on our first shoreline sighting of the bluff and cottage. I had noted earlier that several others of the group were dying and severely leaning outward from the circle, soon to go. The squadron had stood lonely guard there for more than six decades, likely even before the coming of William and Erna, but the end of the tour of duty for all seemed to be in sight.

Instead of going on to the beach and the water as usual, I turned right and to the north, after ten paces, for a stroll through the extensive

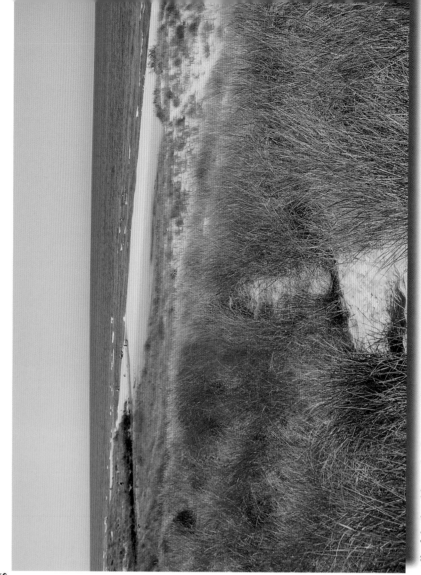

All of the land here, looking southwest toward the park (and the Little Flower Creek outlet, in the upper left), did not exist during our early lakeshore residency. During late 1986 and into the following year, this view would have shown only sea.

foredunes that Gretchen and I had gratefully watched emerge and expand outward from the bluff during the 1990's and into the new century. Twenty-four years ago, upon our arrival here, I would have been roughly eight feet lower and wading in water at least up to my knees had I then attempted walking in this location. In recent years, the lakeward expansion of foredunes had halted, and even retreated some, but there were still some one hundred yards of the new terra firma stretching beyond me and the front of the bluff.

Beside the sea of blue beyond the shore, I now made my way through a green sea of Marram grass riding the dry, rolling, sandy land. The march of this aggressive pioneer species had been relentless during the past two decades, hand in hand with the new, evolving foredunes. Like a broad field of still-green wheat, this particular variety of grass blanketed the foredunes up and down the shoreline and the once-bare bluff slope, even advancing in the opposite direction, up and over the bluff top and into the swale behind. So rampant a covering of vegetation here was something new, at least for more than a half century. For in that 1960s photograph of the newly built Chalet and the beach scene in front, no thick sea of Marram draped the extensive, hilly foredunes of that low water period, only clumps here and there.

This early morning, I was mainly on a quest—going in search of the Pitcher's Thistle, the "threatened" dune species that Maxine had eagerly and proudly shown Gretchen and me some seventeen years before. Both ladies were now gone, the ninety-one-year old Maxine having passed away three years ago. But had specimens of her early discovery survived these two women of the dunes, still there on land that was now in the older one's estate and up for sale?

To my surprise, I came across on my left a semi-hidden path that Gretchen and I had never noticed before. Less than a foot wide, this well-worn route through the thick growth of the sand-stabilizing Marram

grass had been tramped out by White-tails, I realized. A "nature trail" in the fullest sense of the term, I could make out that this deer pathway, paralleling the shoreline, extended from the park area north to Big Flower Creek. Here was new White-tail territory. When there had been little or no foredunes, Deer were occasionally seen coming down to the narrow beach and the lake, but then they shortly returned up the bluff to the forested back dunes, for there was nothing in between of interest to them. The subsequent development of wide, vegetated foredunes had changed that.

In my morning's progress northward, I found, amidst thinner areas of the Marram, a range of plant types other than those identified by Gretchen years back, during the early formation of the foredunes. The tentative advance of woody plants well into this zone was the most surprising change here, for there were several shrub species sparsely scattered about, the most prominent being small stands of low, spreading Sand Cherries. The deer path led to some of these shrubs, and I observed that they had been heavily browsed. Fortunately, Deer are generally not grazers, for how long would the Marram grass last, if they were?

Unexpectedly, I was to find, in one long stretch of foredunes, that every sixty to one-hundred feet, coming out of the forest and down the high dune slopes, there were minor deer trails advancing to the beach, crossing the long, north-south foredune path. It was like the long dunal deer-highway had a dozen or so east-west street crossings, routes to the water. Extensive, vegetated foredunes, now inviting White-tails to travel and feed in the low-light hours, was certainly a substantial geomorphological and ecological transformation here.

A small plant found fairly consistently amidst the dominating "beach" grass I later identified as Sand Cress, with dainty white flowers on extremely slender stems. Previously, Gretchen had found it only sparingly in the early foredunes. And then I came upon several sparse stretches of the brilliantly yellow Hairy Puccoon along an area near the bluff base. Formerly, we had only seen a few scattered groups of the delightfully bright Puccoons along the bluff tops. But they had now advanced to the "lowlands," and in numerous spots. Wormwood, previously only found in conjunction with the bluff as well, was now appearing throughout the more inland area of the foredunes.

With the advent of a variety of new plants in this maturing terrain, and especially the woody shrubs, we had been in the presence of an excellent example of succession since the late 1980s. The formerly species-poor, virgin landscape of wind-assembled ancient rock granules was now exhibiting many of the habitat characteristics of the "older," further-inland bluff top area. If there were to be no major disturbances of the foredune formations in the years ahead, it wouldn't be long before a few trees would be entering the setting, bringing further change along this lakeside environment. Indeed, several young specimens of Balsam Poplar and Red Oak were currently advancing down the bluff slope near the deck, with one small tree already at the bottom.

But as it stood now, the expansive foredunes gave appearance of a rolling prairie, for the dominant plants were waving grasses. Of course, the Marram overwhelmed everything, but there were other grass species as well, and they were, unlike the Marram beachgrass, primarily prairie species. Here and there, were the tall Sand Reed Grass, the Little Bluestem, and Canada Wild-rye, all once a little more plentiful in the dunes, but now mostly overcome by the Marram. Gretchen had written how the expanding bare beach and the emerging embryo foredunes that followed the receding high lake levels of some twenty years ago had strong aspects of a desert in summertime. As most of the widening beach then transformed into rolling foredunes, summer "desert" substantially morphed into "prairie" landscape. Water, desert, prairie, forest—all closely gathered together. A most unusual arrangement, an amazing environment.

After a few hundred yards of searching, I was beginning to think that the Pitcher's Thistle hadn't survived as the foredunes developed and became more heavily vegetated. But that concern was gratifyingly dispelled with my advance to the far end of Maxine's property and into an area close to the higher dune base where the Marram grass was not so thick. There it stood out, the light green, thin foliage of a twelve-inch tall specimen of the desired plant. Not yet in bloom, the Thistle had several large, round flower buds that soon would be opening. Further along, it was a delight to spot specimen after specimen; most, however, were small and without flower buds and therefore not yet of the adequate age of seven to eight years for them to bloom—and then die. Clearly the Pitcher Thistles were prospering in our area. Maxine and Gretchen would have been thrilled with the substantial expansion of this unique western Great Lakes species here in their foredunes.

Other treats were in store as I continued my morning exploration of this regaling shoreline stage. While facing inland photographing the yellow Puccoon, a strange mechanical whistling sound emerged behind me. Turning lakeward, I saw two Swans flying just ten feet above the water, near shore, and approaching very fast. As they passed by, the duo turned west and then curved around to head back south for some reason undetected by me, disappearing in the direction from whence they came.

The next morning, while I was sitting on the bluff deck, there was to be a quick repeat of that strange sound as approximately ten Swans flew over me and the frontal dune treeline. Speeding on north, they may have turned into the Big Flower Creek wetland. The whistling-like sound of their flight strongly suggested these fast-moving white waterbirds were Tundra Swans (or Whistling Swans), but this late into the spring, they should have already been at, or near, their breeding grounds in the northernmost Canadian tundra. The Mute Swans that stay in this area are larger and have a deeper flight sound, so, I really don't know. (How often this "not knowing" frustrated us amateur naturalists!)

Traveling on over the undulating ground, I was beginning to get glimpses of the fanned-out mouth area of Big Flower Creek, and from the marginal height advantage of the foredunes, would train my binoculars on the modest, sprawling outlet. Moving nearly to a full view of the stream's entry into the lake, I was briefly able to watch several Great Blue Herons feeding in the shallow water. However, when they detected my movement in the dunes, although I was yet hundreds of yards away, one by one, they rose aloft and headed back into their marshland sanctuary.

Remaining in the outlet area, though, was a flock of nearly three dozen Gulls on the sandy peninsula, with more gliding out over the calm lake. Scanning the loose assemblage through the binoculars, all appeared to be the monotonous Ring-billed species. But, no, there was an exception in their midst, after all, spied upon my getting closer to the flock. A little smaller than the Ring-bills, this delicate Gull sported a black hood and bill with a white neck collar against its slightly darker, light-gray body. Years before, Gretchen and I had seen a small, lone stranger briefly tagging along on the beach with the larger resident Gulls here. Like this fellow, it was a Bonaparte's Gull.

In spring, Bonaparte's Gulls are stopovers on their way to breeding in Canada. It was quite unexpected to learn that this "sea gull," as most people would call it, nests in boreal spruce trees, the only arboreal gull species. Before making their way back south at the end of summer, the black hood breeding plumage will disappear during a summer molt of feathers, transforming to a white head—and making it harder to pick out any stray unmasked Bonaparte's Gulls from the dominant Ring-bills, should there be a rare and temporary mixing as we have seen.

But what is a "Bonaparte" doing on this Great Lakes beach anyway? Turns out this gull species was given its common name in honor of Charles Lucien Bonaparte, a nephew of Napoleon Bonaparte, and a prominent French ornithologist who lived in America during the 1820s.

Leaving the deer path as it turned in towards the forest and the wetlands and faded out, I descended from the foredunes to arrive at the creek outlet for my half-mile return hike along the beach. There was no company to greet me as the Gulls had just been scattered by an early morning beach walker and her dog. I had lingered back in a low area of the terrain till she and her companion had reached the stream and then turned around. No sense scaring this woman by having a man unexpectedly come out of the dunes towards her. I had sometimes worried when Gretchen, diminutive and attractive, had taken her long beach hikes entirely alone.

Sunlight was now beginning to rise above the high-up dunetop trees and reach the nearshore as I headed back south along the narrow dry strand of sand, beside the gentle in-and-out wash of the lake water. Still a quiet morning, the solar warmth would soon be energizing the lake. A beautiful stretch ahead, like so often in the past. But this is not the way it should be, a beach walk without her, the one who absorbed the greatest pleasures from it. So many changes, abounding in so many ways, so many places. I encounter one almost immediately upon leaving the creek outlet, Chalet-bound.

On my inland side is a 5-foot-high cliff of sand where rougher water of the recent past had advanced inland and sheared off a 50-foot-long stretch of foredune. Into that vertical bank, dozens of two-inch-diameter holes had been excavated to a depth of a foot and more in between the exposed dangling roots of Marram grass. Above and around me swiftly flew an array of five-inch-long Bank Swallows going after aerial insects, some swooping into their nesting tunnels, others leaving. Out here along the beach, these graceful fliers were another of the area's many seasonal songbird species—and another cavity nester, although,

unlike most other avian cavity users, the Swallows excavated their own, but in sand, not trees. (And we humans think *we* are creative and adept.)

Gretchen and I had never before found these sleek, dark grayish-brown birds of white throat band and undersides establishing their nesting cavities in a sandbank along the shoreline, although there had been plenty of such available foredune cut-outs in the past. Previously, these notched-tailed Swallows had always "banked" along the creek's connecting channel, but upon returning last month to this coastal area from wintering in South America, the swallow colony had found altered conditions. That creekside sandbank had become rounded off and no longer provided the necessary vertical wall formation for their nest-tunnels. Upon arriving, these social birds had had to adapt to a new—and more precarious—location, one directly facing the dynamic lake and volatile weather conditions. A strong storm with prolonged wave action could quickly wipe out the whole colony's procreation effort. The necessary adoption of a risky location was a change the Bank Swallows had to live with. Somewhat later it occurred to me that a beach was a most unusual habitat for either a songbird or a cavity nester.

Ten more minutes of walking, with the sun now beating down on me and the beach-foredune area, and more change was brought to mind, with a studied glance up at Maxine's old house. Set up high and back on the frontal dune ridge facing the lake, partly hidden by trees, the modest dwelling that Maxine's successor had changed into a show compound was his no more. A year or two back—Gretchen and I never knew quite when—he had sold to another Grand Rapids party, second-home people we have never met or even yet seen. Word was, though, they were quiet

236

and liked the natural setting. No jet-skis, snowmobiles, or motorcycles. We were grateful for that change. A change laden with irony, as now both easement-way antagonist and protagonist were gone.

The finale to my morning's solitary outing was the passing in the low haze far out over the water of two line-forming squadrons of honking Canada Geese. While I headed south, these fast flyers were pointed uplake, the lead skein not much above the water's surface, the second one coming a little later and much higher up. Outside of certain other waterfowl species, few migrating birds fly in orderly formation. Sky parades of large Canada Geese flock formations are the most spectacular—although the growing numbers of Sandhill Cranes also have similar "V" traveling formations. The distant company of the moment seemed to be on late migration further north, for the geese assemblages continued on out of sight into the faraway misty sky behind me. A reminder that this coastal length is a long-used highway and flyway.

After an extended shoreline walk, Gretchen and I (sometimes with company) would normally finish with a rest on our small, bluff-perched deck. We had found that to cease activity and silently observe for a while the scene just traveled occasionally provided a reward of more than physical recovery. And I was not denied this morning, sitting thoughtfully and gazing back toward the lake expanse after having been gone for two hours. A young family, having made a sunny morning's appearance at the park beach just to the south, was occupied with the languid flow of Little Flower Creek. But my attention was turned northward to the unpeopled land and waterscape just visited. And there in the distance, seventy-five feet out from the shoreline, was a mother Canada Goose with five youngsters in a line behind, paddling in my direction. They had come out of Big Flower Creek, evidently, as I was finishing up my tour, and were making good time against the slightest of current out of the southwest. As I watched the small floating procession come nearer, a distant

motorboat was heard coming from out of the south, perhaps a thousand feet away from the shore. As the large, fast-moving craft approached well out beyond the goose family, the young ones suddenly panicked and tried to flee shoreward. Frantically flapping their immature wings and almost running along the water's surface, the goslings fled diagonally away from the noisy intruder, while Mother stood her ground (water), facing the moving boat. Without the slightest motion of retreating, she resolutely stayed between her brood and the craft as it sped on past. With the perceived threat receding, the goslings quickly circled back to crowd in close to Mom once again.

I continued to watch the reassembled family as it came closer and was granted a landfall, as Mother Goose led her entourage ashore some three hundred feet down in front of me. As she left the water, Mother stretched upward to force the liquid to drain off her body and then rapidly flapped her wings to complete the shedding. In the cutest fashion, the five young ones imitated their parent's action. While adult geese are a combination of light grayish brown, black, and white, the goslings are entirely light to medium brown and more furry-looking than feathered—having a roundish, cuddly looking body.

The beaching was for nourishment, for Mother led the youngsters across the 50-foot-width of flat sand into the foredune edge and proceeded to walk the area, nibbling here and there on tips of Marram grass. Gretchen and I had not known Canada Geese were grazers, for we were familiar with them stretching their long necks down, or tipping up, like dabbling ducks, to feed in the shallow waters of places such as Big Flower Creek or along the shoreline. We had also seen them in grassy areas along ponds, but thought their field foraging was only for insects and such. (Some follow-up reading on the matter revealed that these geese are very much grazers, sometimes destructively eating grass down to its roots. And as their numbers have greatly increased in the past half century, Canada Geese have taken to human contrived "habitats," becoming the bane of many parks, golf courses, pastures, and large lawn areas, such as manicured corporate landscapes. In the process, many of these waterfowl have turned their feathered hind sides on the demanding migratory business and taken up permanent residency in the newer lush geese habitats.)

The land-based snacking on the tough, course greenery was soon called to an end, with Mother leading the goslings back into the water for a return float trip home to complete the youngsters' morning exploration into the wider world. Had I, perhaps, been given the honor of observing the little ones' introductory venture onto the big lake?

It was during the family's land feeding that a third skein of geese in two segments—well over a hundred birds—came flying by, hundreds of yards out from shore. And I wondered, what were the mother's feelings as many of her species passed by, sending out their ongoing honking call? Although she was well ahead of them in having produced offspring and familial ties, was there any tug in her to be off and flying with the journeying crowds that she would so often hear going to breeding waters further north? Or was she perfectly satisfied here with her brood and location? And as I was thinking, there came overhead, just sixty feet above me and not much higher than the tops of the frontal dune trees, another dozen geese honking their way northward.

As almost all species of geese mate for life, where was the other parent during this morning's outing? Back in the marsh feeding? Not likely, as both parents as a rule accompany all family activities, which is what we've seen before. Having recently succumbed to a predator, caught unawares or defending his family while they escaped? Very possible. Perhaps there was a "divorce," which occurs occasionally in unsuccessful pairing, although this seems unlikely here, as breeding did take place. And as size and plumage coloring are the same for both genders, how could I actually know if the parent leading the gosling procession was indeed the mother, and not the father? Either way, with the permanent

pair bonding of Canada Geese, only the demise of the other mate would send this one off in search for another—but not until next spring, for the young ones normal stay with the parents for many months. Is it as wrenching for them to find and then loose a mate as it is for us humans, I have wondered. I hope not.

What a location this shoreline area is. In one short morning's visit, I encountered local and migrant shore birds, waders, and breeding songbirds and waterfowl. I saw colonial nesters and privacy-loving ones. Parent and offspring. And then there were those majestic birds on the move overhead to their breeding grounds further on. Just inland from the beach and foredunes, beginning only a matter of yards away from the bluff top, there were now in residence a range of seasonal forest songbirds having recently joined the year around avian residents for their summer procreation efforts.

It was then well past time for a delayed breakfast. As with the geese, my nourishment would be primarily of grass origin—processed and vitamin-fortified cereal seeds, in my case. Heading up the sandy path between the trees to the Chalet, I was suddenly aware of something oddly different occurring. Stopping, I detected a distant, muffled crashing sound coming out of the south, evidently along the shoreline. Quickly returning to the bluff deck and facing the park beach, I saw in the distance small, low waves washing up against the shore, the leading edge decidedly progressing northward. Strangely, the low, slightly white-capped waves emerged only yards away from the shoreline, with the rest of the lake surface remaining calm. As the leading edge of the wave action rapidly advanced closer and closer, the low-level crashing sound grew in volume, although never really loud. The steady march of waves passed in front of me, and as it proceeded onward, I felt a delayed breeze following behind the advance.

Within approximately five minutes, this unusual process had come out of the south and progressed up the shoreline as far as I could detect. The action then diminished from whence it had come, gradually quieting in front of me, with the faint crashing sound off to the north persisting for a few minutes more before fully fading away. As the phenomenon ended, there remained only a light cooling breeze and the gentle slapping sound of short rippled waves against the shore.

What had happened? While Gretchen and I have experienced many weather fronts moving in over the lake quite suddenly, they would at least materialize with a growing wind, rolling clouds, and some building of waves across the lake surface, not just develop in the immediate shore area. Normally, there would be a noticeable temperature drop, as well. None of that usual frontal activity occurred with this clear, calm, sunny-day event. Moreover, weather fronts moving in from the lake did not settle down in just a matter of minutes to conditions existing before the front event developed.

Had this been an extremely small-scale *seiche* brought on by a change of barometric pressure—where water "tips" toward one side of the lake while lowering on the other side? Water level suddenly rising out of the southwest and being pushed against the beach edge might have created those miniature waves in just the proximity of the shoreline as a very modest rise of lake water advanced up the coast. I wasn't cognizant of any rise of water, other than the miniature waves coming a little farther up into the beach swash zone. Whatever the explanation, the experience was a strange and fascinating phenomenon that Gretchen and I had never encountered in the past.

How fortunate that this one morning of engagement offered so much. It is not always so, but there is never a total paucity of "entertainment" on any morning along this inland sea. That is something that doesn't change.

What had changed, and in a remarkable fashion—and certainly the most notable one of our prolonged lakeshore experience—was the lowering of the historically high Lake Michigan water levels and the subsequent extended development of foredunes along the shoreline. Totally bereft of foredunes, and nearly so of beach, when Gretchen and I first came, the major transformation of this shoreline after our first few years here was simply astounding. As water receded, a widening band of dry, sandy flat land emerged, followed by the steady conversion of the inner beach to spacious foredunes—a virgin landscape, soon replete with diverse vegetation and inhabited "permanently" by little creatures and intermittently by larger ones.

As "organic" gardeners, schooled in the importance of incorporating lots of organic matter into our garden soil, Gretchen and I had found it very surprising to observe vegetative life emerging almost immediately out of the wholly mineral medium of sand, freshly conjured up, to boot. Here was an example of what's called "primary succession," whereby life becomes established on barren, "raw" ground that has no biological legacy—such as with the physical landscape left by a retreating glacier or laid down by a volcanic lava flow. We watched such an extraordinary growth of new terrain and biota that, after a handful of years, its lakeward advance seemed like it wasn't going to stop. How often is there a new world created amidst one's presence?

Shortly after we parted ownership with the cottage in 2002, that ongoing foredune building did come to a halt. Lake levels, after spurting up in 1996 and 1997, began a substantial descent in mid-1998 that proceeded into a more or less normal up and down annual swing. But ever since, that generally normal rise and fall situation has remained consistently, month after month, year after year, below the long-term average for the lake level amounts. Indeed, for well over a decade now, since late 1998, not a single month has seen the Lake Michigan water level rise to its historical average.

A quarter-century ago, with the extended, historically high lake levels of the mid-1980s, newspaper stories interviewing experts carried warnings that we should probably get used to higher water levels than had been normally experienced in the past. That forecast, so far, has been greatly off its mark. In fact, not since the period from 1930 to 1942, years that included the extensive "Dust Bowl" droughts, has Lake Michigan remained this long below its historical average.

In the second half of 2010, a new development emerged with the normal water decline for that time of year becoming somewhat dramatic. And by the end of December, the lake's level had dropped to a point barely eight inches above the historical low mark for that month. Through 2011, the ongoing low period continued, portending a new record, and by the end of the year, Lake Michigan-Huron was in its longest stretch of continuously below average water levels since such records have been kept. The upper and largest of the Great Lakes, Superior, has also been going through an extended period of low levels and set two monthly lows in 2007. And this lake, too, is now in its longest period, historically, of below avarage monthly levels.

Although the two "downstream" lakes had generally been following their historic monthly average water levels in recent years, they began dipping as 2012 progressed, and by mid-year all five of the Great Lakes (as well as, the "not-so-great," Lake St. Clair) measured in below their average historical water levels. In conjunction with the low water levels, the first half of 2012 saw the surface temperatures of all the lakes—the largest fresh water system in the world—being above average, for that time of year, for the record keeping of the last twenty years. And along with the elevated temperatures, evaporated moisture has become increasingly a much greater percentage of the water that leaves these inland seas.

As 2012 came to a close, a new low record was set for Lake Michigan-Huron for the month of December, going slightly below the previous record set a half century before. And then January 2013 came within a fraction of an inch of setting an all-time record water low for anytime of the year. While the three largest Great Lakes will certainly continue lengthening their record-setting low periods—now over thirteen years long—for some time to come (at least on into 2014), how much longer the phenomenon will last no one can tell. For if there's one thing we've learned living beside an inland sea, it's difficult to predict how things will go here and turn out accurate. In the historical time frame, Great Lakes water levels have undergone dramatic fluctuations on our watch. And the question must be raised: are the current lengthy, record low water periods of three of the world's largest lakes connected to the current and recent past record-setting high earth temperatures?

The persistent lower-than-normal lake volume has continued to have its serious impact upon the Big Flower Creek wetland. Four and one-half months after my lakeshore hiking quest, I investigated that hydrologically associated watery terrain. Looking out over the marshland on a gray October afternoon, I saw another significantly changed environment. Descending from the higher forested area on the west side, I edged out onto the flat expanse that contained the winding watercourse Gretchen and I had quietly canoed years ago. But I did not encounter *wet* land. Moving cautiously toward the stream, I expected to begin treading on squishy soil, to feel my foot possibly disappear into a muddy hole with a misplaced step, but that was never the case. Right up to the creek bank the ground was solid. I ended up walking south a thousand feet between the flowing water and the upland ground, coming to where the creek's exiting channel turned west to deposit the stream's land-draining waters into the lake. But only occasional slight depressions in the flat ground surface ever gave any indication of sogginess.

Diminished in width and depth, Big Flower Creek winds its way through a low-lying marshland, now mostly dry and overrun by a monolithic alien grass.

Absent the spread out water coverage of the past, the varied, native wet-meadow vegetation had retreated, been defeated, likely. In its place was a monoculture of Reed Canary-grass with its very slender leaves on long stems two to three feet tall, and seed stalks a little higher. This spindly, alien perennial, literally moving by the aggressive growth of underground rhizomes, had colonized so densely that rarely did the soles of my boots ever actually make contact with soil. Traversing over the raised-up plants with high steps was like walking on a tall, but very forgiving, mattress. Only in short sections along the stream bank was

there anything but the exotic Reed Canary-grass. It was strange to see so exceedingly few of the native grasses, sedges, and Cat-tails that had once stood so tall and proud, rising well above our heads as Gretchen and I had floated along the watercourse. What had this past summer's Red-winged Blackbirds done without their sturdy meadow perches? Where did they place their cup nests, which are typically woven to the tall stalks of Cat-tails?

Indeed, had there been any Red-wings? Clearly, the richness of other wildlife that had made this landscape its home was absent. No Muskrats swam the water, nor were there any of their water-surrounded lodges. The River Otters who had played ice hockey had not been seen for some six years, I was told by friends from whose home along the marsh shoreline I had started my hike.

I saw perhaps three dozen ducks in several groups, seeming all of the same species, but could not get close enough to identify them. I spooked two Great Blues in the far distance (soon to be migrating south). And that was all I observed of wildlife residents. It was well into the migration season, so there should have been a number of bird species spending some time here on stopovers had there been a more normal and suitable wetland situation.

With the double stress of lengthy droughty conditions and the entrenched occupation by an alien vegetation that tolerates no accompanying flora diversity, the inhabitants of the marsh's various niches could not survive. The "marshiness" of the wetland was gone, its biological makeup drastically changed, and it is likely that even the return of higher water levels will not be sufficient to restore this wetland's ecological integrity. While there have been severe droughts evergreens powered by the year-around green, photosynthesizing needles and leaves, absorbing the greatly subdued, but still life-perpetuating sunlight.

The ubiquitous lichen partnership of fungi and algae might be mostly dormant for the winter, but it carried on adorning every living tree we passed. And hidden fungal filaments stayed alive in decaying standing trees and prostrate logs, and underground, along with billions of other and varied tiny organisms, all beyond our sensual awareness. Thousands, if not millions, of buried bulbs, tubers, corms, and rhizomes lived in suspended animation just inches below our feet, waiting patiently to send new growth above ground with the return of enhanced sunlight. And there were innumerable eggs, cocoons, pupas, nuts and other seeds, unnoticed latent progeny waiting for spring to burst forth, heralding a new generation. We may not have seen the year-round resident fauna, but

More life can exist in and on a tree when dead than when it stood in its prime.

before, it may be that recoveries during the past century have been on a sliding scale downward—and that the aggressive Reed Canary-grass, which had been introduced as a pasture plant, this time has displaced native vegetation too thoroughly. Extended periods of this persistent and dominating non-native can eliminate the seed banks in the ground of native species, overwhelming the beneficial impact of water-level fluctuations. This drastic change of the marshland and its unpromising future is disheartening.

Six weeks after my investigation of the dry wetland, on the morning of December 2, 2010, I met two young staff members of the Land Conservancy of West Michigan who had just driven in from Grand Rapids for the annual inspection of our conservation easement property. Like the monitor meeting of eight years earlier that concluded Gretchen's final chapter, this gray day had a little snow to greet us.

Nealy and Josh had not visited the property before, so I led them up and down, in and out, and around the general perimeter of the woods landscape, down through the Sanctuary, and then out through the woods' middle on the reciprocal easement pathway. We followed no trails, other than short portions of a deer path and the old two-track, for Gretchen and I had become so familiar with this undulating terrain that we never had need to create any.

Except for us two-legged visitors, life seemed absent from these dunal woods on this cold, gray, still day. Silence prevailed and nothing appeared to stir. But as Gretchen and I had well learned, life abounded here everywhere, in many forms, even in winter. Trillions of living cells existed in tissues inward of the bark of the woody structures the three of us weaved our way through—and in the long-lasting evergreen foliage. The activity of cell division, though slowed, continued on in the roots of at least some of the trees. Fluids still sluggishly flowed in the veins of the undoubtedly some of those furred and feathered creatures spied us from their hiding and nesting spots—or heard our voices, or felt our footsteps above their burrows, and silently fled away from our advancing presence.

Perhaps a few White-tails had been browsing or traveling nearby, but quietly slipped out of sight upon hearing or smelling the intruding human fauna. It mattered not where we hiked, the vitality of life, some resting for the moment, always existed within inches of where we stood or walked.

Yes, it would have been the customary human view that we are the most important measure of what living is all about to have assumed that our moving presence constituted what defined life here in this quiet winter forest community. Second after second, day after day, century after century, varied living entities have flourished here throughout all seasons for thousands of years since the northerly retreat of the last glacier—diminished only by the coming of techno-fauna.

The forest we were ambling through that day was a denser, more complex, and "messier" one than when Gretchen and I had first roamed and explored it. A near quarter of a century of more growth (tons of it) and death presented us visitors with what is called a "century forest," an arboreal landscape with many trees 80-180, or so, years old. And there were some, perhaps dozens, of the superstructures that Gretchen and I had learned were somewhat older. This woods of uneven-aged trees is not yet (again) an "old growth" forest, but as the current century wears on, this varied and complex forest community, now protected from exploitation, will become

that. For it will match the U.S. Forest Service's old growth definition as a "forest stand at least 180 to 220 years old with moderate to high canopy closure [and a] high incidence of large trees, some with broken tops and other indications of old and decaying wood...."

In the period since Gretchen's passing and her descriptive writing about our woods, I've traveled to most of the forested duneworks along the southern half of the Western Michigan coast that are similar in size to the woods or of a greater extent—treed dunal areas large enough

Having fallen across a driving passageway not far from the Chalet, this wind thrown Beech of the woods revealed in its dismemberment annual growth rings totaling some 150 years. And two Hemlocks, wind thrown recently, tallied in at over 180 years of age for one, and the other at approximately 250 years.

and biologically diverse enough that they can be classified as forest ecosystems. She and I had already made tentative explorations of the neighboring forested areas on the north side of our woods and the rugged duneworks in the southern portion of Meinert Park and a little beyond—both a continuation of the woods' dune ridge system.

By comparing various criteria, it appeared that our forty-three acre tract, along with its immediate extensions lakeward and a little south into Meinert Park—and that would be all of the dunal area once owned by the Hustons—is a little different from that of neighboring forested

areas. And the thought occurred that, perhaps, our dunal forest was even somewhat unique along the central Lake Michigan coast. It short, the many exploratory visits suggest to me that the woods appears to be more of a century forest than any of the other forested areas, with a somewhat greater array of characteristics showing definite and sooner progress to returning to old growth.

This wooded area is generally biologically somewhat denser and more diverse in its biota. The number of tree species is generally greater, with slightly more large trees than most other areas, and appears to have the oldest trees, particularly with the Hemlock species. It is usually a messier landscape, with more extensive leaf litter, greater amounts of decaying accumulated woody debris, and more trees in various stages of drunkenness leaning against their companions—some still alive, others totally out of it. Unlike with some other dunal forests, the absence of leaf litter here and there does not reveal tannish sand, but some degree of brown humus, with many rich brown mounds of long-ago decayed tree stumps and logs. The extent of bright green moss on the ground, logs, stumps, and even up the trunks of trees is greater in our woods than found elsewhere, at least from what I have observed. The same is true regarding the number of fern and evergreen trailing clubmoss patches. And then there are the fungi and lichens, greater in both extent and diversity in our woods, as best I can tell.

With their dense foliage year around, the large number of Eastern Hemlocks (young, middle-aged, and old) existing here also gives a more closed in feeling and a greater richness in landscape appearance. During a springtime rain, a walk in this aging woods, observing a moss shrouded "nurse log" sprouting a baby Hemlock atop it, surrounded by ferns and lush new greenery, there is the appearance of a Temperate Rainforest. At the same time, there is much that connects this woods to a Boreal Forest of the north. I have not found such diversity elsewhere.

However, there may be one exception to our woods being

The richness of the woods' biota is displayed in part by the many varied fungal species, with new ones being found throughout the seasons. Discovered in early April is this spongy jelly fungus, called "Witch's Butter," coming through the dark, scaly bark of a Black Cherry log. Interestingly, it grows parasitically on the mycelium of another fungus that does the actual feeding on the dead wood, and the colorful, gelatinous fruiting body is edible by humans.

somewhat the most unique biologically of the various dunal forests, and that would be the magnificent 1100-acre P.J. Hoffmaster State Park, surely the crown jewel of the Lake Michigan coastal forested duneworks.

In its extensiveness, and with the spectacularly steep ridges and deep valleys, this landscape exists on a far grander scale than our woods—and certainly includes more varied species. There is a greater percentage of large trees, some approaching one hundred feet in height. But I did not see specimens that, in age, seemed to match or surpass some in our woods (and its adjacent extensions). But a forest is more than an arboretum, and here in Hoffmaster (some twenty-five miles to our south), I did not find the more concentrated array of non-tree species as in our woods. I saw no clubmosses, for example. However, with such a large landscape, there is need to return and spend many, many more hours amidst its magnificence to determine its true diversity.

Interestingly, the Western Michigan shoreline dune system extends, in a very narrow interrupted strip, the Northern Hardwood Forest in Michigan farther south than inland. This forest type contains various species common to the Boreal Forest to the north. And it is the existence of the cool weather Hemlocks particularly, along with the White Pines, that separates the lake's dunal forests from the more deciduous Beech-Maple Forest type away from the coast. In their modest display of Boreal Forest species—characteristics seldom existing outside the dunal areas—the limited duneland forests are thus exceptional. And, our woods (and its immediate extensions), with its substantial number of Hemlocks and its association with the adjacent Little Flower Creek Cedar Swamp, seems to be somewhat more boreal-like than the other observed dune forests. This all may seem a little like a parent saying how his/her child is superior to all the other children, but I think that the woods is somewhat special among the exceptional (still too much the parent?).

Why this forest (and its adjoining dunal extensions) somewhat stands out is impossible to know for sure. But it may very well have to do with a difference in the history of the human interactions with the various forested dunescapes that survive and I have analyzed. All of the vast Michigan forests were exploited in the past for their timber, including

Among the many colors of fungi in the woods is that of a blue stain fungus with a scientific name as exotic as its unusual hue: *Chlorociboria aeruginascens*. In processing the nutrients in decaying hardwoods, the filaments of this saprobic organism leave a trail of blue-green pigment wherever they grow, the color coming from materials in the colonized wood itself.

Research into property ownership records and other sources indicates that dunal parcels both to the immediate north and south of the Huston tract were never settled on until long after their timber exploitation (not until generally the second half of the twentieth century, and then mainly for second/vacation homes). In the past, those wooded landscapes had experienced a "cut and run" approach, as did so much of the Michigan forests. And my observations of other forested dune areas along the coast suggests the same. The historical treatment of that which is now our woods seemingly was different, though, with the woods landscape (both above ground and subterranean) undergoing a little less physical and biological damage in its exploitation—and apparently leaving a more intact legacy of interrelating biota and retaining more of its ecological integrity. And it was that passed down and enhanced integrity that Nealy, Josh, and I were checking on that typically gray December morning.

As had been the case over the previous fifteen years, there were no observed violations of the easement agreement, no damage to the conservation values of the dunal landscape. That there was no change in that status was deemed good by both parties. It was good also that we found no evidence of vehicular traffic along the reciprocal easement pathway—a welcomed situation that had been holding for nearly a decade. As the years passed since Gretchen and I had left the scene as cottage residents, we were increasingly pleased that Maxine's successor had refrained from carrying out his early intentions for a built-up roadway through the woods and beyond. We had had a chanced occasion to tell him so several years back—and I continue to be very grateful for his change of heart. With him now gone, would there ever be another lakeshore owner wanting a long access drive out through the woods, I wondered? Hopefully, the impracticality of such a nonessential route will

the shoreline dunal areas—voluminous historical information speaks to that, and one can see that today there is no old growth forest in existence. (A small portion of Hartwick Pines State Park, in the north-central part of the state can be considered an exception to that situation.) However, I now think that the woods (and its adjacent extensions that were once part of the Huston parcel) did not experience as heavy an exploitation as other comparable dunal forests.

While the Hustons came to the area for timber harvesting (immediately after others had already done some "lumbering" there), they very soon after settled upon the parcel, close-up to the duneworks, making it their home for twenty years. It's reasonable to assume that, unlike absentee owners of forested areas who came temporarily and merely for full-scale (and, likely, reckless) exploitation of the timber resources, the Hustons viewed their newly acquired home land in a more sustainable way. Moreover, they were a very small-scale operation, not an outfit coming to the land for rapacious large-scale resource extraction, which damages all aspects of a forest ecosystem, some rather permanently.

The Huston interaction with their duneland forest would therefore very likely have become one of selective harvesting of trees, leaving many for on-going use, such as, providing for later cutting and for hunting and maple sap tapping, while generally protecting smaller trees from harvesting damage—thus leaving a somewhat intact forest system. The family came to host community picnics, and their beach area became a local recreation spot. That Charles and Mary retained ownership of their large parcel after they left for the "big city," and returned for family reunions, strongly says that they loved their varied coastal landscape. They undoubtedly treated it differently than those who had no connection to "their" property. And the tenure of William and Erna, even with their carving out of small cabin lots in the southwest corner of the woods, did not change the character of the overall forest.

be seen by everyone from now on—and be forever a saving grace for the woods.

A conservation easement arrangement can be a stewardship strategy for preserving certain natural features. But it can't protect against various biological forces that can alter the living landscape in ways we normally consider detrimental. The impact of White-tailed Deer on the forest vegetation is one example. Another is the invasion of exotic pests. In our woods inspection, on the southwest corner of the parcel, the three of us found a handful of Beech trees with blotches of white waxy material speckling the gray bark—the consequence of an infestation of a tiny, yellow, sap-feeding scale insect, ones related to aphids. Beech Scale, introduced accidentally into Nova Scotia from Europe over a hundred years ago, has since gradually moved east and south, and was first discovered in northern Michigan counties in 2000. The tell-tale white secretion is a protective covering of the parasitic insects—and the first noticeable sign a Beech tree is in trouble.

Serious damage, however, only results when the minute wounds caused by the feeding activity of the tiny Beech Scale insects enable fungi to invade, sending microscopic filaments spreading into the tree. The feeding of *Nectria* fungi damages the inner bark, the cambium layer, and the interior sapwood, weakening the Beech tree. Often enough, this parasitic relationship becomes pathogenic and the infected host dies. It is not known yet if there has been a *Nectria* invasion of the white-speckled Beeches, but if small reddish clusters of spore-producing bumps (fungal fruiting bodies) on the bark succeed the white Beech Scale coating, then, the woods will have entered a new stage in its existence—with a fungus playing a major role.

American Beech is a defining tree species of this forest community. While it has been learned that in other regions some trees are fully or partially resistant to Beech Scale infesting, it is a very small percentage. So our dune forest composition is likely to undergo a

The recent infestation of Beech Scale insects, exuding a white waxy coating on the exterior of bark, has turned numerous Beeches of the woods into "ghost" trees while they are still living.

We had come on that sunny summer day to each spread a portion of the cremation ashes of wife, mother, and grandmother here, and at the cottage and on the beach, as well—the multifaceted landscape that had engaged the heart and mind of this wonderful woman. I came now to sprinkle a thimbleful of saved remains among the trees and the aged stumps. I intend to do that each year as long as I live—and then have my ashes join hers.

This is a diminished stand of Paper Birches from when we first stumbled into its delighting presence nearly two decades ago. Never great in number or thickly grouped, the white-clad wooden pillars are much reduced now, and only a few of those still standing seem to be hanging on to life. There are no young ones to carry on when the current generation fully succumbs, for the canopy of larger and longer-living species is filling in above, intercepting the sunlight needed for new Birches to sprout and grow. Nor is there the advantage of recent fire to help out, as had once occurred here in the somewhat distant past. In another decade or so, the Birch grove will no longer be recognizable for what it had so graciously offered. Sadly, for some years now, the white columns strewn upon the ground have outnumbered the still standing ones.

Already the new and old corpses, many lying amidst soft moss patches, are returning to the soil from which, as promising seedlings, they arose. Their brief time over, these pioneer plants, in their decaying stage, have moved on to nourishing those longer-lived of other species that are following. Now, these decomposing woodland denizens, who had previously nourished the soul of that lady who was so enchanted by them, are joined by her in their task.

In our struggle over whether to offer the woods for sale to the county as a park addition, Gretchen had written that it was an especially difficult decision for her because the landscape "was now a part of me." From here on, no matter who "owns" these woods in the future, Gretchen,

significant change, with Beech trees becoming much fewer. Mortality of trees will, on the one hand, increase deadwood denning habitat available for certain wildlife, but, on the other hand, Beech nut production will decrease, diminishing an important food crop for many animals and birds. Dead trees open the leafy canopy, allowing sunshine to reach the ground and understory levels, encouraging the sprouting of new seedlings and the growth of young trees. But if White-tails are eating all new vegetative growth within reach as soon as it appears, then the forest density will suffer. Another lesson in how one biological change can have far-reaching reverberations, especially with an invasion of an exotic organism. As always, there is on-going drama in a forest—and an unknowable future.

After a pleasant two-hour tour, Nealy and Josh departed for another monitoring job, heading twenty miles further north into Oceana County. In 1995, our conservation easement had been but one of just a few held by the Conservancy; now, the growing organization has, here into the second decade of the new century, approximately seventy-five, spread out in eight Western Michigan counties to oversee each year.

Now alone as the morning of this overcast day ended, I needed to return to the woods. Walking back up the tree-lined access two-track from the park, on past the driveway to the Chalet, I turned right into the forest and up the ridge that in its undulating way leads to the Birches that Gretchen and I had discovered in pursuit of fawn and Fox, several years before purchasing the woods. I've been to that alabaster grove in the heart of the easement tract many times since Gretchen's passing. The first, in August of 2009, shortly after her death, was with son Derek and wife Emily and their delightful young children, Ava and Dane, now living in Louisville, Kentucky, after two sojourns in California.

Now comes the mineral legacy of the Birch Lady to give assist in the resurrection of a new presence of Pines in this special locale—and to be resurrected herself. For if these new Pines arise to be anything in height like their magnificent predecessors of this dunal forest, then, Gretchen can announce from their glorious tops to the surrounding forest community below, "I, who walked among you and struggled to keep your home intact, who wrote about you and your many companions of the millennia, am here with you still."

On that August visit, we placed Gretchen's hiking shoes in the center of the largest pine stump among the Birches, its aged gray sides barely still standing. Like the remaining, aging alabaster columns, the collapsing, relic stumps will be gone in the not too distant future. More than anything else, it was their discovered presence that had the two of us dig deep into finding the stories of this forested landscape, its people, and so much more. We owe them a lot for that adventure.

Today, I checked under the covering layer of fallen brown leaves inside that special wooden vessel to see the shoes there. They, too, are now part of the landscape.

who loved them so much, will be a part of them forever. She will live on in the Oaks, Maples, Beeches, and even the scattered young White Pines that are currently succeeding the wonderful Birches along their ridge. In one research study, it was discovered that the minerals released from the decaying remains of Birch leaves, and later their carcasses, provided a soil-enriching benefit to the growth of White Pines.

And forever, Gretchen will hike "the woods," and walk the shoreline, basking in the sunset panoramas—and have the lake wind eternally sweep over her, as it first blew against the two of us on the beach that fateful March day years ago beside this wondrous inland sea.

POSTSCRIPT

As 2010 was coming to a close, Meinert County Park on the south side of our woods received an addition of ninety-five acres of backdune terrain on its south flank. The Land Conservancy of West Michigan was instrumental in the acquisition negotiations between the parcel's private owners and Muskegon County officials, and in raising the funds to purchase this outstanding tract of rugged forested dune ridges and deep valleys and two, small, isolated pond-wetlands within. Two years later, the Land Conservancy, after years of negotiations with the owners, acquired a parcel of eleven acres of duneland, adjacent to our woods on the northwest, that also has 900 feet of shoreline. It becomes one of nearly a dozen nature preserves owned by the Conservancy.

With these additional preserved areas, there is now a protected corridor of wooded duneland, having but minor development within, extending from the north edge of our conservation easement tract west to the lake, and south from the woods through the park, for a total length of a mile and a quarter.

The landscape protection all started in 1936 with a small, 16-acre section out of the Huston homestead. Today the total is more than 220 acres in some form of preservation. Hopefully, this protected green corridor can be extended north into the Big Flower marshland and even further south of the expanded park, through ongoing public and private party vision and actions, to hold at bay any further fragmentation of this area's wonderful coastal environment.

Like our woods, the parkland and adjacent areas are a landscape recovering from the logging era, when the pre-settlement arboreal vegetation was dramatically thinned and downsized. But, fortunately, these remnants of one the most magnificent forest areas of the world were not totally demolished. In an age when substantial acreage of the world's forests is vanishing, it is of great importance to assist in the conservation and restoration of forests wherever we can, as they perform valuable ecosystem services.

It is an ongoing struggle between the age-old utilitarian view of forests as economic units providing raw materials and additional space for cultivation or home sites and the newer environmental understanding of forests as providers and protectors of soils, water, climate, and special communities of diverse living organisms (many of which we know little or nothing about). And then there is the aesthetic benefit of woodlands as places of repose, uplift, inspiration, rejuvenation, and pleasant physical activity, as we and many others have found. Putting forests "back together," a "re-wilding" of sorts, as human "development" marches on in relentless expansion, is also a gift to many songbirds and other creatures—in reality, it's a return of that which was once actually theirs.

Not everyone can directly protect natural areas. But there are many ways to be involved in the exciting work of land conservancies that will contribute to landscape/wildlife preservation and restoration. Opportunities abound. By contacting a conservancy/land trust and joining with others who are carrying on this very important mission, your donations and/or your volunteer actions will beneficially reverberate far into the distant future.

For information about and location of a conservancy in your area, contact the Land Trust Alliance, 1660 L Street NW, Suite 1100, Washington, DC 20036. www.landtrustalliance.org

251

ACKNOWLEDGEMENTS

Over the more than two decades of experiencing and learning about our Lake Michigan coastal world, I have consulted innumerable printed and Internet sources and listened to and spoken with many helpful individuals. I am so indebted to the valuable work done by others.

I especially wish to acknowledge and thank the following people for providing very helpful information:

Professors George Parker (retired) and John Barney Dunning, both of the Forestry and Natural Resources Department of Purdue University, West Lafayette, Indiana.

Dr. Kim Chapman, Principal Ecologist at Applied Ecological Services, for notes of his plant observations in our cottage area.

Stu Kogge, Coastal Wetlands Biologist, Michigan Department of Natural Resources, for providing his report, "Documentation of Proposed Environmental Areas, Lower Big Flower Creek, Muskegon/Oceana Counties," published 1997.

John (Bob) and Carole Hanna, Bob and Toni Johnson, Elsie Rosander, and Roger Scharmer. Paul Neis (great-grandson of Charles and Mary Huston) for providing Huston family information and photos in Chapter 15, "Stories."

The staffs of the White Lake Community Library, Whitehall, Michigan, and the Tippecanoe County Public Library, Lafayette, Indiana. Montague Museum and Historical Association, Montague, Michigan.

My deep appreciation to the following for their very helpful editorial suggestions: Dave Cress, Beth Dahl, Kay Dexter, Kim Harden, Dale and Joyce Rothenberger, Elaine Schear, Jo Sullivan, and my

dear friends and colleagues of the Women's Creative Writing Group (Lafayette, Indiana), especially Kathy Mayer and Nancy Patchen, for their wonderful support, encouragement, and contributions.

I have taken short quotes or near-quotes from several publications that were of wide use and special value to me:

The direct quotes about sand in Chapters 10, "Succession," and 11, "Duneworks," are from Michael Welland's outstanding study, *Sand: The Never-ending Story*, Berkley, CA : University of California Press, 2009.

The National Audubon Society sponsored, *The Sibley Guide to Bird Life & Behavior*, Chris Elphick, John B. Dunning, Jr. and David Allen Sibley, editors; New York, NY: Alfred A. Knopf, 2001, an outstanding collection and presentation of information, was particularly useful in Chapters 7, "Spring;" 12, "Woods;" 13, "Flowers;" 15, "Connections."

An exceptionally important book, *Mycelium Running: How Mushrooms Can Save the World*, Paul Stamets; Berkeley, CA: Ten Speed Press, 2005, provided much for particularly Chapter 12, "Woods."

The three books mentioned above are highly recommended for their very interesting and illuminating reading.

Inside Wood: Masterpiece of Nature by William M. Harlow, Washington, D.C.: The American Forestry Association, 1970, provided the direct quote about wood in Chapter 12, "Woods," and much interesting information about trees.

253

the US Army Corps of Engineers, Detroit District, have provided us with continuous data about "our" inland sea and have been invaluable in the telling of the lake level narrative.

[As I, Doug, was finishing the editing and filling out of Gretchen's last manuscript draft, I was fortunate to come across a newly published book that enabled me to enhance the "Woods" chapter in several areas, especially regarding the vast extent of underground biodiversity and activity. This most interesting and enlightening study by biologist David George Haskell is entitled, *The Forest Unseen, a Year's Watch In Nature*, New York, NY: Viking Penguin, 2012.]

To my husband and partner in this wonderful adventure of ours and to all others who have provided help and encouragement in some way, my heartfelt thanks.

[And, on behalf of Gretchen, a final and special thank you to publisher, Susan Bays, for her fine crafting in bringing Gretchen's work into final form — Doug]

Other books on avian information were also helpful and need special note: *The Migration of Birds: Seasons on the Wind* by Janice M. Hughes; Buffalo, NY, Firefly Books, 2009. *Silence of the Songbirds* by Bridget Stutchbury; New York, NY: Walker & Company, 2007. *Songbirds: Celebrating Nature's Voice* by Ronald Orenstein; San Francisco, CA: Sierra Club Books, 1997. *The Wisdom of Birds* by Tim Birkhead; New York, NY: Bloomsbury, 2008.

Useful in several chapters was *The Secret Life of the Forest* by Richard M. Ketchum; New York, NY: American Heritage Press, 1970; *Deep Woods Frontier* by Theodore Karamanski, Detroit, MI: Wayne State University Press, 1989; *The Great Lakes Forest: An Environmental and Social History*, Susan Flader, editor, Minneapolis, MN: University of Minnesota Press, 1983; and *A Field Guide to the Ferns and Their Related Families* by Boughton Cobb, Boston, MA: Houghton Mifflin Company, 1963.

For a quarter of a century, the "Monthly Bulletin of Lake Levels for the Great Lakes" and the periodic "Great Lakes Update," both published by

A QUARTER OF A CENTURY LATER IS THE GLORIOUS SCENE THAT CHANGED OUR LIVES, MODIFIED WITH LITTLE FLOW-ER CREEK NOW REACHING THE ENGAGING SEA ACROSS AN EXPANSIVE PARK BEACH, WITH GRASSY FOREDUNES IN THE BACK-GROUND, AND A DIMINISHED STAND OF BALSAM POPLARS ON THE BLUFF (EXTREME RIGHT), LEAFY-TOPPED SENTINELS THAT ONCE CALLED TO DOUG AND ME WITH A BECKONING COTTAGE-FOR-SALE SIGN. WE ANSWERED AND THE ADVENTURE BEGAN.

Educator, naturalist, writer, Gretchen Paprocki was born in Chicago, Illinois and raised in urban settings, but came to spend much of her adulthood with her husband in the more natural settings of rural Indiana, the mountains of western North Carolina, and along the west Michigan coastal area. In addition to owning property in these locations, she and her family visited and/or camped in numerous natural areas across the continent. Engaging and enjoying the ecological richness of those varied environments, she became a naturalist-conservationist by avocation.

With Bachelor's and Master's degrees in education from Purdue University and an elementary school teacher for 27 years, Gretchen integrated ecological concepts into classroom curriculums, initiated the establishment of a school outdoor learning center, and was chosen as "Indiana Elementary Geography Teacher of the Year," 1993-94. She and her husband, a fellow conservationist, have 2 sons and 2 grandchildren. In 2009, Gretchen died of cancer at age 65 in Lafayette, Indiana.

Along Little Flower Creek winding through the duneworks.

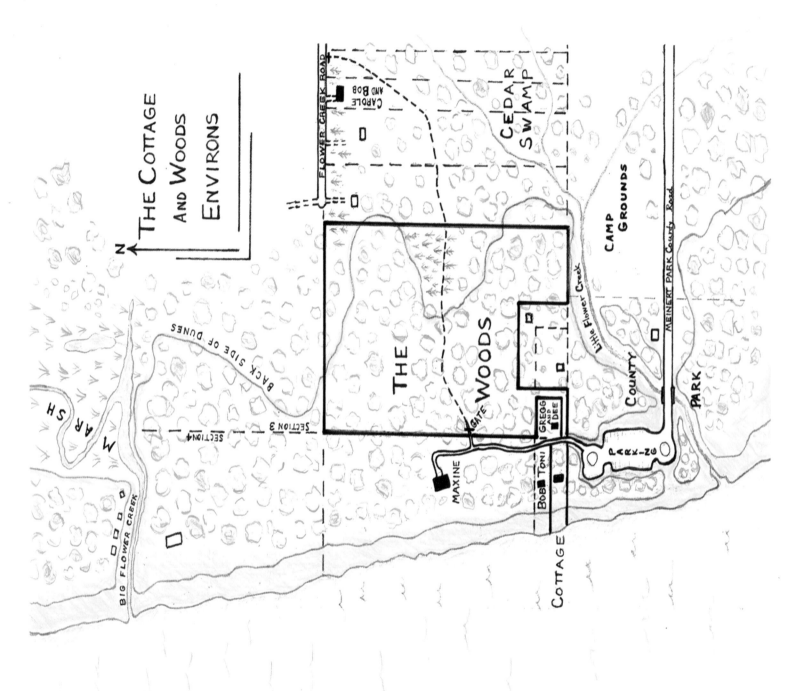

THE COTTAGE AND WOODS ENVIRONS

N